THE ALTERNATE ROUTE

The Alternate Route
Nuclear Weapon–Free Zones

Thomas Graham Jr.

Oregon State University Press   Corvallis

Cataloging-in-Publication data is available from the Library of Congress.

∞ This paper meets the requirements of ANSI/NISO Z39.48-1992 (Permanence of Paper).

First published in 2017 by Oregon State University Press
Printed in the United States of America

Oregon State University Press
121 The Valley Library
Corvallis OR 97331-4501
541-737-3166 • fax 541-737-3170
www.osupress.oregonstate.edu

Contents

Acknowledgments

My purpose in writing this book was to examine the proposition that the cause of nuclear disarmament might take an alternate route, given the collapse of the traditional route of working with Russia. Another path is necessary because the United States and Russia appear no longer able, at least for the foreseeable future, to work together on nuclear disarmament. US-Russia relations have fallen into a seriously negative state, worse than anything since the end of the Cold War.

I must first recognize and thank Frances Eddy, a longtime colleague who worked closely with me throughout the manuscript process. Second, Mary Eddy did a superb job in copyediting the entire text and then laboriously and effectively verified each endnote. In addition, I thank Jeffrey Cornell for his diligence and careful input on the text. To Frances, Mary, and Jeffrey I owe this completed volume in its current form.

Next I would like to thank three outstanding colleagues whose proofreading and suggestions added considerably to this book. First, Krupa Patel (recently graduated from American University Law School) read completely through, thought about, and, where appropriate, commented on the text. Second, Lianet Vazquez (a former staff member of the British American Security Information Council and recently in receipt of a master's degree from the Institute of Political Science, Paris, one of France's finest schools) made creative and far-reaching suggestions for improving important sections of this book. Lastly, Hannah Elizabeth Haegeland (a master's degree graduate from the University of Washington and a former student of mine who is currently involved in several security projects at the Stimson Center in Washington, DC) made several important contributions.

I would also like to express my gratitude to Mary Braun, acquisitions editor at Oregon State University Press, who gave me support and encouragement to take on this project and carry it through. She has also given me helpful advice along the way. In addition, comments from members of the OSU Press editorial board were meaningful for me after the first review by an anonymous reader.

Several thoughtful people, whose opinions I value, upon learning of this book have encouraged me to pursue it in the belief that it would be a worthy addition to the existing literature on nuclear arms control, non-proliferation, and disarmament. I hope that this volume lives up to their ideas and concepts about the impact a book on this subject can have on the effort to verifiably eliminate nuclear weapons worldwide. It certainly has been a culturally rewarding and educational experience for me to write this book. I hope readers will enjoy it and find some insights therein. The cause of worldwide nuclear disarmament is so important it deserves everyone's best and most creative thoughts and efforts.

Acronyms and Abbreviations

ABACC	Brazilian-Argentine Agency for Accounting and Control of Nuclear Materials	DCC	Defense Committee of the Cabinet (Pakistan)
ACDA	US Arms Control and Disarmament Agency	DPRK	Democratic People's Republic of Korea
ACRS	Arms Control and Regional Security	DRDO	Defense Research and Development Organization (India)
AEB	Atomic Energy Board	EEZ	Exclusive Economic Zone
AEC	Atomic Energy Commission	ENCD	Eighteen-Nation Committee on Disarmament
AFRICONE	African Commission on Nuclear Energy	ERL	Engineering Research Laboratories (Pakistan)
ASEAN	Association of Southeast Asian Nations	ExComm	Executive Committee (Cuban Missile Crisis)
BARC	Bhabha Atomic Research Center	FATA	Federally Administered Tribal Areas
CANWFZ	Central Asian Nuclear Weapon–Free Zone	FMCT	fissile material cut-off treaty
CCD	Conference of the Committee on Disarmament	GCC	Gulf Cooperation Council
		HEU	highly enriched uranium
CD	Conference on Disarmament	IAEA	International Atomic Energy Agency
CFE	Conventional Armed Forces in Europe Treaty	ICAN	International Campaign to Abolish Nuclear Weapons
CIA	Central Intelligence Agency	ICBM	intercontinental ballistic missile
CIS	Commonwealth of Independent States	IMS	International Monitoring System
COPREDAL	Preparatory Commission for the Denuclearization of Latin America	INF	Intermediate Range Nuclear Forces
CTBT	The Comprehensive Nuclear-Test-Ban Treaty	ISI	Inter-Service Intelligence Directorate (Pakistan)
CWC	Chemical Weapons Convention	JCPOA	Joint Comprehensive Plan of Action

KRL	Khan Research Laboratories		(NPT)
LoC	line of control (Kashmir)	PPNN	Programme for the Promotion of Non-Proliferation
MENWFZ	Middle East nuclear weapon–free zone	ROK	Republic of Korea
MTR	materials testing reactor	SALT	Strategic Arms Limitation Talks
NATO	North Atlantic Treaty Organization	SDW	Special Development Works (Pakistan)
NNWS	non–nuclear weapon states (NPT)	SEANWFZ	Southeast Asia Nuclear Weapon–Free Zone
NORAD	North American Aerospace Defense Command	SPNWFZ	South Pacific Nuclear Weapon–Free Zone
NPT	Nuclear Non-Proliferation Treaty	START	Strategic Arms Reduction Treaty
NRL	Naval Research Laboratory	WMDFZ	weapons-of-mass-destruction-free zone
NSC	National Security Council		
NSG	Nuclear Suppliers Group	WMDs	weapons of mass destruction
NWFP	North-West Frontier Province	UAE	United Arab Emirates
NWFZ	nuclear weapon–free zone	UN	United Nations
NWS	NPT nuclear weapon states	UNGA	UN General Assembly
OAS	Organization of American States	UNMOVIC	UN Monitoring Verification and Inspection Commission
OAU	Organization of African Unity	UNSCOME	UN Special Committee
OPANAL	Agency for the Prohibition of Nuclear Weapons in Latin America	ZOPFAN	Zone of Peace, Freedom, and Neutrality
PAEC	Pakistan Atomic Energy Commission		
P-5	the five permanent members of the United Nations Security Council: China, France, Russia, the United Kingdom, and the United States		
PD	Presidential Directive		
PDD	Presidential Decision Directive		
PHWRs	pressurized heavy-water reactors		
PNE	peaceful nuclear explosive		
PRC	People's Republic of China		
PrepComm	Preparatory Committee		

The Alternate Route

Introduction

Arms limitation has a long history. There was an effort by the pope in the Middle Ages to outlaw the crossbow, but this measure was soon made obsolete by the firepower of the canon. There was an agreement between the United States and Britain in the nineteenth century to limit firepower on the Great Lakes, observed more in the breach than in the observance. Since the beginning of the nuclear age there has been a widespread desire to limit and eventually eliminate nuclear weapons before they destroy civilization. And much progress has been made: world nuclear arsenals are a fraction of what once existed, but there still are far too many such weapons. The strategic arms control process includes many treaties and agreements; the Strategic Arms Limitation Talks (SALT), leading to the SALT I (the Interim Agreement on Strategic Offensive Arms and the Anti-Ballistic Missile Treaty) and SALT II (the Salt II Treaty) Agreements; the Strategic Arms Reduction Treaty (START); the Intermediate Range Nuclear Forces (INF) Treaty; and the New START Treaty all represent highly important progress. But this process has always depended on close cooperation between the United States and Russia (formerly the Soviet Union).

There must be more progress in nuclear disarmament, and the world community should not lose sight of eventually eliminating nuclear weapons worldwide. But the US-Russian approach is now blocked, perhaps for a long time, because of the ongoing highly negative relationship between these two countries. An alternative route to nuclear disarmament is needed. The nuclear weapon–free zone (NWFZ) movement, little heralded in conferences on nuclear policy around the world, might be such an alternative. Through this process, the Southern Hemisphere as well as important parts of the Northern Hemisphere have been largely made nuclear weapon–free. Thus nuclear weapons are effectively legally banned from Latin America, the South Pacific, Africa, Southeast Asia, and central Asia.

This book examines existing NWFZs and looks ahead to other regions that must play a role in this process if the free zone movement is to move forward: the

Middle East, northeast Asia, and South Asia. If someday in the longer-term future these regions could move in the direction of becoming nuclear weapon–free areas, the remaining areas—China, Russia, and the states of the North Atlantic Treaty Organization (NATO)—might then become nuclear weapon–free themselves, bringing to a successful conclusion the long effort to achieve the complete elimination of nuclear weapons worldwide. Thinking about, examining, and perhaps pursing this process is a tall order, but it is far better than putting aside the ultimate objective of a stable, verifiable, nuclear weapon–free world.

Chapter 1
Another Way Forward

August 6, 1945, began as a beautiful summer day in Hiroshima. The director of the Hiroshima Communications Hospital began his diary entry of the morning, "The hour was early, the morning still warm, and beautiful. . . . Shimmering leaves, reflecting sunlight from a cloudless sky, made a pleasant contrast with shadows in my garden."[1]

The atomic bomb exploded at 8:16 a.m. local time, 1,900 feet above the courtyard of Shima Hospital, and 550 feet southeast of the Aioi Bridge. As one crew member on the bombing mission described it, "Where we had seen a clear city two minutes before, we could no longer see the city. We could see smoke and fire creeping up the sides of the mountains." In the words of another crew member, the city looked like "a pot of boiling black oil." Still another said, "The mushroom itself was a spectacular sight, a bubbling mass of purple-gray smoke, and you could see it had a red core in it and everything was burning inside."[2]

As a Japanese study explained, it was not only human beings that died in the scores of thousands at Hiroshima:

> In the case of an atomic bombing . . . a community does not merely receive an impact; the community itself is destroyed. Within two kilometers of the atomic bomb's hypocenter, all life and property were shattered, burned and buried under ashes. The visible forms of the city where people once carried on their daily lives vanished without a trace. . . . The atomic bomb had blasted and burned hospitals, schools, city offices, police stations and every other kind of human organization.
>
> The whole of society was laid waste to its foundation.[3]

It is not easy to overstate the impact of an atomic bomb on a community, a city, or a country. The atomic bomb "has the power to make everything into nothing." Richard Rhodes in the *Making of the Atomic Bomb* articulates the full emotional impact:

Destroyed . . . were not only men, women and thousands of children but also restaurants and inns, laundries, theater groups, sports clubs, sewing clubs, boys' clubs, girls' clubs, love affairs, trees and gardens, grass, gates, gravestones, temples and shrines, family heirlooms, radios, classmates, books, courts of law, clothes, pets, groceries and markets, telephones, personal letters, automobiles, bicycles, horses—120 war horses— musical instruments, medicines and medical equipment, life savings, eye glasses, city records, sidewalks, family scrapbooks, mementos, engagements, marriages, employers, clocks, and watches, public transportation, street signs, parents, works of art.[4]

The United States conducted its first atomic weapon test in July 1945. The nuclear attacks against Hiroshima and, three days later, Nagasaki would take place in early August only a few weeks following this successful first test. The Hiroshima bomb, called "Little Boy," was a crude device based on the gun assembly principle. It was later largely abandoned by the nuclear weapon states in the development of their nuclear arsenals, but the gun-type design was pursued at Los Alamos Laboratory and used on Hiroshima in part because of high confidence in its reliability.

The United States chose Hiroshima as the first target of a nuclear weapon because, unlike most other Japanese cities, it had been left relatively free from air attack, which could allow the United States to judge the effects of the bomb. The results were utter decimation. The immediate effect of the blast and heat combined with the lingering effects of radiation resulted in the deaths of approximately 200,000 of the nearly 400,000 people who lived in Hiroshima. Of the 76,000 buildings in the city, 70,000 were damaged or destroyed, 48,000 completely. And this was a small bomb. Soon after the end of World War II, as a central symptom of the Cold War, a vast nuclear arms race between the United States and the Soviet Union would come into being.

The second atomic bomb, which was used against Nagasaki, was based on the implosion principle and employed plutonium rather than highly enriched uranium (HEU). It was called "Fat Man" because of its shape. It was essentially the same device that had been tested in New Mexico in July. Later, to a large degree, the US nuclear weapon stockpile would originate from this design, a circumstance not difficult to foresee given that those involved in the Manhattan Project believed using this weapon was important.

The B-29 carrying the implosion bomb left Tinian Island Airfield early on the morning of August 9, 1945, just three days after the Hiroshima bombing and before the Japanese government was able to react fully to the first atomic bomb. The primary target was Kokura Arsenal, and the secondary one was

Nagasaki. The B-29 bomber encountered a problem at Kokura—a ground haze that obscured the target—so the bombing mission, running somewhat low on fuel by that time, headed for Nagasaki. Upon arriving over Nagasaki and finding it obscured by cloud coverage, the US bomber commander decided to attempt a radar approach rather than jettison the enormously expensive bomb into the sea. But at the last moment, a hole opened in the clouds, revealing a city area several miles from the planned aim point; the bombardier dropped the bomb through the hole in the clouds.

The implosion bomb detonated with a force of 22 kilotons (equivalent to 22,000 metric tons of TNT) as opposed to 12.5 kilotons for the Hiroshima bomb. Although the mountains surrounding Nagasaki somewhat reduced the impact of the bomb, 70,000 people were killed instantly, and approximately 140,000 more died over the next five years. Like the survivors at Hiroshima, the survivors at Nagasaki spoke "with equal eloquence of unspeakable suffering. A U.S. Navy officer visited the city about a month later reporting . . . 'the general impression, which transcends those derived from our physical senses, is one of deadness, the absolute essence of death in the sense of finality without hope of resurrection. And all this is not localized. It's everywhere, and nothing has escaped its touch.'"[5] As Rhodes further explains, even though the Japanese had not yet surrendered, President Truman called a halt to atomic bombing the next morning; the decision came none too soon, as a third bomb was being prepared to be sent to Tinian Island Airfield to be available for delivery against Japan by August 17 or 18.[6] The emperor announced Japan's unconditional surrender on August 15, ending the hostilities.

Upon the end of the Second World War, the emerging bipolarization of power, accompanied by the world's alignment into the new Cold War mentality, made the resulting arms race between the United States and the Soviet Union almost inevitable. The destructive power of the newly invented nuclear weapon contributed not only to the idea of increased vulnerability by states lacking this weapon, thus calling for nuclear parity, but also to the belief that great power status could not be achieved without the possession of such a device. The Soviet Union had to pursue the bomb if it wanted to challenge the United States, or at least such was the mind-set at the time.

Thus the Soviet Union carried out its first nuclear test in 1949, four years after the bombing of Hiroshima and Nagasaki. The device bore a close resemblance to Fat Man, reflecting the contribution of Soviet spies in the United States. This test touched off the nuclear arms race and galvanized the United States to build the hydrogen, or thermonuclear, bomb to stay ahead of the Soviet Union. The Soviets soon followed suit. So, by the mid-1950s, nuclear weapon test explosions were in the megaton—not kiloton—range, which is 1 million tons of TNT equivalent and more. The United States developed a bomber nuclear weapon warhead of 25 megatons of explosive yield, or roughly two thousand times more powerful than the bomb that destroyed Hiroshima. The Soviet Union developed a comparable warhead for their SS-9 intercontinental ballistic missile. The United States in the early days of the nuclear arms race developed and deployed an intercontinental ballistic missile with a 9-megaton warhead. It was said that one of those warheads, if placed at the foot of the Washington Monument and detonated, would devastate Washington, DC, out to the Beltway in all directions, a 15-mile radius. Mankind had developed a weapon with which it could truly destroy itself and the world.

During the Cold War and thereafter, the United States built some 72,000 nuclear weapons, and the Soviet Union built around 55,000. At their peaks, the United States had 32,500 weapons in its stockpile and the Soviet Union approximately 45,000. Additionally, there was a perceived risk that these weapons might not remain in the sole possession of the polarized superpowers, but might simply spread all over the world. This risk became a reality when Britain tested its first nuclear device in 1952, France in 1960, and China in 1964. During the Kennedy administration, there were predictions that, by the end of the 1970s, up to two dozen states could integrate nuclear weapons into their national arsenals. President Kennedy, in response to a reporter's question at a March 1963 news conference, said, "personally I am haunted by the feeling that by 1970 . . . there may be ten nuclear powers instead of four, and by 1975, fifteen or twenty. . . . I regard that as the greatest possible danger and hazard."[7]

The Cuban Missile Crisis dramatically and publicly demonstrated the dangers associated with the existence of nuclear weapons. This acute and hugely threatening confrontation took place over fifty years ago, but it continues to haunt all who contemplate nuclear policy and the continuing presence of nuclear weapons. It highlights how easily events can spiral out of control. This has significant meaning for the United States and Russia, who still, twenty-five years after the end of the Cold War, essentially threaten one another with large numbers of alert-status nuclear weapons mated with highly accurate long-range ballistic missiles. Thus the dangers of these weapons linger.

On January 25, 1995, several years after the end of the Cold War, a team of Norwegian and American scientists launched the Black Brant XII rocket to study the aurora borealis.[8] It flew in a trajectory similar to a US strategic ballistic missile aimed at Moscow, and its radar signature was similar to that of a US Trident II submarine-launched strategic missile. Russian radar operators at the Olenegorsk early warning station near Murmansk interpreted what they were seeing on the radar as possibly the first stage of a surprise nuclear weapon attack on Russia by the United States. A full alert was passed through the military chain of command, and the "nuclear briefcase" or "football" (known in Russia as "Cheget," apparently named after Mt. Cheget) was brought to Russian president Boris Yeltsin. He was informed that he had five minutes to decide whether to launch Russia's strategic nuclear missiles—a decision with the potential not only to devastate the United States but also to ensure Russia's destruction in return. Yeltsin activated his "nuclear keys"; it was the only time this had happened since the beginning of the nuclear age. Urgent radio contact was made with Russian submarine commanders, and the Russian military issued orders to its strategic forces to prepare for the possibility of receiving the next command, which would have been a launch order. Fortunately, Yeltsin's doubts that the United States would launch such a surreptitious attack prevented him from making a rash and potentially apocalyptic decision. For four long and tense minutes, Russian commanders waited for the order to launch. Ultimately, the order to stand down and not to launch was given once the Russian radar crew observed the objects associated with the US rocket fall into the sea. Hours later, the Russian leadership learned that this had been a scientific experiment and not an attack. Weeks earlier, some thirty nations, including Russia, had been notified of this experiment, but the message had not made it to the radar crew. A small, seemingly simple yet critical miscommunication had almost resulted in overwhelming devastation.

This incident took place well after the end of the Cold War, when tensions between the United States and Russia had allegedly eroded. Nevertheless, the specter of nuclear war is endemic and not exclusive to US-Russian relations. Nine countries currently possess nuclear weaponry, including India and Pakistan, who have fought three wars in the past and been on the brink of war several times in recent years. The lack of proliferation of nuclear weapons to other countries can largely be attributed to the success of the Nuclear Non-Proliferation Treaty (NPT), which currently has 190 parties, as well as the associated extended deterrence (nuclear umbrella) policies of the United States and the Soviet Union for their allies during the Cold War. NPT state parties have agreed under the treaty's terms to uphold the three pillars of non-proliferation, disarmament, and support of civilian nuclear technology programs. If the NPT regime should ever fail, there could be many other states acquiring and producing nuclear weapons, as President Kennedy so greatly feared. Even if the NPT regime is maintained as is, accompanied by the continued lack of progress on nuclear disarmament commitments by the nuclear weapon states and contravened by programs of modernization of nuclear weapons, additional misunderstandings, near misses, or even nuclear war could result. Likewise, the treaty's lack of compulsory universality—which allows states like India, Israel, North Korea, and Pakistan to possess nuclear weapons without a legal obligation to dismantle their programs in the future—begets similar challenges.

The Cuban Missile Crisis presents a microcosm of the risks present when nuclear weapons are involved in confrontations and is worthy of intensive study. As former secretary of defense Robert McNamara has said, the Cuban Missile Crisis was the best-managed major crisis of the twentieth century, but the world got through it by luck. Experts have written that "October 27, 1962, when the Cuban missile crisis peaked, was the most dangerous day in recorded history."[9]

Late on Friday, October 26, 1962, two messages came in from Soviet leader Nikita Khrushchev. The first appeared to have been written by a man under great stress; it was long and rambling but urged a peaceful solution. It was a private message, and it proposed the withdrawal of Soviet missiles in exchange for a US pledge not to invade Cuba. The second message was diametrically opposed to the first in tone—harsh and unyielding. It seemed to be a crafted policy statement written by a group, rather than a message from a man. It asserted that Soviet missiles would remain in Cuba until the United States removed its comparable missiles from Turkey, a NATO ally. This message was made public. The United States could accept the offer in the initial private message, but the second public demand was much more complicated; accepting it would amount to bending under pressure.

Time was running out. The joint chiefs and congressional leaders were pressuring the president to invade Cuba and remove the missiles. His military and intelligence advisors assured President Kennedy that there were no operational missiles in Cuba at that time. But to quote Secretary McNamara in 2002:

> These events seemed dangerous at the time. But it wasn't until nearly thirty years afterward that we learned . . . that the nuclear warheads for both tactical and strategic nuclear weapons had already reached Cuba before the quarantine line was established—162 nuclear warheads in all. If the president had gone ahead with the air strike and invasion of Cuba, the invasion forces almost surely would have been met by nuclear fire, requiring a nuclear response from the United States.[10]

The critical moment in the crisis came when one of Kennedy's advisors, a member of his special committee for the crisis working in secret—known as the Executive Committee, or ExComm—former ambassador to the Soviet Union Llewellyn "Tommy" Thompson, spoke up. Ambassador Thompson was a man of vast experience with the Soviet Union, and he knew Khrushchev personally.

McNamara also said in his 2002 comments,

> I still quake when I read those lines [from the ExComm transcript]. On the one hand, here was the president, with time running out, looking for a way to resolve the crisis peacefully but confused by the dual communications from Khrushchev. On the other was Tommy Thompson, a senior-level foreign service officer but, in terms of rank, one of the lowest-ranking members of the ExComm, advising the president. But so great was the president's belief in Tommy's expertise—his empathy with Khrushchev and the entire leadership in Moscow—that he put the question to Tommy, then and there, to vote it up or down. And Tommy proved to be exactly right. I thank God we had a president who was determined to find a way out of the crisis short of war and an adviser like Tommy, so full of empathy for our Soviet adversary.[11]

The exchange between Kennedy and Thompson likely pointed the way for the United States and the Soviet Union to avoid all-out nuclear war—with vast, almost unbelievable, destruction—by, in McNamara's words, "a hair's breadth."[12]

> PRESIDENT KENNEDY: "We're not going to get these weapons out of Cuba, probably, anyway . . . I mean by negotiation. . . . I don't think there's any doubt he's not going to retreat now that he made that public, Tommy. He's not going to take them out of Cuba."
> LLEWELLYN THOMPSON: "I don't agree, Mr. President. I think there's still a chance we can get this line going."
> PRESIDENT KENNEDY: "He'll back down?"
> LLEWELLYN THOMPSON: "The important thing for Khrushchev, it seems to me, is to be able to say 'I saved Cuba; I stopped an invasion,' and he can get away with this, if he wants to, and he's had a go at this Turkey thing, and that we'll discuss later."
> PRESIDENT KENNEDY: "Alright."[13]

This truly terrifying crisis was resolved peacefully, and, as McNamara noted in 2002, "We're damn lucky to be here."[14]

The Cuban Missile Crisis and the near miss with Russia in 1995 were not the only close encounters with nuclear war, however; there were several serious and highly dangerous incidents in the years in between. In November 1979, President Carter's national security advisor, Zbigniew Brzezinski, was awakened in the middle of the night by his military advisor, General William Odom. Brzezinski

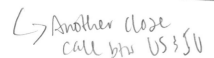
Another close call btw US & SU

was informed that the Soviet Union had launched 250 nuclear weapon–armed strategic ballistic missiles at the United States in a surprise attack. Minutes later, the number had increased to 2,000 Soviet intercontinental ballistic missiles headed toward the United States. Brzezinski knew that soon he would have to wake President Carter. Thereafter, President Carter would have ten minutes to decide whether to launch missiles before the incoming Soviet missiles reached the United States. There was no question of evacuating Washington, including the White House, because the city would be incinerated in a matter of minutes. Brzezinski did not wake his wife, as he believed that everyone would be dead in a few minutes. As it turned out, however, the president didn't need to be wakened; a further check clarified that the entire incident was the result of a computer malfunction at NORAD, the North American Aerospace Defense Command. The computer had issued a false alert.

If Brzezinski had awakened President Carter, strategic nuclear war was likely to have followed. The result of such a small act would have been the complete destruction of the Soviet Union and the United States, but also most of the world. Attacks on allied powers, the subsequent radiation, and the nuclear winter effect would have devastated the earth. Smoke, soot, and nuclear debris from the nuclear explosions would spread worldwide, causing the death of most crops, foliage, and animals, with widespread catastrophic famine.

Both the United States and the Soviet Union made much of their "second strike capability"—their ability to ride out a nuclear attack and still respond with devastating force—during the Cold War. They could then argue that the strategic balance was stable and there was no advantage to striking first. But in fact it was far from stable; both sides had launch-on-warning policies, which called for the state to launch its entire strategic nuclear force at the other side once radar and other sensors confirmed that a nuclear attack was on the way, but before it arrived.

Therefore nuclear training exercises were common during the Cold War. For forty-five years, once a week more or less, some variation of the following exercise was carried out. The commander of the Strategic Air Command would telephone the Pentagon on the secure, dedicated line with the notice that several thousand Soviet nuclear warheads had been detected on a flight path to strike the United States—a full-scale thermonuclear first strike. The weapons would arrive in twenty minutes. A secure conference call would be organized immediately, involving the secretary of defense, chairman of the joint chiefs, and the national security advisor or their deputies, perhaps along with a few other officials. The situation would be discussed on the call among the senior participants with a plan to notify the president with ten minutes to go. The president would have ten minutes to decide whether to launch the US strategic force of land- and sea-based missiles and heavy bombers, based on the information presented to him. During the roughly forty-five years of conducting this exercise, when confronted with the information under these circumstances, the president's response was always the same: "launch." So, if Brzezinski had awakened the president and alerted him of the "fact" that 2,000 Soviet strategic missiles were headed toward the United States, it seems highly likely that President Carter would have ordered the launch of nuclear force. Thus a full-scale nuclear war as a direct result of a computer error would have been caused. Perhaps more concerning, this was not the last of the computer errors; other false alerts were sent out on June 3 and June 6, 1980, because of a failed chip and a "faulty message design."

By no means were these fate-tempting incidents confined to the American *happened* side. There was the 1995 incident, but also another dangerous Cold War incident *to the US* on the Soviet side was recorded and narrated by journalist David Hoffman in his *& so* book *The Dead Hand*. At 7:00 p.m. on September 26, 1983, Lieutenant Colonel Stanislav Petrov arrived at Serpukhov 15, south of Moscow, a top-secret missile attack early warning station. He was the senior officer present, with twenty-six years of military service. He considered himself a practical military man. He did not believe that nuclear war would ever happen, the results were too devastating, but he admitted that the present was a dangerous period with hostilities flaring on both sides. The job of the station was to closely follow the reports of five specially designed satellites that were constantly monitoring US Minuteman intercontinental ballistic missile fields. Petrov knew that the satellites had been built in a hurry and deployed hastily, as was often the case in the experience of the early warning center. The satellite system had been put in place in 1982, even though it was not ready. Its purpose was to give Kremlin leaders an added ten to twelve minutes of warning time if Minuteman launches were to occur, during which time they would decide the best course of action.

Although there were more signals from the satellites than usual, this night was routine for Petrov. But at 12:15 a.m., the thin, silent panel across the top of the control room suddenly lit up, flashing with the word "LAUNCH." A siren wailed. Petrov stood up at his desk so that he was visible to all the officers in the control room and ordered that the system be fully checked, which would take approximately ten minutes. If this had been a real attack, the system check would have used up all the extra warning time. Petrov scrutinized the monitors, including an optical telescope. There was no sign of a missile, and the other monitors did not indicate a missile launch. If it was a report of just one missile, this was not, he thought, an indication of the start of a nuclear war. He picked up the telephone to call his commanders. He had not completed his checks, but this could not wait. He reported a false alarm to the duty officer. The duty officer replied, "Got it!" While the phone was still in Petrov's hand, a series of flashes on the control panel suddenly appeared. A second, third, fourth, and fifth missile launch were reported. An electronic message was automatically sent to higher levels of the military. Petrov felt paralyzed; he had to decide right away. Sirens were sounding and red lights flashing. He made a decision without any confirmatory data. He repeated to the duty officer at the command center, "this is a false alarm." The message went up the chain of command.[15]

Once again, the world had been saved from nuclear destruction because of a steady and courageous man. But there is no certainty that such a person will always be present during these critical moments. US and Russian strategic weapons in considerable numbers are still on alert status many years after the close of the Cold War.

On the American side, in the summer of 1980, President Carter signed two new secret directives on nuclear war. Presidential Directive (PD) 58, signed June 30, called for a new multibillion-dollar program to protect the president and other senior government leaders from nuclear attack. Presidential Directive 59 expanded a president's nuclear targeting choices to focus on Soviet leadership as well as military and industrial targets. PD 59 was developed in part to let the Soviet leadership know something special. According to a senior Pentagon official, they had been "personally placed in the American nuclear crosshairs."[16]

As sort of a pièce de résistance, during the Cold War, the Soviets developed a system called "Perimeter." It was designed to take human beings largely out of the process for ordering retaliatory nuclear strikes. Soviet leaders were worried about their ability to carry out a retaliatory nuclear attack after a decapitating first strike. They drew up plans to guarantee such a strike. The initial idea was a fully automatic system in which a computer alone would issue the order to launch. According to Hoffman,

> It would still function if all the leaders and all the regular command systems were destroyed. Computers would memorize the early warning and nuclear attack data, wait out the onslaught, and then order retaliation without human control. . . [known as the Dead Hand], this system would turn over the fate of mankind to computers. . . . [But] it was eventually abandoned; Soviet designers and leaders could not go that far.[17]

Instead, the Soviets opted for the modified system known as Perimeter. In the early moments of a nuclear crisis, the system would be activated by the general staff or from an underground command post. It would authorize a small group of officers stationed in deep underground bunkers, surrounded by hardened concrete that could survive a nuclear war, to launch a full retaliatory response. As Hoffman describes it, if the system was switched on, the officers in the deep underground bunkers had a checklist of three conditions: (1) verify that the Perimeter system was activated, meaning that the Kremlin through the general staff had given advance permission to fire; (2) verify that contact with military and political leaders had been lost, indicating that all were dead; and (3) determine whether nuclear detonations were being felt by a system of special sensors. If all three conditions were met, the officers were to fire certain special command rockets hidden on the surface that would fly for about thirty minutes and launch all remaining nuclear-armed missiles at the United States. The system was tested and fully operational by 1984. At the climax of an era of fear and mistrust, one of the superpowers had built a Doomsday machine.[18]

From this brief narrative, the danger of the continued existence of nuclear weapon arsenals by states is blindingly obvious. The 1995 incident shows that even the end of the Cold War was no insurance against a catastrophic exchange of nuclear weapons by the United States and Russia, be it by accident or technical failure. Once launched, nuclear weapons cannot be recalled. Even one small bomb of 10 kilotons (several kilotons smaller than the Hiroshima bomb and less than half of the Nagasaki bomb), if detonated in a downtown area of a city like New York, San Francisco, or Washington, would have devastating effects.

William J. Perry, former US defense secretary, described the effects of such a detonation:

> The downtown area would be obliterated. Just outside the area leveled by the blast, people wounded by flying debris, fires, and intense radiation would have little chance of survival; emergency workers could not get to them because of the intense radiation, and in any event their injuries (burns and acute radiation exposure) would require sophisticated and intensive medical care to offer any chance of survival; only a fraction of them could hope for such care. Further downwind from the detonation point, a plume of radioactive debris would spread. Its shape and size would depend on wind and rain conditions, but the area over which people who did not shelter themselves or flee within hours would receive lethal doses within a day would range from five to ten square miles.[19]

> India & Pakistan war would be much more deliberate

Imagine the effect on Russia, the United States, and the rest of the world if one thousand such weapons with explosive yields of up to fifty times greater had detonated. That event nearly happened in 1995 and could even happen today. India and Pakistan, by contrast, could engage in a nuclear war deliberately, delivering scores of nuclear weapons on both sides. Indian and Pakistani weapons are currently in place and aimed toward each other. The proximity of the two states allows for almost no warning time, and experts believe that an Indo-Pak nuclear war, even if restricted entirely to the subcontinent, could trigger a nuclear winter. The smoke, soot, and debris clouds that would spread around the world would cause the death of most crops, foliage, and animals. The resultant nuclear winter could cause major famines worldwide. It would be the greatest disaster in human history: millions would die, many immediately from blast, heat, and flying debris; many later from radiation poisoning; and huge numbers still later from the nuclear winter effect.

Instability also exists in the Middle East. Today, Israel has a monopoly on nuclear weapons in the region, but that monopoly may not last. Some believe that Saudi Arabia could acquire nuclear weapons from Pakistan, as it helped finance the Pakistani program. Others have alleged that Iran might itself develop nuclear weapons or obtain them from North Korea. North Korea and Iran have cooperated closely for years on developing ballistic missiles capable of delivering nuclear weapons; however, there is now a deal in place between the P-5 + 1 (United Nations Security Council five permanent members plus Germany) and Iran that will prevent independent Iranian development of a nuclear weapons for at least fifteen years. But acquisition of nuclear weapons by Iran from North Korea or Saudi Arabia from Pakistan would likely trigger the broad-scale nuclear proliferation that President Kennedy so rightly feared. The technology, after all, is seventy years old, and the possibility of eventual nuclear weapon use under such circumstances cannot be discounted.

Every US president has spoken of the need to eliminate nuclear weapons in some form. President John F. Kennedy said before the United Nations (UN) in 1961:

> Every man, woman, and child lives under a nuclear sword of Damocles, hanging by the slenderest of threads, capable of being cut at any moment by accident or miscalculation or by madness. The weapons of war must be abolished before they abolish us.[20]

Later, President Ronald Reagan briefly tried to reach an agreement with President Gorbachev on the elimination of nuclear weapons at a meeting in Reykjavik, Iceland, in 1986. The incipient understanding quickly foundered over disagreement regarding missile defense. The following conversation demonstrates how far the two leaders were prepared to go.

> REAGAN: "Let me ask this: Do we have in mind—and I think it would be very good—that by the end of the two five-year periods all nuclear explosive devices would be eliminated, including bombs, battlefield systems, cruise missiles, submarine weapons; intermediate-range systems and so on? It would be fine with me if we eliminated all nuclear weapons."
> GORBACHEV: "We could say that, list all the weapons."[21]

President Kennedy was concerned that nuclear weapons might spread all over the world. He envisioned the possibility of a world in which there could be fifteen to twenty states with nuclear weapons integrated into national arsenals. If his fears had been realized, there could be more than twice his predicted number of nuclear weapon states in existence in the world today simply because the technology is so widely understood. This would create a situation in which every conflict could have a high probability of becoming nuclear. Furthermore, it would be extremely difficult to keep nuclear weapons out of the hands of international terrorist organizations or other nonstate actors, who could use such weapons against vulnerable populations. Luckily, such proliferation has not taken place, and President Kennedy's nightmare has not become reality—at least not yet.

The NPT halted the spread of nuclear weapons and limited their possession to China France, Russia, the United Kingdom, and the United States, the states that possessed such weapons by 1967, one year before the treaty was signed. Thus some 185 states have pledged to never acquire nuclear weapons in exchange for the sharing of peaceful nuclear technology and gradual nuclear disarmament by the states allowed by the NPT to keep nuclear weapons. Unfortunately, the NPT is weakening because the nuclear weapon states, particularly the United States, continually fail to meet their own disarmament obligations under the treaty. Moreover, the NPT's basic bargain is beginning to come apart as India, Israel, and Pakistan remain outside the treaty with nuclear weapon stockpiles. North Korea has left the NPT to build nuclear weapons. Iran perhaps has been trying to acquire nuclear weapons while remaining within the treaty, although the agreement between the P-5 + 1 and Iran should prevent any such development for many years.

The NPT is ultimately supposed to be a disarmament treaty. As Hans Blix notes, "Fulfillment by all parties of the bargain underlying the Non-Proliferation Treaty is required if the treaty is to remain viable. . . . It is a contract in which all parties commit themselves to the goal of a nuclear-free world."[22] If the NPT does not hold and further proliferation is not prevented, then nuclear weapons will never be eliminated.

Into this situation came the four statesmen in 2006: former secretary of state George Schultz, former secretary of state Henry Kissinger, former secretary of defense William Perry, and former chairman of the Senate Armed Services Committee Sam Nunn. They organized a project at the Hoover Institution on the campus of Stanford University to advocate for the abolition of nuclear weapons. They wrote joint articles published in the *Wall Street Journal* and elsewhere, organized conferences, gave congressional testimony, and made speeches to promote their objective. Advocating a nuclear weapon–free world had always been considered a nonserious quest in the corridors of power in Washington, DC. The first article written by the four statesmen and published in the *Wall Street Journal* changed this sentiment overnight. The elimination of nuclear weapons as a policy goal became and has remained a serious subject in Washington. A few excerpts from this 2007 article, titled "A World Free of Nuclear Weapons," set the tone.

> The world is now on the precipice of a new and dangerous era. . . . Unless urgent new actions are taken, the U.S. soon will be compelled to enter a new nuclear era that will be more precarious, psychologically disorienting, and economically even more costly than was Cold War deterrence.

> Rajiv Gandhi, addressing the U.N. General Assembly on June 9, 1988, [proclaimed that] nuclear war . . . will mean the extinction of four thousand million: the end of life as we know it on planet Earth.

> Ronald Reagan called for the abolishment of "all nuclear weapons," which he considered to be "totally irrational, totally inhumane, good for nothing but killing, possibly destructive of life on earth and civilization." Mikhail Gorbachev shared this vision.

> We [the four statesmen] endorse setting the goal of a world free of nuclear weapons and working energetically on the actions required to achieve that goal.[23]

This movement blossomed for a while and continues, but it has faded as of late with the return of President Putin to power in Russia and particularly the crisis over Ukraine. And the repercussions of this crisis could affect other countries, as there is also the issue of negative security assurances and the importance of nuclear weapons in nuclear security arrangements. In 1994, the Budapest Memorandum on Security Assurances, shared among the Russian Federation,

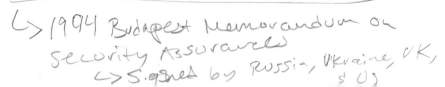

Ukraine would relinquish its nuclear arsenal

Ukraine, the United Kingdom, and the United States, was agreed on. This agreement established that Ukraine would relinquish its nuclear arsenal—at the time, it had the third-largest nuclear arsenal in the world, as a considerable part of the former Soviet arsenal was located there—and join the NPT in exchange for a commitment from Russia to respect Ukraine's existing borders, to refrain from the threat or use of force against its territorial integrity, or to enact any other types of pressure against the country.

With the invasion of Crimea, the question that arose was whether this invasion would have occurred had Ukraine kept its nuclear weapons. Beyond the fact of invasion, the link between disarmament and the abrogation of assurances to respect Ukraine's territorial integrity was also destabilizing. The United States and Russia together possess around 90 percent of the nuclear weapons that exist and, by a huge margin, possess the world's largest nuclear weapon arsenals. It has been axiomatic since the 1960s that progress in nuclear non-proliferation and nuclear disarmament critically depended on close cooperation between the United States and Russia (Soviet Union). That cooperation no longer exists. There appears to be little prospect of joint US-Russian progress on the reduction of nuclear weapons, quite possibly for many years. Does this mean that the elimination of nuclear weapons is now a lost cause? Must this essential effort be put aside?

It need not be. There is another way, one that has never received much attention: the nuclear weapon–free zone (NWFZ) process. Some argue that a nuclear weapon convention like the Chemical Weapons Convention should be pursued, under which an immediate ban on all nuclear weapons would be negotiated. But the states with nuclear weapons have made clear they would never agree to such a ban. Describing the achievements and the potential of the NWFZ movement, including the degree to which it could reasonably be considered as an alternate route toward zero nuclear weapons, is the objective of this book. Over the years, pursuant to the Strategic Arms Limitation Talks (SALT) and the Strategic Arms Reduction Talks (START), dramatic US-Russian strategic arms reductions have been achieved, but there are still perhaps 12,000 nuclear weapons left. While this progress is an improvement over the depths of the Cold War, reductions must not end here.

In 1963, following the Cuban Missile Crisis, the government of Mexico was concerned that there might be another such crisis one day, again involving Latin America. It decided to do something to reduce the risk of that possibility. Mexico had little influence over the two superpowers, the United States and the Soviet Union, during the Cold War, but it could try to keep nuclear weapons out of Latin

Good Question

US & Russia together possess 90% of nuc. weapons

Alt Route - NWFZ process

Still so many nuces left

→ Why we need alternate solution

America. There had already been some action in this regard at the United Nations. In mid-1962 even before the crisis, the Brazilian representative to the UN General Assembly proposed making Latin America an NWFZ, and during the crisis in October of that year, a draft resolution calling for such a zone was introduced by Brazil and supported by Bolivia, Chile, and Ecuador. This draft resolution was not put to a vote, but in April 1963 the president of Mexico and the presidents of four other Latin American countries (Bolivia, Brazil, Chile, and Ecuador) announced that they were prepared to sign an international agreement that would make Latin America an NWFZ. Many Latin American nations became interested in this initiative, which resulted in much discussion and negotiation among them. Many of these countries wanted to ensure that there was no possibility of ever again being caught up in a confrontation between superpowers like during the Cuban Missile Crisis. In November 1963, this declaration received the support of the UN General Assembly, with the United States voting affirmatively.

At a conference in Mexico City in November 1964, the Preparatory Commission for Denuclearization of Latin America was established with a mandate to prepare a draft treaty. The driving force behind the Mexican effort for an NWFZ treaty for Latin America was Ambassador Garcia Robles. In 1982, Ambassador Garcia Robles shared the Nobel Peace Prize with Sweden's Alva Myrdal in recognition of his efforts to create an NWFZ in Latin America. In February 1967, at a regional meeting for Latin American states at Tlatelolco—the region of Mexico City where the foreign ministry is located—the Latin American nuclear weapon–free zone treaty, also known as the Treaty of Tlatelolco, was signed. In December, the UN General Assembly endorsed the treaty by a vote of 82 to 0, with twenty-eight members abstaining. The United States voted in favor.

In designing this treaty, Garcia Robles faced many complexities. There were many differences regarding nuclear issues among Latin American states. In addition, there were two potential nuclear weapon programs in the region, in Argentina and Brazil. Robles designed a treaty structure that permitted all Latin American states to be associated with the Treaty of Tlatelolco from the start, but to become bound by it gradually. This strategy was successful. In 2002, when Cuba became the last Latin American state to become bound by the treaty, the treaty effectively was brought into force. Since that date, all of Latin America has been legally nuclear weapon–free.

The next region to pursue nuclear weapon–free status was the South Pacific. There was concern among the then ten members of the South Pacific Forum about the possible storing and dumping of nuclear waste in the South Pacific and about the French nuclear weapon test program in the region. In 1983, Australia made a treaty proposal to the forum, and in 1985 the South Pacific Forum endorsed the South Pacific nuclear weapon–free zone treaty, known as the Treaty of Rarotonga. The treaty was opened for signature on August 6, 1985. It entered into force for the land area of the South Pacific nations when Australia became the eighth country to ratify on December 11, 1986. All members of the forum are now parties to the treaty.

On April 11, 1996, forty-eight African states signed the African nuclear weapon–free zone treaty, known as the Treaty of Pelindaba. (Pelindaba was the location most associated with the South African nuclear weapon program abandoned by President de Klerk in the early 1990s.) There was also the issue of Libya, the Qaddafi regime purchased the technology for a nuclear weapon program from the rogue Pakistani proliferator A. Q. Khan around the year 2000; it was subsequently abandoned and destroyed. Early on, signatories were many, but ratifications were slow. Some years passed before the requisite twenty-eight parties ratified the treaty, allowing it to enter into force. The Treaty of Pelindaba became effective in August 2009 and currently has fifty-three signatories and thirty-six ratifications. Steady progress is finally being made toward a nuclear-free African continent. The entry into force of Pelindaba in conjunction with the Tlatelolco and Rarotonga treaties potentially places virtually the entire Southern Hemisphere off limits to nuclear weapons. Also noteworthy, Libya has ratified the Treaty of Pelindaba and is now a party.

The Treaty of Bangkok, agreed among the ten Association of Southeast Asian Nations (ASEAN) members established Southeast Asia as an NWFZ on December 15, 1995, with the treaty entering into force in March 1997, when Thailand became the seventh nation to ratify. Today the treaty has been ratified by all ten of the ASEAN states, but because of a long-running dispute over its application to maritime areas, the protocol to the treaty designed specifically for the nuclear weapon states of the NPT has not been signed by any of those nations.

Finally, after many years of discussion, the central Asian nuclear weapon–free zone, or Treaty of Semipalatinsk, was agreed upon in 2005 and signed on September 8, 2006, in Semipalatinsk, Kazakhstan (the location of the former Soviet test site). It entered into force on February 20, 2009, when the fifth of the five central Asian states deposited its instrument of ratification.

All these treaties have a protocol or protocols attached to the treaties for the NPT nuclear weapon states to sign and abide by. These protocols provide that the nuclear weapon states are obligated to respect the zone established by the treaty

Significance of these NWFZ s.

and to never use or threaten to use nuclear weapons against parties to the treaty. In some cases, as for Rarotonga and Pelindaba, a pledge not to test nuclear weapons in the zone is also included.

There is a separate protocol in the Pelindaba, Rarotonga, and Tlatelolco treaties for outside parties that have territory in the zone to place those territories under the nuclear-free status of the treaty zone. All the nuclear weapon states as well as all other relevant outside powers have become party to the appropriate protocols of the Tlatelolco treaty. Thus, for example, Puerto Rico and the Virgin Islands are legally nuclear weapon–free under the Treaty of Tlatelolco. The result is not so complete with the other free-zone treaties, but the NWFZ movement is approaching the achievement of a nuclear weapon–free Southern Hemisphere, along with substantial parts of the Northern Hemisphere. Additionally, some 111 countries have now adhered to one of the NWFZ treaties.

Further effort should be applied to this process, particularly to obtain US Senate approval for the protocols to the Rarotonga, Pelindaba, and Semipalatinsk treaties, which the United States signed in 1995, 1997, and 2014, respectively. Because the protocols are in effect mini treaties (attached to a larger treaty), for the United States to be obligated thereunder, Senate advice and consent to ratification must be obtained. In the cases of Rarotonga and Pelindaba, the United States is the principal holdout. President Obama finally sent the protocols to Rarotonga and Pelindaba to the Senate in 2011 and to Semipalatinsk in 2014.

The next steps in the free-zone process will likely take many years to pursue, but they may be possible and, importantly for this analysis, do not depend significantly on Russia. The creation of NWFZ treaties in the Middle East, northeast Asia, and South Asia would be the next logical step toward fulfilling the mandate of the NPT and eliminating nuclear weapons. These treaties will be far from easy to negotiate or implement, as each region is plagued with its own uniquely complex political and legal challenges. Yet such achievements are not impossible. Taking northeast Asia as an example, the main challenge facing the establishment of an NWFZ in the region would be North Korea, which unilaterally withdrew from the NPT in 2003 and has since developed an active nuclear weapon program with confirmed nuclear tests in 2006, 2009, 2013, and two in 2016. But history has demonstrated that over time the Korean problem can at least be addressed; President Clinton had almost solved it shortly before he left office. The agreed framework was still functioning, cutting off North Korean access to the plutonium route to nuclear weapons. North Korea had done little with the centrifuge equipment acquired from A. Q. Khan, the Pakistani proliferator of

Next steps in NWFZ

What needs to for happen NE Asia

the technology of mass destruction, and thus was not pursuing a uranium bomb. They had accepted in principle a comprehensive agreement on missiles and had suggested they might be prepared to conclude a Korean War peace treaty and to establish normal diplomatic relations with the United States. The George W. Bush administration threw the agreement aside on the grounds it was something President Clinton had done. Japan and South Korea are already NPT members, so the challenge lies in persuading North Korea—a daunting task, but with some successful precedent.

The Middle East presents similar challenges. There have been many proposals and attempts to achieve an NWFZ in the region, but its resolution will likely depend on the enormously complex and frustrating Middle East peace process. The idea of establishing an NWFZ in the region was first proposed by Iran in 1974. In 1990, under Hosni Mubarak's leadership, Egypt broadened the concept to include other weapons of mass destruction, including chemical and biological, as part of a weapons-of-mass-destruction-free zone (WMDFZ). Despite calls by many nations in the region to create either a WMDFZ or an NWFZ, disagreements regarding the terms, duration, and implementation have prevented progress. The 1995 NPT Review and Extension Conference adopted a resolution on the Middle East asking that states take practical steps toward the creation of a WMDFZ in the Middle East. This resolution was reaffirmed again at the 2000 NPT Review Conference, the 2003 International Atomic Energy Agency (IAEA) General Conference, the 2006 WMD Commission Report, and the 2010 NPT Review Conference. NPT parties attempted to respond to the 1995 resolution at the 2010 NPT Review Conference. They agreed to hold a nonnegotiating, as opposed to a diplomatic, conference on a WMDFZ for the Middle East in 2012 involving all Middle East states. The meeting did not occur, however, and this outcome largely caused the subsequent failure of the 2015 NPT Review Conference. Although Israel is not a NPT member, the United States seemed to imply at the 2010 Review and Extension Conference that Israel would attend if the conference were made a nonnegotiating conference. But in the end Israel blocked this effort by refusing to come. Iran announced it would come shortly after Israel's refusal.

Although several difficulties remain, which will be described at length in chapter 9, this resolution might over time help to persuade the Middle East states to consider a process for an NWFZ treaty. A favorable outcome in the region will hopefully have little to do with the US-Russian dynamic and more to do with the geopolitical atmosphere in the region and cooperation among the Middle Eastern nations.

→ What needs to happen for the ME

The resolution of the nuclear impasse in South Asia, closely linked in one way or another to the nuclear program in China, may have to await the time when the five NPT nuclear weapon states are prepared to seriously consider nuclear disarmament. But Pakistan follows India to a considerable degree on this issue, and India waited until 1998 to do tests supporting weaponization, more than thirty years after China. So, someday a South Asian NWFZ might be conceivable, as India does not reflexively follow China.

Regardless of the possible roadblocks, creating a world where there are additional significant nuclear weapon–free geographic locations could bring the world closer to the prospect of zero nuclear weapons worldwide. This could be the effect even if the nuclear weapon competition in South Asia continued. These treaties and the creation of NWFZs can be accomplished outside of the influence of the US-Russian relationship, which, while integral to the disarmament process is of limited importance when creating NWFZs across other sovereign state areas. Additionally, these types of arrangements for northeast Asia, the Middle East, and South Asia would have to be negotiated on the road to zero even if close US-Russian cooperation in nuclear non-proliferation and disarmament had continued.

This book analyzes the five NWFZ regimes that exist, discusses in depth the prospect and eventual way forward in northeast Asia; addresses the concept of how a nuclear weapon–free Middle East might be achieved; and examines the issue in the South Asia context. As noted, there was an agreement at the 2010 NPT Review and Extension Conference to hold a nonnegotiating conference on a WMDFZ among all Middle East states, including Israel and Iran, in 2012. It was the major issue in 2015 to permit agreement on a final document of the conference. Consistent with international practice in this and other areas, final documents of NPT review conferences, to be considered official, must be adopted by unanimous consent, in other words, without objection. But agreement on this specific issue was not achieved in 2015, as it was in 2010, and the conference failed. How a Middle East NWFZ can be established and what factors are necessary for success will be addressed at length herein. Also examined in depth are the South Asia nuclear situation and the likelihood of progress in the region, even with an existing arsenal in China. Finally, there will be a serious look at how success with the free-zone movement might one day be brought to bear on pushing the nuclear arsenals of the five NPT nuclear weapon states toward zero. Given the situation the world community faces today, this might be the best and most effective way to keep the goal of a nuclear weapon–free world alive in the current political atmosphere.

Chapter 2
The Nuclear Non-Proliferation Treaty and Nuclear Weapon–Free Zones; Russia and Disarmament

There is an apocryphal story that has been around for years attributed to Carl Sagan, the great scientist, astrophysicist, and philosopher. The story goes that, at one of his presentations, an audience member asked why we have not heard from any other worlds when Sagan had claimed that many other worlds likely exist in the universe. Sagan's response was that the more primitive civilizations don't know how to reach us, and those sufficiently advanced to make contact have probably already destroyed themselves. The world community began to fear such an outcome after the US military's use of atomic weapons against Japan, and the subsequent vast nuclear arms race between the United States and the Soviet Union. Furthermore, the proliferation of nuclear weapons to nation-states beyond the United States did not stop after the first Soviet test in 1949. The United Kingdom followed suit in 1952 and France in 1960. In the early years, there was some lip service paid to preventing proliferation, but after the failure of the Baruch Plan in 1946, there was little real sentiment in the world community for stopping the apparently inexorable spread of nuclear weapon technology. The Baruch Plan was the United States' attempt immediately after World War II to prevent nuclear weapons from spreading. Under the proposal, nuclear matters would be the province of the United Nations (UN), not individual nations, but the United States would retain its technological capability. The Soviet Union would have none of it. Nuclear weapons came to be regarded by many as simply another development in weapon technology. Sweden had a potential nuclear weapon program beginning not long after World War II. Twice by national referendum, the Swiss public voted to keep the option open for Switzerland to acquire nuclear weapons.

By 1960, the United States and the Soviet Union were building huge numbers of nuclear weapons and placing them on hair-trigger alert. They also built long-range ballistic missiles capable of delivering nuclear weapons on target in thirty minutes or less. After the advent of the fourth state with nuclear weapons, France, it appeared that nuclear weapons might simply sweep the world. Thus sentiment began to change.

In 1961, Ireland introduced a resolution into the UN General Assembly (UNGA) calling on all nations to negotiate and conclude an international agreement prohibiting the transfer or acquisition of nuclear weapons.[1] More specifically, the Irish Resolution called for an international agreement whereby "the nuclear States would undertake to refrain from relinquishing control of nuclear weapons and from transmitting the information necessary for their manufacture to States not possessing such weapons, and . . . States not possessing nuclear weapons would undertake not to manufacture or otherwise acquire control of such weapons."[2]

The United States and the Soviet Union introduced non-proliferation proposals at the Eighteen-Nation Committee on Disarmament in Geneva (ENCD, later the Conference of the Committee on Disarmament, or CCD, and for many years now the Conference on Disarmament, or CD). But despite unanimous General Assembly support for the Irish resolution, nothing happened for several years. At the twentieth session of the UNGA in 1965, the subject was pursued again. Another resolution was introduced, this time by Sweden and India, and it was adopted as well. More specific than the Irish resolution, it proposed an international treaty to halt the proliferation of nuclear weapons based on five principles:

1. The treaty should be void of loopholes that might permit nuclear or non-nuclear powers to proliferate, directly or indirectly, nuclear weapons in any form.

2. The treaty should embody an acceptable balance of mutual responsibilities and obligations of the nuclear and non-nuclear powers.

3. The treaty should be a step toward the achievement of general and complete disarmament, more particularly nuclear disarmament.

4. There should be acceptable and workable provisions to ensure the effectiveness of the treaty.

5. Nothing in the treaty should adversely affect the right of any group of states to conclude regional treaties in order to ensure the total absence of nuclear weapons in their territories.[3]

In August 1965, the United States submitted a draft non-proliferation treaty to the ENCD. The Soviets followed suit shortly thereafter in the UNGA in September. The United States tabled amendments to its draft in the ENCD in March 1966. This was followed by private talks on the subject between the United States and the Soviet Union in the fall of 1966. An agreement was reached at the end of the year on the basic nontransfer and nonacquisition provisions of a draft treaty on nuclear non-proliferation and on several other related provisions.

Considerable disagreement existed between the United States and the Soviet Union on the issue of nuclear weapons and US alliance arrangements with NATO, but both sides recognized the importance of an agreement on non-proliferation. Pressure from non-nuclear states to do something continued to grow as well. This was evident at the 1964 African Summit Conference and at the Cairo Conference of Nonaligned Countries the same year. A series of resolutions passed the UNGA that urged priority attention to non-proliferation. A resolution unanimously passed the US Senate in May 1966 supporting continued efforts to negotiate a non-proliferation agreement.

The United States undertook a long and difficult series of consultations with its NATO allies where questions were asked about the draft treaty. The United States gave its interpretation on various issues in response, particularly asserting that the draft treaty covered nuclear weapons, not delivery vehicles; that it would not prohibit NATO consultation and planning on nuclear defense; that it would not prohibit the deployment of US nuclear weapons on the territory of NATO non–nuclear weapon states with their consent; and that it would not bar succession of a new federated European state to the nuclear status of one of its members. The questions and answers were made available to the Soviet Union, which entered no objections.

On August 24, 1967, the United States and the Soviet Union submitted separate, identical texts of a draft treaty on nuclear non-proliferation to the ENCD. The principal articles in this draft text covered nontransfer and nonacquisition of nuclear weapons by the nuclear weapon states (NWS) defined in both the draft and final treaty as states that had manufactured and exploded a nuclear weapon or other nuclear explosive device prior to January 1, 1967, in effect China, France, the Soviet Union, the United Kingdom, and the United States, and by the non–nuclear weapon states (NNWS), respectively. There was also an article on safeguards and other less important provisions, as well as a final paragraph in the preamble that was essentially the same as that of principle (e) of the Swedish-Indian UNGA Resolution of 1965. The idea of an article in the emerging NPT on the right of states to establish nuclear weapon–free zones originated at the same time. Both ideas came from Mexico. By 1967, this idea of NWFZs became more pressing; on February 14, 1967, the Treaty of Tlatelolco was opened for signature. This was the reason that the two co-chairmen of the NPT negotiations, the United States and the Soviet Union, had included a reference to NWFZs in the preamble of the identical draft NPT texts. According to Ambassador Mohamed Shaker in his treatise, however, Mexico promptly insisted that this provision be transferred to the body of the treaty, and this was done in the identical treaty drafts of January 18, 1968.[4]

Between August 24, 1967, and January 18, 1968, intensive negotiations took place between the co-chairmen and the non–nuclear weapon states that were members of the ENCD. The NNWS insisted on the application of principle (b), balanced obligations, from the 1965 resolution as well as principle (c), disarmament, and therefore held to the position that their renunciation of nuclear weapons must be accompanied by a commitment from the nuclear states to reduce and eventually eliminate their nuclear arsenals and to make progress on comprehensive disarmament measures. This commitment meant at a minimum:

1. the negotiation of a comprehensive test-ban treaty—the most important objective— the central quid for the quo of giving up the most powerful weapon ever created;

2. deep reductions in existing nuclear arsenals;

3. legally binding security assurances; and

4. additional NWFZs and a fissile material cut-off treaty (FMCT).

The NNWS lobbied the co-chairmen to include these interim goals toward nuclear disarmament, which was itself understood as a far-off-in-the-future objective, in the text of the NPT. Their objective was not realized; they succeeded only in obtaining a reference in the preamble to a comprehensive test-ban treaty. In the end, the NPT was constructed on a basic bargain whereby the NPT non–nuclear weapon state parties agreed to foreswear nuclear weapons in exchange for a pledge from the NPT nuclear weapon state parties to eventually eliminate their nuclear arsenals, as well as unfettered access to the peaceful use of nuclear energy (a sine qua non for many states, such as Belgium, Germany, Spain, and Switzerland). The latter obligations on peaceful nuclear energy are found in Article IV of the treaty and the disarmament obligations in Article VI. The preservation of the right to negotiate NWFZs eventually became Article VII.

So, Article VI includes the idea that one of the interim steps—made clear in the negotiating record—is the pursuit of more nuclear weapon–free zones (beyond Tlatelolco), and Article VII explicitly preserved the right of NPT parties to establish such zonal arrangements.

In 1968, the NPT was given a term of only twenty-five years by the negotiating parties even though most multilateral arms control treaties have an unlimited duration. This was because three of the negotiating states—Germany, Italy, and Sweden—were uncertain whether the agreed safeguards would put their nuclear industries at a competitive disadvantage; that the nuclear weapon states would in fact deliver on their side of the balanced obligations, principally the disarmament obligations; and that the lack of guarantees or security assurances would ensure that the renunciation of nuclear weapons would place them at a permanent military disadvantage. A clause was added that twenty-five years after entry into force, the state parties could meet in a conference and by a majority vote and on a one-time basis, without reference to national legislatures, extend the NPT for an additional fixed period or periods or indefinitely. In persuading the then 178 NPT parties at the 1995 NPT Review and Extension Conference, to extend the NPT indefinitely, the NPT nuclear weapon states made the same pledges they made in 1968, even though during the first twenty-five years little progress had been made in realizing those pledges. And some of them were made a little sharper (and of course they were now a formal NPT-agreed document); for example, a comprehensive test-ban treaty was to be negotiated in one year.

In addition, the five NPT nuclear weapon states joined a UN Security Council resolution agreeing to never use nuclear weapons against any NPT non-nuclear state party in good standing. But this pledge by each nuclear weapon state was made in the form of a national statement attached to the Security Council resolution and as such was not legally binding. It was only a policy statement. In 1995, the NPT document "Principles and Objectives for Nuclear Non-Proliferation and Disarmament"—part of the political price for NPT indefinite extension and adopted by the NPT parties to accompany the resolution on indefinite NPT extension—urged steps to assure the non-nuclear states against the use or threat of nuclear weapons. The document states: "These steps could take the form of an internationally legally binding instrument."[5]

The document further called for the establishment of nuclear weapon–free zones and affirmed that such arrangements strengthen "global and regional peace and security." It goes on to say that "the development of nuclear-weapon-free zones, especially in regions of tension, such as in the Middle East . . . should be encouraged as a matter of priority." The document concludes with a call for "the cooperation of all the nuclear weapon states and their respect and support for the relevant protocols [to nuclear weapon–free zone treaties]" and states that such support "is necessary for the maximum effectiveness of such nuclear-weapon-free zones and the relevant protocols."[6]

The United States is a party to the two protocols to the Treaty of Tlatelolco, which will be discussed later in this book. As previously stated, the United States has signed the relevant protocols to three other NWFZ treaties in 1995, 1996, and 2014, which will also be discussed later. The first two were submitted to the Senate for advice and consent to ratification in 2010, and the third shortly after it was signed in 2014. No Senate action has been taken on any of the three to permit the United States to become a party. There is a fifth (including Tlatelolco) NWFZ treaty whose protocol none of the NPT nuclear weapon states have signed because it contains provisions that some consider contrary to the international right of freedom of the seas. As a matter of policy, the United States will only support such treaties by becoming a party to the relevant protocol or protocols if: the transit of nuclear weapons through the zone established by the treaty is unaffected, individual state parties are free to permit or deny port calls by US warships (regardless of their weapons), and there is no infringement upon the international law of the sea. Among the guidelines established by the United Nations for these treaties are requirements that: they establish an effective verification system, provide for all states parties to accept International Atomic Energy Agency (IAEA) safeguards, be of indefinite duration, and provide for the NPT nuclear weapon states to agree to legally binding protocols that prohibit the use of nuclear weapons against an NWFZ treaty state party.

Upon the initiative of Finland, the UN General Assembly in 1974 commissioned a comprehensive study of NWFZs. The study was conducted and completed by a group of experts at the CCD in 1975. The study conclusions set forth multiple criteria:

- Obligations related to the establishment of a nuclear weapon–free zone may be assumed not only by groups of states, including entire continents or large geographical regions, but also by smaller groups of states and even individual countries.

- Zonal arrangements must ensure the complete absence for the present and future nuclear weapons in the region covered by the treaty.

- The initiative for the zonal treaty must come from within the region concerned.

- If the zone is intended to embrace a region, the participation of all militarily significant states, and preferably all states, would be important.

- The zonal treaty must have an effective system of verification (the experts were of the view that the viability of the nuclear weapon–free zone will largely depend on this).

- The treaty established must be of unlimited duration.

"Most of the experts [involved in the study] also agreed that the zone members should not exercise control over nuclear weapons outside the zone" and "that any arrangements for the establishment of such a zone must provide for appropriate guarantees by nuclear weapon States not to use or threaten to use nuclear weapons against zone members."[7] Historically, an NPT negative security assurance was to be a legally binding commitment against the use of nuclear weapons by an NPT nuclear weapon state party against an NPT non–nuclear weapon state party, to match the legally binding foreswearing of the possession of nuclear weapons by all NPT non–nuclear weapon state parties. NWFZ treaties from the beginning have added an additional legal obligation for the nuclear parties to the NPT not to threaten to use nuclear weapons against any zonal treaty state party.

The UNGA considered this expert study at its thirtieth session in 1975 and commended it to the attention of all governments. Ambassador Shaker offered these details:

Upon the initiative of Mexico, the General Assembly defined the concept of a nuclear-weapon-free zone as follows:

"'A nuclear-weapon-free zone' shall, as a general rule, be deemed to be any zone, recognized as such by the United Nations General Assembly, which any group of States, in the free exercise of their sovereignty, has established by virtue of a treaty or convention whereby:

(a) The statute of the total absence of nuclear weapons to which the zone shall be subject, including the procedure for the delineation of the zone, is defined;

(b) An international system of verification and control is established to guarantee compliance with the obligations deriving from that statute."

The General Assembly also addressed the obligations of NPT nuclear weapon States toward nuclear weapon-free-zone treaties recognized by the UNGA. In every such case, NPT nuclear weapon states should undertake, in an international legally binding instrument, the following:

"(a) To respect in all its parts the statute of total absence of nuclear weapons defined in the treaty or convention, which serves as the constitutive instrument of the zone;

(b) To refrain from contributing in any way to the performance in the territories forming part of the zone of acts which involve a violation of the aforesaid treaty or convention;

(c) To refrain from using or threatening to use nuclear weapons against a State included in the zone."[8]

Summing up the issue of nuclear weapon–free zones in his monumental treatise on the NPT, Shaker concludes that the inclusion of a separate article in the NPT codifying the right to establish nuclear weapon–free zones—as recommended by the 1965 UNGA Resolution—was the right thing to do.

> The NPT itself needs to be bolstered by further arms control measures not only on the part of nuclear weapon States but also on the part of non-nuclear weapon States. . . . A nuclear-weapon-free zone as a feasible objective would be the most suitable remedy for those States not expected to adhere to the NPT because of its discriminatory nature.[9]

This reference relates to the anticipated long-term possession of nuclear weapons by five states—the five permanent members of the UN Security Council—and no one else. In justifying its refusal to join the NPT, India has long denounced the NPT as establishing a "nuclear apartheid."

In 1998, in a *Foreign Affairs* article titled "Against Nuclear Apartheid," India's then senior advisor to the prime minister on defense and foreign affairs, Jaswant Singh, explained India's opposition to the NPT and the CTBT:

> While the end of the Cold War transformed the political landscape of Europe, it did little to ameliorate India's security concerns. The rise of China and continued strains with Pakistan made the 1980s and 1990s a greatly troubling period for India. At a global level, the nuclear weapons states showed no signs of moving decisively toward a world free of atomic dangers. Instead, the Nuclear Non-proliferation Treaty (NPT) was extended indefinitely and unconditionally in 1995, perpetuating the existence of nuclear weapons in the hands of five countries busily modernizing their nuclear arsenals. In 1996 after they had conducted over 2,000 tests, a Comprehensive Test Ban Treaty (CTBT) was

opened for signature, following two and a half years of negotiations in which India participated actively. This treaty, also, was neither comprehensive nor related to disarmament but rather devoted to ratifying the nuclear status quo. India's options had narrowed critically.

India had to ensure that the nuclear option, developed and safeguarded over decades, was not ended by self-imposed restraint. Such a loss would place the country at risk. Faced with a difficult decision, New Delhi realized that its lone touchstone remained national security. The nuclear tests it conducted on May 11 and 13, 1998, were by then not only inevitable but a continuation of policies from almost the earliest years of independence. India's nuclear policy remains firmly committed to a basic tenet: that the country's national security in a world of nuclear proliferation lies either in global disarmament or exercise of the principle of equal and legitimate security for all.[10]

Ambassador Shaker expressed the hope that the nuclear weapon–free zone process offers the opportunity to bring into the nuclear disarmament process states that did not join the NPT because of its discriminatory nature, such as India. It is true that this process treats all parties as equal, unlike the NPT, but only those in the region. That would not be enough for India. India's present polices on this issue are global. India sees itself as a great power and therefore retains the right to be a nuclear weapon state, like the five permanent members of the Security Council. Since the earliest of days in the nuclear era, India has thought about acquiring nuclear weapons. There are no indications that India is interested in nuclear disarmament, not so long as China has weapons. But we can hope that, over time, this may change as the nuclear weapon–free zone process moves forward. India has nuclear weapons that could arguably counter those of China, but those of Pakistan counter those of India. Furthermore, Pakistan has a significant Taliban insurgency that could come to power someday. Even if the Taliban's coming to power is unlikely, it is a possibility—a possibility that creates real concerns. If that were to happen, India would be in a truly desperate situation given Pakistan's sophisticated and growing nuclear arsenal. Thus nuclear weapons have made India less, not more, secure.

It is possible that, sometime in the future, India may change. India's nuclearization is different from that of other states. India's first nuclear weapon test was in 1974. But India did not take steps toward weaponization (building a stockpile of weapons) until the late 1980s and did not truly build a stockpile until after the 1998 test series. For fifteen years, India lived in a situation where China had several hundred nuclear weapons, but India did not build them.

So, "if the NPT can be matched by the establishment of denuclearized zones all over the globe, the proliferation of nuclear weapons would then cease to be a cause of concern."[11] The great Mexican diplomat—and father of the Treaty of Tlatelolco—Alfonso Garcia Robles had the following to say about all this:

> We should attempt to achieve a gradual broadening of the zones of the world from which nuclear weapons are prohibited to a point where the territories of Powers, which possess those terrible tools of mass destruction, will become "something like contaminated islets subjected to quarantine."[12]

Ambassador Garcia Robles has identified the central point in this effort. Without the NPT nuclear weapon states, through the NWFZ process, the world community can move toward zero nuclear weapons. If the nuclear weapon states are involved at least to some degree, even if not all of them participate, the world community can come even closer to the goal of the worldwide elimination of nuclear weapons. Since the beginning of the disarmament effort, the idea was to limit, control, and ultimately reduce and eliminate nuclear weapons. The United States and the Soviet Union (Russia) would reduce to relatively low levels, and then the others would join the process. This idea evolved because the United States and the Soviet Union were the first nuclear weapon states and throughout the Cold War possessed well over 95 percent of the world stockpile of nuclear weapons. Even today, with perhaps a 75 percent reduction in nuclear weapons from its Cold War high for Russia and a nearly 85 percent reduction for the United States, the two countries together possess over 90 percent of the nuclear weapons in the world.

To be more specific, the strategy for disarmament has always been to first reduce the US and Russian nuclear weapon arsenals to something in the range of one thousand total weapons and then bring in the other three NPT-recognized nuclear weapon states—China, France, and the United Kingdom—for a five-sided negotiation to continue to reduce to low levels. At this point, account would have to be taken of the four outliers—India, Israel, North Korea, and Pakistan—who together possess between three and four hundred nuclear weapons. The need to take account of Iran is not yet certain. A 2009 speech by President Barack Obama clearly expressed this traditional view:

> To reduce our weapons and stockpiles, we will negotiate a new Strategic Arms Reduction Treaty with the Russians this year. President Medvedev and I began this process in London and will seek a new agreement by the end of this year that is legally

binding and sufficiently bold. And this will set the stage for further cuts, and we will seek to include all nuclear weapons states in this endeavor.[13]

The bilateral US-Soviet negotiations to control nuclear weapons—initially, and for a long time thereafter, limited to strategic or intercontinental weapons only—began as a negotiation to stabilize relations between the world's two superpowers—that is, to establish stability based on parity—to reduce the risk of nuclear war, which could devastate civilization.

In the words of John Newhouse, the author of *Cold Dawn*, one of the first great books on the US-Soviet nuclear disarmament process,

> Still, there was a kind of agreed-upon rationale for SALT. . . . The talks were launched, not from a common impulse to reduce armaments, but from a mutual need to solemnize the parity principle—or, put differently, to establish an acceptance by each side of the other's ability to inflict unacceptable retribution in response to a nuclear attack. . . . Thus, each *may* recognize that an unlimited arms race would undermine deterrence—and, hence, stability—conceivably by allowing one side or the other to acquire a margin of superiority that in turn would create risks of a first strike. But additionally, a failure to set limits could mean sustaining indefinitely the push for more and better nuclear arms, with costs driven constantly upward—possibly at the expense of other priorities. Here, too, stability . . . could be degraded.[14]

Thus, the US-Soviet/US-Russia strategic arms negotiations began as an attempt to halt the out-of-control and dangerous nuclear arms race between the United States and the Soviet Union. The Strategic Arms Limitation Talks (SALT) process in its first phrase (SALT I) established stability based on parity and mutual deterrence; each superpower was, in effect, the hostage of the other. Each country possessed a long-range nuclear weapon arsenal that could survive a first strike and still devastate the other side. This concept was referred to as mutually assured destruction and was memorialized in the Anti-Ballistic Missile Treaty, which kept strategic defenses at a low, almost nonexistent, level. No benefit could thereby be gained by a first strike, because the country being attacked could still devastate the attacker. In this way, stability was established and the nuclear peace kept.

Then, beginning with the second phase of the SALT Process, SALT II, this bilateral process developed into a means by which, beyond the establishment of an uneasy equilibrium that underlay stability, the nuclear stockpiles of the two Cold War superpowers and, then, the United States and Russia could be safely reduced. It strengthened stability and peace and the carrying out of NPT Article VI obligations of the two states. There were many agreements in this process:

SALT II, START, INF, and other less central agreements. All always involved a negotiation between the United States and Russia. Then, beginning in 2006 with the Schultz, Perry, Kissinger, and Nunn effort, hope emerged that a process could be established, first involving only the United States and Russia until their nuclear weapon stockpiles could be brought down as said to around the one thousand weapons level, and then involving the other nuclear states. This could evolve over time into a serious attempt to achieve the worldwide elimination of nuclear weapons, thereby removing this scourge of humankind from our planet. President Obama's 2009 speech also echoed this hope:

> So today, I state clearly and with conviction America's commitment to seek the peace and security of a world without nuclear weapons. I'm not naïve. This goal will not be reached quickly—perhaps not in my lifetime. It will take patience and persistence. But now we, too, must ignore the voices that tell us that the world cannot change. We have to insist, "Yes, we can."[15]

But at least for now, that process cannot be the remedy. The 2010 US-Russia New Start Treaty appears to be the last in this long series, principally because the US-Russia relationship no longer supports such negotiations. This has increasingly become the case since the return of Vladimir Putin to the Russian presidency in 2012. Either the goal of eliminating nuclear weapons must be abandoned, or another path that does not require Russian cooperation must be found.

President Putin of Russia famously said in an April 2005 address to Russia's senior politicians and its parliament:

> Above all, we should acknowledge that the collapse of the Soviet Union was a major geopolitical catastrophe of the century. As for the Russian nation, it became a genuine drama. Tens of millions of our co-citizens and co-patriots found themselves outside Russian territory. Moreover, the epidemic of disintegration infected Russia itself.[16]

During the Russian Empire, there were no formal borders between a "Russian Republic" and a "Ukrainian Republic" or any other republic; such borders did not exist until Bolshevik times. Thus people who think like President Putin may give these borders limited legitimacy; they at least say they think in terms of the "Russian nation," which includes those areas contiguous to Russia today where significant Russian populations live.

It may be that these Russian-speaking populations in many cases would not wish to return to President Putin's "Motherland," not because the Motherland is Russian, but because of President Putin's internal policies. Be that as it may, so long as Putin pursues a policy broadly directed toward reuniting these "co-citizens" and "co-patriots" with Russia, and that seems to be his policy now regardless of its degree of merit, it is certain to place Russia squarely on a collision course with the United States and NATO. In such an atmosphere, US-Russian cooperation on nuclear arms control and disarmament is simply not possible. Rather, rearmament seems to be the objective. In President Putin's words, "A large scale program of rearming the Army and Navy is being successfully implemented, which includes an active development of the aerospace and nuclear forces. This is the guarantee of global parity."[17] And as the crisis in Ukraine continues to unfold, President Putin's popularity seems only to increase, despite international economic sanctions that are greatly damaging the Russian economy. Polls published at the end of November 2014 "showed the approval rating for Russia's leader at 85 percent, just down on the last month's 88 percent, which equaled the record high of 2008."[18]

What preceded Putin's high poll numbers?

In his first two terms in office, from 2000 to 2008, Vladimir Putin made his priority the reestablishment of a strong state. He disempowered disloyal regional governors, crushed the oligarchs who did not heed his insistence that they stay out of politics, and obliterated the leadership of the separatist uprising in Chechnya. He took complete control of the main television channels and neutered any opposing political parties. He established postmodern state symbols and an anthem that combined features of the imperial and communist past.[19]

Yet he did not exhibit such an anti-American posture, as he does now. As David Remnick wrote for the *New Yorker*:

Nor was Putin aggressively anti-American in his first years in power. He craved membership in the world economy and its institutions. . . . He even talked about Russia joining NATO. "Russia is part of the European culture," he told the BBC, in 2000. "And I cannot imagine my own country in isolation from Europe and what we often call the civilized world. So it is hard for me to visualize NATO as an enemy."[20]

Remnick further asserts, however, that such spirit of amity and relative cooperation was short lived. In 2009, after Putin had stepped aside from the presidency in favor of President Medvedev and became prime minister, he hosted President Obama along with his then advisor on Russia, Michael McFaul, soon to become the US ambassador in Moscow. Putin subjected Obama to a long lecture on American deceptions. He insisted that the United States should recognize former Soviet republics—especially Ukraine—as being within Russia's sphere of influence. He said that the United States regarded Russia as weak and believed it could push Russia around, doing things like bombing Belgrade and Kosovo. He also demonstrated concern about NATO's expansion to the east, which since 2004 included seven additional countries: Bulgaria, Romania, Slovakia, Slovenia, and the three Baltic states. Putin took such expansion as not only a geopolitical threat but also a violation of NATO's commitment not to expand to the east, allegedly made to Gorbachev in exchange for his acquiescence to the reunification of Germany. Later in 2004 came the Orange Revolution in Ukraine, which "Putin also saw as a Western project and a foreshadowing of an assault on him."[21] A similar revolution, known as the Rose Revolution, had taken place a short time earlier (in November 2003) in Georgia. Putin saw this in the same light as the revolution in Ukraine, as the brief war in Georgia in August 2008 bears witness.

The current conflict over Ukraine, like the Orange Revolution, which began with the removal of the pro-Russian president of Ukraine, in Putin's view, may be considered another attempt to draw Ukraine into the Western sphere of influence, with the objective of NATO membership, which some American politicians have advocated for years. Putin has long made it clear that this would cross a red line for him.

As Remnick concludes, President Putin has increasingly identified himself with the destiny of Russia. He began to develop the concept of Russia as the center of an anti-Western, socially conservative, bulwark against a menacing America. "This is a conservative position," he admits, but one that does not prevent "movement forward and upward but [rather] prevents movement backward and downward, into chaotic darkness and a return to a primitive state."[22] Ambassador McFaul, some months after he assumed his post in 2013, tried to arrange a summit in Moscow between Obama and Putin to engage on the issues including "arms control and missile defense," but this effort came to nothing.

> Nearly twenty-five years after the fall of the empire, Putin has unleashed an ideology of "*ressentiment*." It has been chorused by those who, in 1991 despaired not of the loss of Communist ideology, but of imperial greatness, and who, ever since, have lived with what Russians so often refer to as the "phantom-limb syndrome:" the pain of missing Central Asia, the Caucasus, the Baltic states; the pain of diminishment. They want revenge for their humiliation.[23]

As McFaul explains, the US-Russia relationship is "at its lowest point since the post-Soviet period began in 1991." McFaul left his position in Moscow after the

Sochi Olympics and returned to Stanford. Two years later, McFaul said that the Malaysia Airlines disaster during the war in Ukraine gave Putin a way out—he could say that the separatists had gone too far and we must deescalate and negotiate. But McFaul assigned a low probability to such an outcome. "More likely is that he [Putin] will not change his course, the U.S. will then increase sanctions, and the war will continue. Neither scenario, however, offers a way to reverse this negative trajectory in U.S.-Russia relations. I really don't see a serious opening until after Putin retires, and I have no idea when that will be."[24]

The extreme negativity surrounding the US-Russia relationship is not limited to the top of the Russian government; it is pervasive throughout Russian society:

> Anger toward the United States is at its worst since opinion polls began tracking it. From ordinary street vendors all the way up to the Kremlin, a wave of anti-U.S. bile has swept the country, surpassing any since the Stalin era, observers say. More than 80 percent of Russians now hold negative views of the United States according to the Levada Center [one of Russia's few independent sources for data about public opinion].[25]

The negative attitude toward the European Union is nearly as high, and only 40 percent of Russians now believe that Russia should try to improve its relationship with the West.[26]

Their list of grievances is long. The country essentially believes it was betrayed by the West. Russians did everything they could—according to this view—to do what the West wanted to be reaccepted as part of Europe. The response was the expansion of NATO to their borders after, again according to this view, Russia was promised that there would be no further expansion of NATO if Russia would agree that East Germany could merge with West Germany and become part of NATO. It seems that this expansion is not intended to stop there, with Western politicians calling for Ukraine and Georgia—constituent parts of the Soviet Union and the Russian Empire before it—to be brought into NATO. In the opinion of Evgeny Tarlo, a member of Russia's upper house of parliament, instead of accepting a Russia that attempted to completely reorient itself toward the West after the Cold War, "the West has been trying to destroy Russia."[27]

In his book *The New Tsar: The Rise and Reign of Vladimir Putin*, Steven Lee Myers, a distinguished *New York Times* journalist, had this to say about Putin's general outlook:

> Each step against Russia he now believed to be a cynical, calculated attack against him. His actions belied a deep sense of grievance and betrayal, sharpened by the crisis that unfolded at the very moment Russia had achieved his Olympic dream. He

was impervious to the threats of sanctions or international isolation because he now believed Russia's views, its interests, would never be respected, as he felt he had never been shown adequate respect, all the more so since he returned to the Kremlin in 2012 after the four-year interregnum as prime minister.[28]

In a *Washington Post* article, Michael Birnbaum points to the NATO bombing of Serbia, a Russian ally; the US invasion of Iraq, another Russian ally; and the Russia-Georgia conflict. When Putin returned to the presidency of Russia, the volume of anti-America antagonism was greatly turned up:

> fed by powerful [denunciation and consistent negativism] on the Russian federal television channels, the main source of news for more than 90 percent of Russians. The anger seems different from the fast-receding jolts of the past, observers say, having spread faster and wider. And all of this took a quantum leap after the beginning of the confrontation over Ukraine, so that now there is broad anti-Americanism at the grassroots level [a new phenomenon.] "What the government knew was that it was very easy to cultivate anti-Western sentiments, and it was easy to consolidate Russian society around this propaganda," said Maria Lipman, an independent Moscow-based political analyst who is working on a study of anti-Western attitudes.[29]

And to give a sense of the attitude of Russian military officials, according to Andre Kondrashev, who made a documentary involving President Putin that was broadcast on March 15, 2015, the defense ministry told him that a military specialist had advised using "all means of deterrence" but that Mr. Putin wanted to avoid anything like the Cuban Missile Crisis. According to Kondrashev, "The president said the situation was complicated and dramatic but the Cold War was over and we did not need an international crisis of the Caribbean type."[30]

Under the Russian constitution, President Putin may serve out his current term and then run for a second six-year term that would not expire until 2024, not accounting for the possibility that the constitution could be changed. He faces no serious opposition from any quarter. And in 1924 he will be only seventy-two years old. But given the broad support for this new ideology of Russia as a bulwark against America, along with recovery of empire, both among the elite and the public, any successor to Putin may share his worldview. Things do change, but sometimes they take a long time in doing so.

Chapter 3
The Treaty of Tlatelolco

The Treaty of Tlatelolco, or the Latin American nuclear weapon–free zone treaty, was the first agreement to prohibit nuclear weapons in a populated area. Although its geographic scope applies to Latin America and the Caribbean, the Treaty of Tlatelolco has been an integral part of the international non-proliferation regime since its creation—it antedated the NPT by a year—and continues to play an important role in world security. The Treaty of Tlatelolco and its protocols, which were included in the treaty text, marked the first time non–nuclear weapon states and nuclear weapon powers agreed on measures proscribing the acquisition and deployment of nuclear weapons, proving such cooperation was possible. The success of this treaty was followed by the completion in 1968 of the NPT negotiations. The NPT provided a global complement to the Treaty of Tlatelolco, and the two treaties have ever since reinforced each other.

The NPT has been the most successful arms control agreement in history. It has come to near universality with 190 parties. Four states have never signed the Treaty (India, Israel, Pakistan, and South Sudan), and one (North Korea) withdrew from the NPT; thus, only five states are not governed by the provisions of this Treaty. But at one point, there were nuclear weapon programs in Latin America. Brazil and Argentina both had projects, and there was a possibility of other states developing new nuclear weapon programs. With the advent and eventual success of the treaty, the likelihood of such an event was considerably lowered. With all states in the region now parties to the treaty, and over thirty states making an additional commitment to refrain from developing nuclear weapons, the likelihood that such a scenario would happen in contravention of the provisions of the NPT was greatly reduced.

The Latin American and Caribbean nuclear weapon–free zone established by the treaty also demonstrated that regional politics were as important, if not more important, than bloc politics. This fact has become clearer since the collapse of the former Soviet Union. For decades, during the Cold War, international politics were viewed by many as consisting of only an east-west or north-south component. The Treaty of Tlatelolco reinforced the idea that non-proliferation is a concern not only to the United States and Russia, but also to the rest of the world. It demonstrated that non-proliferation is an important security concern of developing countries, particularly because it was an incipient initiative by countries within the region. Tlatelolco also served as a model for other regions that wanted to and would later develop comparable regimes. Much of what is in Tlatelolco found its way into other NWFZ treaties, but Tlatelolco was the first. Before its advent, there were treaties banning nuclear weapons in unpopulated areas such as in Antarctica and outer space, but none where real countries existed.

Latin America currently plays an important role in economic and world affairs. As part of this expanding role, there is a general recognition that nuclear power will likely be an important issue in the region. Already, three states have nuclear power plants within their territories—Argentina, Brazil, and Mexico—and they are considering an expansion of their nuclear energy capability. Chile, Peru, Uruguay, and Venezuela have also expressed interest in nuclear power generation. Argentina and Brazil joined the non-proliferation regime in the 1990s, even though they did so after a long period of resisting it.

Latin America has key advantages over some other regions in nuclear power development. It is a de jure and de facto denuclearized region in which several countries that have made considerable progress in nuclear technology are full members of the non-proliferation regime. It is also the first region to have established a broad NWFZ that stretches from Mexico to Tierra del Fuego. "With the exception of Argentina, all Latin American states with nuclear plants and nuclear research reactors have converted to low enriched uranium and are now free of weapons usable material."[1]

Argentina, Brazil, and Mexico are influential states in the region and are thus far the principal states with a nuclear technology capability. A recent report details their nuclear capability in this way: each of these three countries currently has two nuclear power reactors, producing roughly the same portion of national energy production: 4.97 percent in Argentina, 3.55 percent in Mexico, and 3.17 percent in Brazil. Argentina has plans for four more reactors, including two to be built by China and one by Russia. And Chile, with its impressive economic growth, is likely to begin building commercial nuclear reactors. Argentina, Brazil, and Mexico are also involved in nuclear research. Of the 250 research reactors operating in 56 countries, 19 are in Latin America and Caribbean countries, with 6 in Argentina, 4 in Brazil, and 3 in Mexico. Chile and Peru also have 2 reactors each.[2]

As a report from the US Naval Postgraduate School by Arturo Sotomayor describes, Latin America has a considerable interest in nuclear technology:

> Historically, Argentina, Brazil, Chile and Mexico have complied differently with global and regional nonproliferation norms. With the exception of Mexico, the founding father of the nuclear-weapon-free zone in Latin America, all other South American nuclear states are latecomers to the international nonproliferation regime. Argentina, Brazil, and Chile during the periods in the 1960s through the 1980s when they were ruled by military dictators remained adamantly opposed to the NPT . . . and did not ratify the Treaty until the 1990s, following upon their democratization. The two most advanced such states, Argentina and Brazil, developed their nuclear plants under military tutelage, with little civilian intervention, . . . and in the midst of a bilateral military rivalry. Argentina's military government developed a secret ballistic missile project called Condor with Egypt and Iraq.

The Condor would have been capable of delivering nuclear weapons. In Brazil, the military government undertook a parallel secret project of nuclear technology that coexisted with the public nuclear power program. The secret program involved the building of centrifuges to enrich uranium, the ultimate objective of which was the construction of a nuclear weapon.[3]

According to the Sotomayor report, domestic changes, which took place not as a result of US pressure or sanctions but were primarily part of the transition to democratic government, finally brought Argentina and Brazil first into the Tlatelolco treaty and then the NPT. This occurred slowly and progressively through a series of bilateral agreements and confidence-building measures. In 1990, the democratically elected presidents Carlos Saúl Menem of Argentina and Fernando Collor de Mello of Brazil met at Iguaçu Falls, which is part of the common border between the two countries. There they signed an international instrument in which the two countries renounced the development of nuclear weapons and set forth several constitutional arrangements to assure each other that the nuclear establishment of each country would fully abide by the international commitments. Also, a safeguards agreement was negotiated under the auspices of the IAEA. In 1991, the two presidents met again in Mexico to sign an accord on the peaceful use of nuclear energy. This meeting permitted the creation of the bilateral Brazilian-Argentine Agency for Accounting and Control of Nuclear Materials, known as ABACC. Pursuant to ABACC commitments, the two countries were to supply a complete inventory of all nuclear materials to the agency as well as a complete description of any nuclear facilities. ABACC's main task was to verify, through onsite inspections, the information supplied by both governments. This process led Argentina to ratify and become a party to the Treaty of Tlatelolco in 1994 and the NPT later that year; Brazil joined Tlatelolco the same year as Argentina and finally followed suit on the NPT in 1998. Chile also became a party to the Treaty of Tlatelolco in 1994 and the NPT the following year, after its full return to democracy in 1990. "The nuclear reversal process in South America was a notable achievement of the 1990s and has been widely acknowledged as a successful diplomatic story of regional denuclearization."[4] This achievement blazes the trail that one hopes will ultimately lead to worldwide nuclear disarmament.

Both the global and regional non-proliferation regimes are important mechanisms for international security, and they reinforce one another. We live in a world in which nuclear weapons exist. A negotiated regional NWFZ is a step toward limiting and reducing these weapons. The several nuclear weapon–free zones that exist today, taken together, can lead to additional such zones and perhaps eventually toward global nuclear disarmament, making this seemingly distant goal possibly achievable. The Latin American NWFZ, or Treaty of Tlatelolco, is the first such treaty arrangement. Its name derives from "the Aztec name for the district of the Mexican capital where the Ministry of Foreign Affairs of Mexico is located and where the Treaty itself was opened for signature . . . in 1967."[5]

Historically speaking, Latin America has been comparatively free from international war, at least among the Latin American states. Since gaining independence from Spain in the early part of the nineteenth century, the only major international war in the region involving Latin American states was the Chaco War, fought by Bolivia and Paraguay over control of the River Paraguay in the early 1930s. During the Chaco War, more than 100,000 soldiers were lost, which confirmed Paraguay's control. Of course, there have been many incursions into Latin America by outside powers, principally the United States, but also France. Two periods of terrible civil war occurred in Colombia, but by and large the states of Latin America have been able to get along with one another. Perhaps a history of peaceable coexistence was a contributing factor to Latin America's establishing the first NWFZ, encompassing a major continent and populous area.

In the 1950s, an increasing Latin American perception that the US presence in the region was reaching hegemonic proportions along with numerous regional rivalries and suspicions provided the background for an attempt at regional denuclearization in Latin America. But concern about nuclear proliferation cut across Latin America and inter-American regionalism, revealing the potential for developing significant areas of common interest. These concerns were greatly heightened by the Cuban Missile Crisis and the accompanying threat of worldwide nuclear war. Most importantly, the creation and relatively positive performance of a regional NWFZ highlighted the scope for common security in the region and the potential for the establishment of region-wide nuclear weapon–free zones beyond Latin America. It also highlighted the interest in arrangements for regional security.[6]

The concept of a nuclear weapon–free zone, which existed at the time of the negotiation of the Treaty of Tlatelolco—as set forth by Monica Serrano in a significant treatise written at the University of London's Institute of Latin American Studies—was that it should be developed with four main pillars. First, the participating countries must undertake a legally binding international commitment not to produce or deploy nuclear weapons in their territories and not to permit other countries to do so. This obligation remains valid in times of war and in times of peace. Second, the recognized nuclear weapon states must agree to respect such a zone and not to use or threaten to use nuclear weapons against participating states. Third, an international verification system must be included. And fourth, the zone must be established in such a way that it enhances international peace and security. Serrano notes that the first proposals concerning NWFZs were initially proposals of the Soviet Union, aimed at advancing their cause in Central Europe during the Cold War. As such, they were expressions of the US-Soviet conflict in Europe. A second round of proposals in the 1960s, including the efforts in Latin America, were seen as attractive options to advance decolonization and promote national independence, as well as to preserve the non-nuclear status of decolonized states and ensure disengagement from the East-West conflict.[7]

Latin American disarmament measures after World War II took two different routes, one in the Organization of American States (OAS) and the other in the United Nations. In the latter forum, Latin American nations often worked with nonaligned nations from all over the world and pursued general, as opposed to regional, initiatives. In the former forum, initiatives put forth appeared to be so aligned with US interests that they seemed to be US ideas put forward by Latin American proxies. Latin America's reaction to these proposals ranged from open opposition to disinterest. In January 1958 at the Overseas Writers Club in New York, the Costa Rican ambassador (and vice president of the OAS) proposed a special commission to develop a disarmament project for Latin American nations. It was motivated by US Treasury Secretary Robert B. Anderson's suggestion that Latin American states consider reducing their military expenditures.

The Costa Rican plan sought to prohibit Latin American states from manufacturing or acquiring nuclear weapons as well as from buying conventional weapons outside the continent. The United States, for its part, would agree not to transfer nuclear weapons to Latin American states and not to assist in the manufacture of such weapons in Latin America. But the United States retained the right to deploy such weapons in Latin America if necessary for security. This proposal was much in line with US foreign policy interests, as there was already some concern about possible nuclear weapon programs in Argentina and Brazil. Not surprisingly, the proposal was well received by the US Congress. The proposal was sent to other delegations at a regular meeting of the OAS. There it was opposed by the Mexican ambassador, who said, among other things, that disarmament was a global issue, which belonged under the jurisdiction of the United Nations. He sought to mobilize Latin American opinion against the plan, which he said was a plan to "weaken the weak, strengthen the strong," and reinforce US hegemony. Also, the plan's presumption of Latin American inability to produce nuclear weapons, coupled with its suggestion that actual or potential nuclear budgets be allocated to economic development, was interpreted as recognition of a potential regional intent to acquire nuclear weapons.[8] The Costa Rican plan did not go forward, but the concern about nuclear proliferation in the region was real enough. This problem had been perceived for some time by the United States and by some Latin American states.

Argentina began its program in the 1950s with the idea of developing an independent route to the development of nuclear energy. President Juan Perón had begun this program in 1950 in association with other measures to strengthen the Argentine military posture. US-Argentine relations had been frayed for some time, beginning with Perón's declaration of neutrality in World War II. This policy was changed near the end of the war so that Argentina could join the United Nations. Likewise, only the outbreak of the Korean War persuaded Perón to ratify the Rio Treaty (also known as the Inter-American Treaty of Reciprocal Assistance) and bring Argentina into the OAS. He did this and toned down his anti-American policy in order to receive military and other foreign aid that had been severely cut back during World War II as a result of his neutrality policy. But Argentina continued its efforts to pursue an independent nuclear route by developing natural uranium technology to produce nuclear power. Pursuing such technology limited international control over the Argentine program.[9]

Argentina's aggressive program raised Brazilian interest, as Serrano demonstrates. In 1951, the National Research Council was established. It, along with the general staff of the armed forces and the Brazilian National Security Council, controlled uranium deposits. In 1953, Admiral Paulo Alberto, the president of the National Research Council, met in West Germany with a group of German scientists who had been involved with the nuclear project under Nazi Germany. They agreed that Brazil would import uranium enrichment technology and that the Brazilian scientists would be trained in Germany. The United States learned of the deal and blocked it, and Admiral Alberto was forced to resign in 1955. These events, along with the signing of agreements with the United States under the Atoms for Peace program, put an end to Brazil's independent program at that time, which as a result became increasingly dependent on the United States. On the other hand, Argentina continued its "silent march." In 1958, Argentina became the first Latin American state to own and operate a nuclear research reactor.[10]

The Costa Rican plan had failed largely because of Mexican opposition, which perceived it as simple US interventionism. But a second plan was advanced the next year. It began with a proposal by Chilean President Alessandri in the United Nations in November 1959 for a conference to reduce military expenditures in the region. Because this proposal came from within Latin America, it was generally accepted by all countries in the region. The United States approved of the initiative, but concerns about the purchase of arms in Europe by Latin American states led the United States to implement a law making warships available for purchase to "friendly nations." This policy coincided with the fall of many military regimes in Latin America, however, and was seen as weakening the antimilitary front. This soured the atmosphere, and the Alessandri plan came to naught.[11]

The year 1958 marked the entry of Latin America into the disarmament debates at the United Nations. Little had been accomplished over the years in the UN Disarmament Commission. The Mexican ambassador, in a speech, recommended the establishment of a specialized agency to address disarmament issues. In 1959, the United Nations in an effort to bring East and West together in such an organization established the Ten-Nation Disarmament Committee, composed of the United States and several of its prominent allies as well as the Soviet Union and several of its allies. The world community at the time was becoming quite energized over the issue of debris from atmospheric nuclear weapon tests by Great Britain, the Soviet Union, and the United States contaminating the environment and entering the food chain. Strontium-90, a radioactive isotope, which was debris from such tests, was detected in milk in grocery stores. Mothers around the world took to the streets. Radioactive rain fell on Japan from Soviet tests at Semipalatinsk. The Americans greatly underestimated the yield of a thermonuclear weapon test in the Pacific, and radioactive debris fell on a Japanese fishing boat, causing the death of one of the crew. Nations around the world began demanding an end to the tests.

There still was little progress on disarmament, but in response to the public protests, the United States instituted a test moratorium in 1958, which was also observed by the Soviet Union and Great Britain. Even so, it was understood that the decision to observe the moratorium could fall apart at any time. Many states believed that it was necessary to expand the forum established in 1959, both to remove the discussions somewhat from their Cold War context and also to bring into disarmament negotiations nonaligned non–nuclear weapon states. In 1960, a fourth nuclear weapon state, France, conducted its initial tests in the Sahara. Then, in September 1961, the Soviet Union broke the test moratorium beginning with the largest nuclear weapon test of all time, producing an explosion of 58.6 megatons. The United States responded with a vigorous series of tests. In December, the composition of the Eighteen-Nation Committee on Disarmament was agreed and it was created at the United Nations. Brazil and Mexico were included as members. Argentina praised the inclusion of Latin American states while complaining about the selection process. Discussions of a comprehensive nuclear test-ban treaty were taken up at the ENCD for most of 1962. Brazil, Mexico, and other non-nuclear states essentially served as facilitators in negotiations among Great Britain, the Soviet Union, and the United States. France was elected as a member of the ENCD but refused to take its seat. Thus the ENCD was in reality a seventeen-nation body. This remained the case through the 1960s, with the NPT being negotiated at the ENCD. Beginning in 1969 and continuing into the early 1990s, however, the ENCD was gradually expanded into the Conference on Disarmament (CD) with sixty-two members. While other highly important disarmament treaties were negotiated at the ENCD/CD over the years, all productivity seemed to cease after 1996, and the CD entered a status of permanent deadlock much like the UN Disarmament Commission in the 1950s.

While much of the work in 1962 at the ENCD was on the test ban, with Brazil and Mexico as facilitators, Brazil and Mexico also made annual appeals to the nuclear powers in the ENCD to settle their differences. At the ENCD, Mexico affirmed the value of unilateral measures aimed at preserving non-nuclear status through its decision to renounce the possession of nuclear weapons and to prohibit the placing of nuclear weapons on its territory. On September 20, the Brazilian ambassador to the United Nations raised the possibility of establishing a NWFZ in Latin America in a speech in the General Assembly. The next month brought the Cuban Missile Crisis.

In August 1960, Inter-American Conference VII at the OAS under the Rio Treaty (which established the OAS) took place, and at this conference a resolution concerning the "communist presence" in the region and responding to Cuba's increasing isolation and closeness to the Soviet Union was introduced. It proved to be highly controversial. Mexico and other Latin American states had initially supported the Cuban Revolution. The crisis of OAS consensus created by this resolution was overcome only by phrasing the final resolution in abstract terms and avoiding any direct reference to Cuba.[12]

But after the failure of the Bay of Pigs Invasion in 1961, Cuba's dependence on the Soviet Union grew rapidly. Soon, Premier Khrushchev was implying that the Soviet Union was placing a nuclear umbrella over Cuba: "Soviet artillerymen, in case of need, can support the Cuban people with missile fire if the aggressive forces of the Pentagon dare bring intervention against Cuba." Several explanations have been offered as to the rationale behind the actions by the Soviet Union and Cuba in eventually supporting the deployment of Soviet missiles with nuclear warheads in Cuba. For the Soviets, it was a quick route to strategic parity with the United States. For Cuba, it distracted attention from growing domestic difficulties and indicated that Castro could effectively defy the northern colossus. Externally, Fidel Castro asserted that "Russian missiles in Cuba . . . would deter the United States invasion and prevent nuclear war altogether."[13]

But as early as January 1962, Inter-American Conference VIII, due to the increasing radicalization of the Castro regime and the policy now of open confrontation between Cuba and the United States as well as between Cuba and US–Latin American allies, adopted two resolutions calling for sanctions against Cuba and its expulsion from the OAS. These resolutions effected a realignment of Latin America states away from cooperation with Cuba and toward isolation. This shift was epitomized by Mexico as it moved away from its earlier enthusiastic sympathy toward a more cautious diplomatic attitude. The change was a response to the internal character of Castro's Cuba and its alliance with the Soviet Union. For the United States, the principal concern was Cuba's support for revolutionary movements elsewhere in the hemisphere. No one either in the United States or in Latin America thought that the Soviet Union and Cuba would implement a plan to deploy nuclear weapons and ballistic missiles in Cuban territory, 90 miles from America's shores. As late as September 1962, the US Intelligence Board continued to regard Soviet emplacement of missiles in Cuba as a highly unlikely prospect. This estimate helps to explain the surprise of the Kennedy administration when it confronted exactly that circumstance the following month.[14]

The discovery of Soviet missiles in Cuba by the United States on October 14, 1962, presented the Kennedy administration with difficult challenges. Accepting the status quo could serve to reverse the strategic balance. Diplomacy was unlikely to succeed and, in President Kennedy's view, an invasion carried with it too many uncertainties, despite the heavy pressure being placed on him by the US Joint Chiefs of Staff and Congress to invade promptly. Kennedy's concerns proved to be well justified.

Instead, President Kennedy chose to institute a blockade of the island. This strategy offered a firm middle course, placed the responsibility on Khrushchev to escalate to the next step, and enabled the United States to take advantage of its local preponderance of forces. Not least of all, the blockade, or defensive quarantine, was consistent with the Rio Treaty, as such action was authorized by the OAS. Article 52 of the UN Charter permits regional arrangements and regional action "relating to the maintenance of peace and security."[15] The OAS, pursuant to this provision of the charter, could take action under Articles 6 and 8 of the Rio Treaty, including a decision for the use of force, in response to a situation that endangered the peace and security of the hemisphere. Although no actual armed attack was underway, and the legal situation was not free from controversy because of this fact, and despite there being no prior authorization from the UN Security Council, senior US government international lawyers argued that the OAS nevertheless was not only empowered to act, but should act given the gravity of the situation. Their argument appeared to be sound: what could threaten peace and security more than the imminent threat of nuclear war? The fact that the OAS could and did act in this situation, creating the appearance of legality for the US action, was important to the Kennedy administration.

On October 23, 1962, the Council of the OAS adopted a resolution calling for individual and collective measures, including the use of force, to achieve the removal of Soviet missiles in Cuba. The blockade proved successful, enabled the Soviets to clearly read US determination, reduced the risk of miscalculation, and permitted a dignified Soviet withdrawal. As Graham Allison put it in his book *Essence of Decision: Explaining the Cuban Missile Crisis,*

> The United States was firm but forbearing. The Soviet Union looked hard, blinked twice, and then withdrew without humiliation. Here is one of the finest examples of

diplomatic prudence. . . . Having peered over the edge of the nuclear precipice, both nations edged backwards toward détente.[16]

Former secretary of defense McNamara strongly agreed with this assessment.

The US proposal for the blockade in October 1962 was the first resolution ever adopted unanimously by the OAS. But even here several states—Bolivia, Brazil, Mexico, and Uruguay—had reservations about parts of the resolution and, while Mexico definitely supported the need for action, it had doubts about the legality of the blockade.

On October 29, 1962, the day after Khrushchev announced the planned withdrawal of Soviet missiles in Cuba, Brazil again proposed a UNGA resolution supporting the establishment of an NWFZ in Latin America. The resolution was offered both as a solution to the current crisis and as a measure to prevent future dangers of this nature. Thus the debates on this proposal that followed took place in the aftermath of the Cuban Missile Crisis. Cuba expressed sympathy for the proposal while noting that the United States would remain free to deploy nuclear weapons around the hemisphere in places like Panama and Puerto Rico. The US representative said that the United States would support an NWFZ in Latin America if an effective verification system were in place. Several Latin American states expressed support, but there were important abstentions, namely, Argentina, Colombia, and Venezuela. Mexico criticized the hasty introduction of the proposal. This unfavorable atmosphere caused the Brazilian delegation to put aside its proposal for the time being. However, the very next month, in November 1962, the Brazilian proposal was revised and resubmitted to the General Assembly. At the urging of the United States, the reference to a possible nuclear weapon–free zone in Africa was deleted, and the resolution was limited to Latin America. This time, the reaction of Mexico was more positive.

In January 1963, the Brazilian foreign minister, Manuel Tello, sent a letter to the Mexican ambassador in Brazil, Alfonso Garcia Robles, proposing a joint declaration by Mexico, Bolivia, Brazil, Chile, and Ecuador of an NWFZ in Latin America. Mexico's response was a letter from the president of Mexico, Lopez Mateos, to the presidents of Bolivia, Brazil, Chile, and Ecuador making such a proposal. Brazil's response was immediate and enthusiastic, while President Alessandri of Chile expressed his desire "to keep Latin America out of the nuclear struggle." The Argentine private response was that the proposal was "inopportune." US Senator Hubert Humphrey in Washington declared that the negotiation of such a zone should have diplomatic priority in the region. Elsewhere, there was broad support in Washington, with a caveat that the transit of nuclear weapons through the Panama Canal zone be excluded from the obligations of this agreement.[17]

The five supporting states decided to make a public declaration of their intention, and letters were sent in late April to the other Latin American states urging them to adhere. The Argentine reaction now was supportive. Cuba responded by stating that it would not accept any proposal for denuclearization where Puerto Rico and the Panama Canal zone were excluded and the Guantanamo military base remained in US hands. The Central American states made a cautious reply, while Peru and Haiti expressed immediate support. In May, Mexico and Brazil jointly sent the proposal to the ENDC. The official Argentine reaction had also expressed a strong preference for engaging in negotiations at the OAS to establish the proper links to the inter-American framework. This was ultimately the course the Latin American states settled upon. In September 1963, the ambassador of Brazil to the United Nations asserted in the General Assembly that the development of a Latin American nuclear weapon–free zone would not be the result of a UN resolution, but rather an agreement among the states within the region itself. Ambassador Garcia Robles of Mexico stated that the establishment of such a zone in Latin America would represent an affirmation of the independence of the nations of the region. Serrano concludes her account by saying that there is little doubt that the Cuban Missile Crisis was the catalyst that led to the Treaty of Tlatelolco, even though there had been an interest in the development of a nuclear weapon–free zone in Latin America for some years. The negotiation of the treaty was a complicated affair, beginning in 1964 and was being carried out against the backdrop of a new generation of military governments in the region, which affected the policy positions of several key states.[18]

The negotiations on a nuclear weapon–free zone began formally in 1964, after the joint declaration of the five presidents of April 29, 1963. In his Nobel Peace Prize lecture, Garcia Robles said of the declaration:

> In [it] the presidents of Mexico, Brazil, Bolivia, Chile, and Ecuador announced that their governments were "willing to sign a Latin American multilateral agreement by which they would undertake not to 'manufacture, store, or test nuclear weapons or devices for launching nuclear weapons.'"[19]

Garcia Robles further describes how this statement was followed seven months later by a UNGA resolution adding six more Latin American states to the five that promulgated the April statement. Costa Rico, El Salvador, Haiti, Honduras, Panama, and Uruguay were added, and they in turn welcomed the joint

declaration and expressed hope that the states of the region would initiate studies on the obligations that would have to be negotiated to achieve the objectives
of the five presidents. It also requested that the UN secretary general provide
technical assistance as requested. Approximately one year later, on November
23-27, the Mexican government hosted a conference in Mexico City to begin the
negotiating process. At this conference, the creation of an ad hoc organization—
the Preparatory Commission for the Denuclearization of Latin America, known
by its Spanish acronym, COPREDAL—was agreed upon.[20] This proved to be a
decisive step.

In the account of Garcia Robles, COPREDAL held its first negotiating session
in Mexico City from March 15 to 22, 1965. It had been instructed by the November
conference to "prepare a preliminary draft of a multilateral treaty for the denuclearization of Latin America." At this meeting, COPREDAL adopted rules of procedure and established a number of subsidiary working groups. COPREDAL held
four sessions in the subsequent two years, with the fourth and final session taking
place from January 31 to February 14, 1967. At the second session, in the summer
of 1965, draft articles for the verification section of the prospective treaty and the
preamble were prepared. Verification was to be by the IAEA and the implementing body of the treaty either of which could conduct "special inspections." At
the third session, proposals, which included texts for all the draft articles for the
treaty, were agreed upon. In some cases, however, because of differences in views,
two parallel alternatives were developed. At the last session of COPREDAL, the
final text of the Treaty of Tlatelolco was negotiated. The treaty text was unanimously approved on the 12th of February 1967, and at the closing meeting of the
session on February 14, 1967, the treaty was opened for signature. Representatives
from fourteen of the twenty-one participating Latin American nations signed the
treaty at the closing ceremony.[21] Today, the treaty has thirty-three parties representing all the states in Latin America and the Caribbean.

At the fourth session, COPREDAL had numerous issues to address. Two worth
mentioning were approval of the final language addressing peaceful nuclear
explosions and the language of the two subsidiary protocols. The most difficult
question to settle, however, was the article on the entry into force of the treaty,
Article 28.

One of the fundamental concerns of the negotiating parties of the Treaty of
Tlatelolco was the preservation of the right to use nuclear energy for peaceful
purposes. The treaty adopted a comprehensive but precise definition of a nuclear
weapon. The definition provided that "a nuclear weapon is any device which is

capable of releasing nuclear energy in an uncontrolled manner and which has a group of characteristics that are appropriate for use for warlike purposes."[22] Also, Article 17 of the treaty provides that "nothing in the provisions of this Treaty shall prejudice the rights of the Contracting Parties, in uniformity with the Treaty, to use nuclear energy for peaceful purposes."[23] This language safeguards the right to acquire and develop such peaceful nuclear applications as nuclear power reactors, research reactors, and the various medical applications of nuclear technology. This language, however, in conjunction with the second clause of the definition of nuclear weapons, leaves open the option of using nuclear explosions for peaceful purposes. Subsequent NWFZ treaties, the first of which was almost twenty years later, did not include this second clause of the definition. The change can be attributed to an evolution in thinking; by the time other nuclear weapon–free zones were negotiated, it was clear that peaceful nuclear explosive devices were indistinguishable from nuclear weapons. But this was not the case at the time; even though it seems preposterous in modern-day terms, in the 1960s, there still were advocates for using nuclear devices for such things as digging canals and the stimulating of oil and gas production. Accordingly, Article 18 permits the use of peaceful nuclear explosions, but only if a party can demonstrate that the proposed use of such technology is feasible without violation of the other articles of the treaty. Garcia Robles in his 1979 paper says:

> Since the consensus of the experts is that this is at present impossible, it must obviously be concluded that the states parties to the Treaty will not be able to manufacture or acquire nuclear explosive devices (even though they may be intended for peaceful purposes) unless and until technical progress has developed for such explosions devices which cannot be used as nuclear weapons.[24]

The Nuclear Non-Proliferation Treaty, signed the next year, also has an article on peaceful nuclear explosions, which was motivated by Article 18 of Tlatelolco. It calls for the nondiscriminatory availability of benefits of peaceful nuclear explosions in Article V, which have been regarded as a dead letter for many years. Garcia Robles notes that, to remove any doubt that only military denuclearization for Latin America is intended by the Treaty of Tlatelolco, the original name of the treaty was changed by COPREDAL at its last session from "Treaty for the Denuclearization of Latin America" to "Treaty for the Prohibition of Nuclear Weapons in Latin America."[25]

This treaty was the first nuclear weapon–free zone treaty, so its adoption of two additional protocols, one for nuclear states (Protocol II) and one for outside parties that have jurisdiction over territory in Latin America (Protocol I), set an important precedent. Protocol I provides that those extracontinental states, which de jure or de facto are internationally responsible for territories lying within the Zone established by the NWFZ treaty, upon becoming a protocol party undertake to accept the statute of denuclearization established by the treaty for those territories. Protocol I parties would not participate in the General Conference of the parties established by the treaty, but neither would any of the verification provisions apply to them for their territories, except to have safeguards agreements with the IAEA. France, Great Britain, the Netherlands, and the United States are responsible for territories within the treaty zone, and all four have ratified Protocol I. The United States did so in 1981, thereby establishing Puerto Rico and the US Virgin Islands as areas legally free of nuclear weapons. The United States included several "understandings" (formal communications to other parties as to the treaty's interpretation), the most important being that the transit of nuclear weapons through the zone by airplane or ship is not affected by the treaty. This was particularly important to the United States, particularly the US Navy. None of the understandings were ever challenged, and this one concerning transit was made explicit in all subsequent nuclear weapon–free zone treaties.

Protocol II invites the five NPT-recognized nuclear states to respect the nuclear weapon–free zone established by the treaty and most importantly "not to use or threaten to use nuclear weapons against the Contracting Parties." This is the legally binding negative security assurance that the NPT non-nuclear state parties have generally sought since the signing of the NPT. Thus far, the negative security assurance has only been achievable through the NWFZ treaties, all of which subsequently have included this highly important part of the Treaty of Tlatelolco Protocols. Great Britain was a party to Protocol II at the time of the Falklands/Malvinas conflict with Argentina, and therefore was legally obligated not to use or threaten to use nuclear weapons against a Tlatelolco party. Argentina, however, had not become a party to the treaty. Thus Great Britain was under no obligation not to use nuclear weapons against Argentina during this conflict. This situation was not lost on Argentine policy makers.

The treaty also established an implementing organization, the constituent parts of which are the General Conference, the Council, and the Secretariat. This organization of the parties ensures the treaty regime functions properly. Among other responsibilities, through its General Conference, it decides what measures to take in case of serious treaty violations. The name of this organization is the Agency for the Prohibition of Nuclear Weapons in Latin America, and it is referred to it by its Spanish acronym, OPANAL. All subsequent nuclear weapon–free zone treaties have followed this precedent as well. OPANAL was established when the treaty entered into force for Mexico, the eleventh Latin American state, as this action meant that a majority of states in COPREDAL were bound by the treaty's obligations, which is the treaty requirement for its implementing institutions to be established.

The most difficult problem for COPREDAL to resolve was the provision for entry into force. There were two groups among the negotiating parties. The first group argued that the treaty should come into force among those countries that had ratified it once eleven states of COPREDAL had deposited their instruments of ratification, just as with OPANAL and similar to general treaty practice. The second group took the position that the treaty should not come into force until the following four things happened:

1. the signature and ratification of the treaty by all states to which it was opened,

2. the signature and ratification of Protocol I by all states to which it was opened,

3. the signature and ratification of Protocol II by all states to which it was opened, and

4. the conclusion of safeguards agreements with the IAEA by all contracting parties of the treaty and of the protocols.

All of this was the result of the genius of Ambassador Garcia Robles; he formulated the solution to the two distinct views. Article 28 provides that the treaty will come into force only when the four requirements set forth in Article 28, Paragraph 1, are met. Article 28 also permits a state to waive the four requirements by a formal statement of waiver and thus the obligations of the treaty will apply to that party's land area. In practice, each Tlatelolco treaty party has brought the treaty into force for itself by depositing its instrument of ratification and the formal waiver document with the depository, which is the government of Mexico. The fourth condition has never been met and may never be met.

Thus, for many years, Argentina, while a signatory, had not ratified, while Brazil and Chile had signed and ratified but had not waived. Cuba, of course, did nothing for a long time. Ambassador Garcia Robles believed it important to involve all Latin American states in the treaty, some of which were not yet ready to accept its obligations. This was because both Argentina and Brazil had active, independent national nuclear programs that were potentially nuclear weapon programs. Chile went along with Brazil. But by 1994, Argentina and Brazil no longer wished to keep open the nuclear weapon option. Argentina ratified the Treaty of Tlatelolco and waived the four requirements, while Brazil and Chile deposited their declarations of waiver with the government of Mexico.

With the accession of Cuba in 2002, all Latin American states had signed, ratified, and waived pursuant to Article 28 and the treaty as a result applied to the land area of all Latin American states. Also, three of the four requirements had been met. Some small island states in the Caribbean still have not concluded safeguards agreements with the IAEA for cost reasons. But for all intents and purposes, the treaty is in full force. As of now, the treaty's de facto zone of application is the land territory of the parties. If the fourth requirement under the terms of the treaty ever is met, the area of the application of the treaty will expand to a large ocean region surrounding Central and South America and the formal Treaty Zone of Application will be in full force.

From the early days in the nuclear era, both Brazil and Argentina saw nuclear power as a means of lessening dependence on the United States. The establishment of the Balseiro Institute in Bariloche in 1955 by President Juan Perón was potentially a step in that direction. Also, for both countries, the nuclear weapon option for a long time remained in the background. The 1966 military coup in Argentina differed from previous military interventions aimed at a so-called reestablishment of constitutional rule. This coup set the basis for a prolonged military rule that gave the military the opportunity to carry out ambitious programs that in the past had been disrupted by political instability. US restrictions on transfers of sensitive technology led the Argentine military to approach Europe. In 1968, the National Atomic Energy Commission announced its decision to grant Siemens, a West German company, a contract to build Atucha I, Argentina's first nuclear power plant. Argentina chose a nuclear power plant design, which used natural uranium—like Canada's CANDU—rather than a reactor that used enriched uranium, such as in the United States. This allowed Argentina to both consume its uranium reserves and escape international control. Similarly, in Brazil in 1967, a fifteen-year plan was initiated to work toward an independent nuclear program and the complete nuclear fuel cycle. In 1975, Brazil also reached an agreement with Siemens, under which Siemens would build eight nuclear power stations as well as uranium enrichment and reprocessing facilities. There were allegations the same year that 50 kilograms of plutonium had been diverted from the Atucha I power plant in Argentina. Nothing further appears to have come from the assertion.

These developments led to increased pressure for Argentina to join the NPT and the Treaty of Tlatelolco. The Carter administration undertook an ultimately successful diplomatic effort to cancel the Brazil-Germany agreement. In 1977, Canada canceled the sale of an enrichment plant to Argentina because of insufficient safeguards, and Argentina made public through its ambassador in the United States its interest in establishing a joint front with Brazil to resist US opposition to the construction of enrichment plants. More active cooperation began between Argentina and Brazil in nuclear energy and technology. This rapprochement between the two countries was not inhibited by the 1983 announcement by Argentina of its achievement of the capability to enrich uranium. Evidence since the late 1970s indicates a gradual change from competition to cooperation between the two states. The return of civilian rule had an important role in this process.

But Argentina had begun a serious program under military rule to acquire nuclear weapons. The centerpiece of this effort was a successful secret program to develop gaseous diffusion technology (one of the oldest of enrichment technologies, used by the United States in the 1940s). The existence of the plant housing this technology, located at Pilcaniyeu in Rio Negro Province, was kept secret until the restoration of civilian rule. At least initially, this plant was designed to enrich only to 20 percent. The plan was for 500 kilograms of 20 percent enriched uranium per year, but the plant was never operational because of technical problems. A new, much smaller, pilot plant producing only low-enriched uranium was opened in 1993. Government officials confirmed that research carried out at the Balseiro Institute research reactor had yielded the capacity to produce weapons-grade uranium, but the program was promptly cancelled after the return of civilian rule in December 1983.

In the 1970s, during a period of competition with Argentina through technology transfers—which did not require IAEA safeguards—Brazil pursued a covert nuclear weapon program known as the Parallel Program with enrichment facilities (including small-scale enrichment plants, a limited reprocessing capability, and a missile program). In 1981, Brazil's President Sarney announced successful uranium enrichment up to 20 percent. In 1990, his successor, Collor de Mello, symbolically closed a designated test site and revealed the military's plan to develop a nuclear weapon. Brazil's National Congress began an investigation into the Parallel Program. The investigation revealed secret bank accounts used by the National Nuclear Energy Commission to fund the program and found that Brazil's Institute of Advanced Studies had designed two nuclear weapon devices, one with a projected yield of 20 to 30 kilotons and the second with a yield of 12 kilotons.

All this questionable behavior formally came to an end in 1991. On December 13, Argentina and Brazil signed the quadripartite agreement at IAEA headquarters, which created the Brazilian-Argentine Agency for Accounting and Control of Nuclear Materials, allowing, among other provisions, for full-scope IAEA safeguards on Argentine and Brazilian nuclear installations. Three years later, in 1994, Argentina and Brazil joined the Treaty of Tlatelolco and took subsequent steps to join the NPT regime, as said, Argentina in 1995 and Brazil in 1998.

Nevertheless, Argentina continued with its full nuclear fuel cycle program. Brazil officially opened its Resende enrichment plant in 2006, accompanied by a dispute with the IAEA, albeit quickly settled, regarding the parameters of IAEA facility inspections. As noted, Argentina had enrichment capability in place since 1983. As Serrano observes:

> As the Latin American experience indicates, a basis for common security could be an important factor in the perception of a balance favoring the advantages, rather than the costs, of non-nuclear status. Nuclear-free zones could offer a sound framework for promoting and regulating the peaceful uses of nuclear energy through the setting up of systems of control better adapted to the interests of regional states, and the development of regional fuel cycle capabilities and regulations for the administration of the most critical materials. Finally, as the Argentine-Brazilian rapprochement suggests, NFZs could provide the necessary conditions to develop more effective means of cooperation, mediation, and confidence building, and control measures over the direction followed by nuclear energy programs.[26]

The genius of Ambassador Garcia Robles, the commitment to peace of the peoples of Latin America, and the stimulus of the Cuban Missile Crisis combined to create the world's first nuclear weapon–free zone in a populated area. The Treaty of Tlatelolco established many precedents that were followed by subsequent NWFZ agreements, such as an implementing body of the treaty like OPANAL. There was also the precedent of subsidiary protocols for outside states to place territories over which they had jurisdiction under the nuclear weapon–free obligations of the zonal treaty as well as for the recognized nuclear weapon states to pledge respect for the zonal nuclear weapon–free region established by the treaty, while at the same time giving the parties to the treaty a negative security assurance—a solemn and legally binding pledge not to use or threaten to use nuclear weapons against parties of the treaty. It is now broadly established that NPT non–nuclear weapon states can achieve this goal by creating or joining a regional NWFZ treaty.

There were also precedents in the Tlatelolco treaty that were not followed. There has been no subsequent need for the complicated entry into force provision developed by Garcia Robles to cope with the existence of two potential nuclear weapon programs in Latin America at the time of the negotiation of the treaty. Garcia Robles believed that it would be best over the long term if the treaty provided a means by which all Latin American states could have at least some relationship to the treaty zone. Brazil chose to take advantage of this mechanism, but Argentina did not. In the end, both states abandoned the nuclear option and joined the Treaty of Tlatelolco and the NPT. Also, the language of Article 18, on peaceful nuclear explosions, was as forward leaning as Garcia Robles could make it, but the debate was not yet over. Pursuant to Article 18, a potential user had to prove in advance that the peaceful nuclear explosive device in question was distinguishable from a nuclear weapon, which never was possible. But by 1986, when the next NWFZ treaty, the Treaty of Rarotonga, covering the South Pacific, entered into force, the debate was over. By then, it was accepted everywhere that a device for a peaceful nuclear explosion was indistinguishable from a nuclear weapon; hence future NWFZ treaties had no need for an article on peaceful nuclear explosions.

Ambassador Garcia Robles did the world community a great service by leading the effort to create a NWFZ treaty regime in Latin America through the Treaty of Tlatelolco. In doing so, he helped to establish the idea that substantially populated areas of the earth could be made legally nuclear weapon–free. It was a truly a great performance by a visionary worthy of a Nobel Peace Prize.

Chapter 4
The Treaty of Rarotonga

French Premier Pierre Mendes-France made the decision for France to build an atomic bomb in late 1956, in the wake of the defeat at Dien Bien Phu in Vietnam. His successors—particularly Premier Guy Mollet—carried the program forward so that, when General Charles de Gaulle returned to power in 1958, all was in place. The program was pursued vigorously, and the Reggane test center was completed in the Algerian Sahara Desert region in the fall of 1958. The first French test was actually conducted in an area some distance south of the test center in a "remote part of the Sahara."[1] The explosive yield of this first test, designated Gerboise Bleue and carried out on February 13, 1960, was in the range of 60 to 70 kilotons. It was the largest first test explosion for any country. The motivating rationale, as the French made clear from the beginning, was prestige. President de Gaulle promptly declared, "Hurray for France! Since this morning, she is stronger and prouder."[2] Later, in a speech in November 1961, he said that a "great state" that does not have nuclear weapons when others do "does not command its own destiny."[3]

France conducted two more atmospheric nuclear weapon tests in 1960, and a fourth was scheduled in early 1961. By February 1961, however, France was near the point of open rebellion as President de Gaulle prepared for negotiations to end the Algerian War for independence by granting independence to Algeria. On April 21, two thousand armed insurgents gathered in the Forest of Orleans outside Paris, and another four hundred in the Forest of Rambouillet, where preparations were underway for a march on Paris. Fortunately, these groups soon disbanded for lack of orders. The next day, April 22, at 3:00 a.m., four senior generals in Algeria announced a military coup aimed at the overthrow of President de Gaulle and the preservation of French control in Algeria. On April 23, President de Gaulle in a televised address ordered army troops not to obey orders from the rebellious officers and to sabotage their arms. The coup collapsed on April 26 with the surrender of its leader, General Maurice Challe. Nonetheless, the day before, on April 25, French technicians at Reggane had hastily conducted an unplanned nuclear test explosion of a plutonium bomb to prevent the device, which was present at the test site in connection with a nuclear test planned for later in the year, from being captured by followers of General Challe. The yield of the explosion was only about 1 kiloton, but the detonation may have been intentionally compromised. This premature detonation was the last atmospheric nuclear weapon test in Africa. The reaction to the four tests in Africa and around the world convinced President de Gaulle that atmospheric nuclear testing in the Sahara could not be continued. So, the French test program in Algeria went underground.

Geological conditions in the Sahara Desert required that underground nuclear tests be conducted in vertical galleries rather than deep vertical shafts. Nevertheless, France carried out thirteen more nuclear weapon tests in Algeria—all underground—between November 7, 1961, and February 16, 1966. Jeffrey T. Richelson reports in his comprehensive book *Spying on the Bomb* that most of the tests were less than 20 kilotons, but one exceeded 50 kilotons and another produced a level of 110 kilotons.[4]

In the peace agreement between the French government and the Algerian rebels, concluded at Evian on Lake Geneva on March 18, 1962, France recognized Algeria's independence and agreed to cede control of the Sahara to the new government in five years. It had been clear to all, except perhaps die-hard supporters or sympathizers of General Challe and his fellow conspirators, that an independent Algeria would prohibit French nuclear weapon testing, even underground. Thus France would need a new test site, one that could accommodate high-yield thermonuclear device testing. In July 1961, General Jean Thiry, who had been assigned the responsibility to find a new test site, presented to the government a list of four possibilities, one in the South Atlantic and three in the South Pacific: New Caledonia, the Marquesas, and Réunion. Other sites were considered over the following year, and when the selection commission made its decision on March 22, 1962, it decided to locate the test site center (the Pacific Test Center) at Gambier-South Tuamotu in French Polynesia in the South Pacific, which French leaders had preferred from the start. Actual detonation locations could include nearby Mururoa Island and perhaps other islands such as Fangataufa, Maria, Marutea, and Temoe. The decision was made final on July 4, 1962, and it was further decided that the first tests would be atmospheric, with the objective of being operational by 1966, a year earlier than would be possible by preparing a site for conducting an underground nuclear weapon test.[5]

Richelson describes the geological nature of French test sites in the Pacific: "Mururoa is a coral atoll, a ring-shaped coral reef enclosing a lagoon that is the visible rim of an extinct underwater volcano." The atoll is about 6 by 18 miles with a lagoon deep enough for large ships. Its coral ring is between 650 and 985 feet wide, except for a two and a half–mile gap connecting the lagoon to the Pacific Ocean. He further details, "Mururoa is located about halfway between Australia and South America, about 720 miles from Tahiti in the extreme southwest corner of the Tuamotu Archipelago; one of five archipelagos making up French Polynesia, Tuamotu consists of about eighty atolls. In May 1963 the first detachment of [French] engineers assumed control of the planned test site, followed in September by the first group of Polynesian workers." By January, five hundred men were working on Mururoa.[6]

Richelson continues his account with Fangataufa, about 25 miles southeast of Mururoa, which became the secondary Pacific Ocean test site. It measures about 3 by 5 miles and was originally a closed atoll, requiring the French Army to blast a 250-foot gap through the coral ring to permit access from the ocean. A third atoll, Hao, about 280 miles northwest, initially served as a base where nuclear weapon test devices were assembled. Here, the French military built one of the longest runways in the South Pacific, where device components arrived from France by plane. Later the assembly function was moved to Mururoa. In early July 1966, France began atmospheric nuclear weapons testing in the Pacific. On July 2, 1966, in the presence of senior French officers, on a barge in the Mururoa lagoon, a pure plutonium device was detonated, producing an explosive yield of 30 kilotons. Less than three weeks later, a 60-kiloton device was detonated at Fangataufa via airdrop.[7]

Three more tests followed in September and October. President de Gaulle was present for the September test, which had an explosive yield of 120 kilotons. Later in the month, the French conducted a test of a boosted fission device of 150 kilotons yield, which was a significant step toward a hydrogen thermonuclear weapon. At the beginning of France's active test program, President de Gaulle had been willing to wait until 1970 for a French thermonuclear weapon capability. But by 1966 he had a different view; he demanded a thermonuclear weapon by 1968, asserting to his new minister for research and atomic and space affairs, "of the five nuclear powers are we going to be the only one which hasn't made it to the thermonuclear level? Are we going to let the Chinese get ahead of us?" Thus by 1968 it must happen. The French program did make this date with some technical help from the British. On August 24, 1968, the French carried out their first thermonuclear weapons test at Fangataufa. The 3-ton device was detonated from a balloon at almost 2,000 feet, producing an explosion of 2.6 megatons. De Gaulle proclaimed this test "a magnificent scientific technical and industrial success, achieved for the independence and security of France by an elite of her children." But the radioactive contamination from this test was so severe and extensive that Fangataufa was declared off-limits for six years. Two weeks after this test, a second thermonuclear explosion took place on Mururoa, yielding 1.2 megatons.[8]

Richelson explains that the French testing program took a year off in 1969, the French claiming budgetary limitations, but many suspected contamination as a cause as well. Between 1970, when the program restarted, and September 15, 1974, France conducted twenty-nine tests, all of them in the atmosphere. Twenty-eight were on Mururoa and one was on Fangataufa. The most notable of eight tests in 1970 was a one-megaton test on July 3. Six hours after the detonation, French officials returned to the atoll, and Defense Minister Michel Debré, who would live twenty-six more years and die at the age of eighty-four in 1996, took a swim in the lagoon. The French finally bowed to international pressure, however, and ended their atmospheric test program in the South Pacific after their test on September 15, 1974.[9]

The French test program continued underground in French Polynesia off and on for twenty-two more years. It ended in 1996, after the NPT was made permanent at the 1995 Review and Extension Conference. The French, shortly after the decision to permanently extend the NPT, in 1996 restarted their test program after a moratorium of several years. But after a few tests they again bowed to highly intense international pressure and completely terminated their test program, including the closure of their test site, after several months.

It was the notoriety of the French atmospheric nuclear weapon tests and the extensive contamination that was created that led to widespread antinuclear agitation in Australia, New Zealand, and the Pacific Island states—most significantly in New Zealand and in French Polynesia—in the 1960s and 1970s. This ultimately was followed by the successful negotiation of the Rarotonga Treaty, establishing the South Pacific as a nuclear weapon–free zone in the 1980s under the leadership of Australia.

Nuclear testing in the Pacific began in 1946 by the United States. From 1946 to 1958, the United States conducted sixty-seven nuclear and thermonuclear bomb tests at Bikini and Enewetak Atolls in the Marshall Islands, accounting for one-third of all US atmospheric tests. In the 1960s, there were twenty-four more atmospheric tests at Christmas (Kiritimati) Island and nine at Johnston (Kalama) Atoll, all conducted by the United States. The United Kingdom conducted twelve atmospheric nuclear weapon tests at the Monte Bello Islands and Maralinga and Emu Field in Australia, and then nine more nuclear and thermonuclear weapon tests in the late 1950s at Kiritimati and Malden Islands. Malden Island, called Independence Island in the nineteenth century, is a low, arid, uninhabited island in the central Pacific Ocean, about 39 kilometers (15 square miles) in area. It is part of the Republic of Kiribati in the central Pacific. These tests also were an important factor in provoking antinuclear public reaction in the South Pacific, but the French tests were the primary motivator. Between 1966 and 1996 in French Polynesia, France conducted 193 atmospheric and underground nuclear tests at Mururoa and Fangataufa atolls, all organized from its Pacific Test Centre. But from nearly the beginning of the nuclear age there were community protests in the South Pacific, scarcely a year into the nuclear age after the first test was carried out in the Pacific at Bikini.

The International Campaign to Abolish Nuclear Weapons (ICAN), a worldwide coalition of nongovernmental organizations, chronicled some of the resistance to nuclear testing and nuclear arms buildup. In 1950, a prominent Tahitian political leader, Pouvanaa a Oopa, a veteran of the French Army in both world wars, collected signatures for the Stockholm peace appeal. In 1954, Marshall Islanders lodged a petition with the UN Trusteeship Council opposing US nuclear testing. In 1956, Western Samoa (then still a trust territory of New Zealand) petitioned the Trusteeship Council to halt British nuclear tests being planned for Christmas Island. In 1957, the Fijian newspaper *Jagriti* noted, "Nations engaged in testing these bombs in the Pacific should realize the value of the lives of the people settled in this part of the world. They too are human beings, not 'guinea pigs.'"[10]

In 1975, the Pacific Conference of Churches joined with the Fiji Young Women's Christian Association and the antinuclear group Against Testing on Mururoa to host the first Nuclear-Free Pacific Conference in Suva, Fiji. The conference delegate from the New Hebrides stated, "The main objective of this conference is to end nuclear tests in the Pacific, but the more we discuss it, it becomes obvious that the main cause is colonialism." ICAN, further noting the success of the campaign, reports that by 1980 the nuclear-free and independent Pacific movement had established a secretariat in Hawaii: the Pacific Resource Centre. This movement campaigned against nuclear testing, the transport of nuclear materials through Pacific fishing grounds, and the mining of uranium on indigenous land. In the 1980s, churches, trade unions, and community organizations lobbied, eventually successfully, for the creation of a South Pacific nuclear weapon–free zone and also supported nuclear weapon–free zone legislation in countries such as Vanuatu, Palau, and New Zealand, where it was particularly effective.[11]

A recent case study details the environmental impact of the test program:

> The exact effects of the French nuclear tests will not be known for years. The French government is very secretive about releasing information about environmental hazards associated with nuclear testing. There is lack of statistical research to assess the risks to the people in the South Pacific. Due to pressure from the European Union and the scientific community, France has conducted several tests to assess the health and environmental risks associated with the nuclear tests. Working with the French government, Jacques Cousteau and his team explored damage to the Mururoa atoll for six days in June 1987. Cousteau, however, had limited time, resources, and access. In February of 1996 France invited the United Nations organization, the International Atomic Energy Agency (IAEA), to officially release all nuclear security data. . . . In 1994 the IAEA set a resolution for all states to fulfill their international responsibilities to ensure that nuclear testing sites have no detrimental health or environmental impacts.

> France's nuclear testing in the South Pacific, especially in Mururoa, has inflicted long-term environmental damage to the geographical structuring of the atoll. Radiation has seeped into the fissures of the atoll. A French map from 1980 shows that years of nuclear testing have cracked the atoll. Several scientists have concluded that previous nuclear testing caused fissuring . . . by destroying the coral and altering land plates. Dr. Murray Matthews from the National Radiation Lab in New Zealand discusses the spread of radioactive material from windstorms and rains. Pierre Vincent, a volcanologist, stated that "further tests could rupture the rock and release radionuclides from underground cavities." The long-term effects increase the risk of landslides and tsunami, seismic tidal waves. Future shocks from underground explosions could induce a tsunami that could submerge all of Polynesia. Radioactive leaks also increase the risks to aquatic life in the surrounding area.[12]

And the bitterness continues. Reverend François Pihaatae, general secretary of the Pacific Conference of Churches, put it this way:

> For almost 70 years since the United States' first Pacific nuclear test in Bikini in 1946, church members have been forced to live with the legacy of this menace. Three of the world's major powers—the U.S., Great Britain and France—conducted nuclear tests in the Pacific with blatant disregard for human life and the environment. This unwanted activity has maimed generations of Pacific people and hundreds of European servicemen and their families.[13]

And another commentator put it this way:

Seeking "empty" spaces, the Western powers chose to conduct Cold War programs of nuclear testing in the deserts of Central Australia or the isolated atolls of the Central and South Pacific. . . . Since the 1950s, churches, trade unions, women's organizations and customary leaders in the islands have campaigned for an end to nuclear testing and the abolition of nuclear weapons.[14]

France did not take these criticisms very well. The first French test in July 2, 1966, in Mururoa, was carried out over the objections of thirty members of the Polynesian Territorial Assembly. Weyler asserted that it sucked all the water from the atoll's lagoon, "raining dead fish and mollusks down on the atoll," and there were reports that it spread contamination across the Pacific as far as Peru and New Zealand.[15]

Much later, after the French tests in the South Pacific had gone underground, a serious problem developed with respect to a test in Mururoa on July 28, 1979. France had abandoned atmospheric testing in 1974 and moved underground in response to world pressure led by New Zealand. The underground tests were conducted in deep shafts drilled into the volcanic rocks underlying the atolls. Some cracking of the atolls was discovered, leading to concerns that leaks of radioactive material could occur. In the 1979 test, the nuclear device became stuck halfway down the 800-meter shaft. The detonation caused a large submarine landslide on the southwest rim of the atoll, which resulted in a significant piece of the outer slope of the atoll to break loose. A 2-kilometer-long and 40-centimeter-wide crack appeared in the atoll.[16]

In 2013, the French newspaper *Le Parisien* claimed that, after reviewing recently declassified Ministry of Defense documents, it was clear that French nuclear tests in the South Pacific had been far more toxic than previously acknowledged. A vast swath of Polynesia was subjected to radioactive fallout. *Le Parisien*, as reported in *The Guardian* newspaper in the United Kingdom, asserted that the documents revealed that plutonium fallout hit the whole of French Polynesia (a much broader area than previously admitted) and that Tahiti, the most populated island, was exposed to five hundred times the maximum accepted level of radiation.[17] In 2015, the Assembly of French Polynesia was considering a resolution demanding financial compensation for "major pollution" caused by the 193 nuclear tests carried out by the French government at the Mururoa and Fangataufa atolls of €754.2 million ($930 million). In addition, the resolution called for a payment of €132 million for the continued occupation of the two atolls.[18]

France conducted forty-three atmospheric nuclear tests at Mururoa and one at Fangataufa between 1966 and 1974. During these nine years, numerous protests were lodged by the South Pacific community. New Zealand was a leader of these protests, three of which were formal protests by the South Pacific Forum Organization (with members Australia, Cook Islands, Fiji, Gilbert Islands, Nauru, New Zealand, Niue, Papua New Guinea, Solomon, Tonga, and Western Samoa) filed with the French government during this time. Australia also made several separate protests. In 1973, New Zealand and Australia filed actions with the International Court at The Hague on the grounds that insofar as the French atmospheric nuclear tests in the Pacific modify the physical conditions of their respective territories, measurably increase pollution of the seas, and interfere with navigation of the high seas and the air space above them, "they constitute a breach of France's international legal obligations to the countries and peoples affected."[19] The court issued injunctions prohibiting further atmospheric nuclear testing by France in the area. France ignored the order and continued to conduct such tests at Mururoa. But in 1974, France made a public announcement that no further atmospheric tests would be conducted in the Pacific. The court by a vote of nine to six held France to the pledge made in this announcement and therefore dismissed the New Zealand and Australian case as moot.[20]

Regional protests were led by New Zealand and to a degree by Australia. In a sense, the negotiation of the Treaty of Rarotonga represented the third of three waves of South Pacific regional interest in the nuclear-free zone concept and protest against nuclear weapon tests in the region. The first period of protest and policy proposals was in 1962-63, just before the commencement of French testing. It involved proposals by the opposition Labor parties in Australia and New Zealand for a nuclear weapon–free zone in the Southern Hemisphere. The second period was in 1974-75, when New Zealand and the South Pacific island states gained support in the United Nations for the establishment of a nuclear weapon–free zone in the South Pacific.[21]

The first wave of regional interest and proposals emerged in the context of increasing international concern and objections to nuclear weapon testing in the late 1950s and early 1960s, when nuclear weapon testing by the then-nuclear states was being conducted almost exclusively in the atmosphere. Radioactive fallout particles appearing in the food chain—strontium-90 in milk—were a particular focus. All of this was happening against a Cold War background. Australia and the Pacific islands became important sites for nuclear testing. Public concern in Australia over radioactive fallout intensified, particularly after Great Britain moved its test program from Christmas Island to Maralinga on the Australian continent.[22]

Michael Hamel-Green, author of *The South Pacific Nuclear-Free Zone Treaty: A Critical Assessment* and other publications, explains that during this time the first proposal for a regional nuclear weapon–free zone was advanced in the Australian Parliament by the leader of the opposition Labor Party, Arthur Calwell. He proposed that the 1959 Antarctic Treaty nuclear weapon–free zone (which among many other things, such as declaring the entire Antarctic landmass free from claims of national sovereignty, also prohibited nuclear weapons in the Antarctic) be extended north to the equator in all directions. Calwell also called for the convening of a conference of Antarctic Treaty members as well as other countries to discuss making the entire Southern Hemisphere a nuclear weapon–free zone. This was strongly opposed by long-serving Australian Prime Minister Robert Menzies, a firm supporter of NATO and the Cold War Western Alliance. He dismissed the Labor Party proposal with the words that Australia should not "permanently contract herself out of permitting nuclear weapons to be used in war or defense . . . on her soil" and asked, "Have we reached the very ecstasy of suicide in Australia?" This of course reflected the Cold War thinking of the time. Australia wanted protection against communist China. Calwell's proposal was adopted at the May 5, 1962, Labor Party Federal Executive meeting shortly before his presentation in parliament, and it was reaffirmed at the July 5 meeting of the Labor Party leadership group. In subsequent months, many peace activist and nuclear disarmament nongovernmental groups got behind the Labor Party initiative, and the New South Wales Peace Committee organized a petition in support of the Labor Party proposal with over 200,000 signatures. Calwell used the proposal in his 1963 election policy approach, much to the Labor Party's delight. Following the Labor Party's defeat in the 1963 election, however, the party did not pursue this initiative after 1964.[23]

In New Zealand, Hamel-Green notes, civil society disarmament activists were successful in encouraging the New Zealand Labor Party to accept the Southern Hemisphere nuclear weapon–free zone proposal as policy in 1964. In both Australia and New Zealand, nuclear disarmament activists lobbied opposition Labor parties to adopt nuclear weapon–free zone policies in case the parties were to come to power. A prominent member of the New Zealand Labor Party noted, "Public concern about [French testing's] harmful effect was widespread."[24]

The New Zealand Labor Party came to power in 1972, led by Prime Minister Norman Kirk. It responded to public concern by sending two frigates into the test zone in July 1973. The Australian Labor Party, also elected in 1972, led by Prime Minister Gough Whitlam, along with New Zealand brought the case against French testing at the International Court of Justice. However, France continued underground testing in the South Pacific, going on to conduct 147 additional tests between 1975 and 1996.[25]

The Pacific island states are normally divided into three groups based on ethnic affinity. According to Hamel-Green, Micronesia includes the "small" islands in the mid-Pacific between the equator and 20°N: the Federated States of Micronesia, Guam, Kiribati, the Marshall Islands, Nauru, and the northern Mariana Islands. Melanesia, the "black" islands, which are situated in the southwest Pacific, includes Fiji, Irian Jaya, New Caledonia, Papua New Guinea, the Solomon Islands, and Vanuatu. And Polynesia, the "many" islands in the southeast and southwest Pacific, includes the Cook Islands, Easter Island, French Polynesia (Fangataufa, Mururoa, Tahiti, and many others), Hawaii, Niue, Samoa, Tonga, Tuvalu, and Western Samoa. All these islands share a colonial history dating to the nineteenth century, when the major European powers progressively colonized the Pacific. This area was one of the last to be decolonized, with most islands achieving independence or self-governance in association with a major metropolitan state in the last fifty years. With the exception of Papua New Guinea and Fiji, all the independent island states are microstates with populations of less than 250,000. Regionally, most of the states and territories are members of the South Pacific Commission, established in 1947 as a regional agency to promote economic and social development. In 1971, responding to frustration over not being able to address regional political issues—most importantly French nuclear weapon testing at Mururoa—within the framework of the commission, some of the newly independent island states together with New Zealand and Australia formed another regional body, the South Pacific Forum, within which the Rarotonga treaty was negotiated.[26]

The initial group of forum states included Australia, the Cook Islands, Fiji, Nauru, New Zealand, Tonga, and Western Samoa. By 1985, when the Treaty of Rarotonga was opened for signature, additional members consisted of Kiribati, Niue, Papua New Guinea, the Solomon Islands, Tuvalu, and Vanuatu. States added a few years later were the Federated States of Micronesia and the Marshall Islands, after they achieved self-government (along with Palau) under the Compact of Free Association with the United States. These three states are associated states with observer status pursuant to the Rarotonga treaty although they are NPT parties. While the formal initiatives for the treaty came from Australia and New Zealand, much of the impetus came from the island countries, as it was in some of those territories that most of the nuclear weapon testing in the Pacific by France, Great Britain, and the United States was carried out. Both the 1975 New Zealand initiative under Prime Minister Kirk and the 1983 Australian South Pacific Nuclear Weapon–Free Zone (SPNWFZ) proposal, which led to the Rarotonga treaty, were put forward in the context of long-standing island state support for regional denuclearization.[27]

As in Australia, the New Zealand Labor Party had a long history of support for regional and global disarmament proposals. In 1963, Norman Kirk suggested a Southern Hemisphere nuclear weapon–free zone to be established by international agreement. Kirk became prime minister in the new government, and his government and the Rowling government after Kirk's death in late 1974 pursued this idea until the defeat of the Labor Party in the 1975 election. Kirk's proposal called for a South Pacific nuclear weapon–free zone extending from 60°S (the Antarctic Treaty boundary) to the equator, with the eastern and western boundaries to be negotiated. The first step of the Kirk government was to take the New Zealand proposal to the mid-1974 ANZUS Council meeting with Australia and the United States. ANZUS refers to the defense treaty among Australia, New Zealand, and the United States. Presentation of the proposal led immediately to confrontation with the United States. The US secretary of state was attending the meeting, and he refused to permit the New Zealand initiative to be included in the final communiqué of the meeting.[28] The United States at the time was in the depths of the Cold War with the Soviet Union, and while it no longer conducted nuclear weapon tests in the Pacific or atmospheric tests anywhere, pursuant to the Limited Test Ban Treaty of 1963, it sympathized with France, its Cold War front-line ally. Also, the United States did not want to create a precedent for proposals for the establishment of nuclear weapon–free zones in places it considered inappropriate, such as Central Europe. One free zone—Tlatelolco—was enough.

The next step by the Kirk government was to seek a hearing for its proposal in the South Pacific Forum. There it was supported by all the island states and Australia, which was still under the Whitlam Labor government. The forum emphasized "the importance of keeping the region free from the risk of nuclear contamination and involvement in a nuclear conflict" and "commended the idea of establishing a nuclear weapon-free zone in the South Pacific as a means of achieving that aim." Despite continued US opposition, New Zealand, joined by Fiji and Papua New Guinea, introduced the New Zealand proposal as a resolution in the UN General Assembly. On December 11, 1975, the General Assembly adopted the resolution, and all members were enjoined to carry forward consultations about ways and means of implementing the proposal. The vote was 110 to 0, with twenty abstentions, which included four NPT nuclear weapon states (France, the Soviet Union, the United Kingdom, and the United States). China voted in favor of the resolution.[29]

Under the New Zealand National Party government, which took office after the 1975 election, the New Zealand South Pacific nuclear weapon–free zone proposal was allowed to lapse. Like the new government in place in Australia after the loss by Labor, this New Zealand government viewed SPNWFZ proposals as likely to create complications for ANZUS and relations with the United States. Between 1976 and 1984, there were a total of thirty-four port visits by US ships believed to be fitted out with nuclear-capable weapon systems after the government revoked a ban on nuclear warship (nuclear powered or nuclear armed) entry, in force even before the preceding Labor government. Public opposition to visits by nuclear ships increased, and from 1978 on, the Labor Party position included a ban on nuclear warship entry along with continuing support for a regional South Pacific nuclear weapon–free zone. In 1983, the Labor Party's annual conference adopted a proposal that called for a "total nuclear-free zone in the Pacific" and a ban on nuclear-armed ships in New Zealand's territorial waters, along with a renegotiation of the ANZUS treaty to ensure that New Zealand's non-nuclear status was recognized. In July 1984, Labor returned to power in New Zealand. But there was division within Labor's leadership on the SPNWFZ. The Labor Party also had returned to power in Australia in 1983 under Prime Minister Robert Hawke and as said had raised the SPNWFZ initiative at the South Pacific Forum in August 1983. The Hawke government followed up at the August 1984 meeting with a proposal containing guidelines and the establishment of a forum working group. Some in the New Zealand Labor Party, such as former Prime Minister Sir Wallace Rowling, thought the Australian proposal was "weak" because it did not address the problem of nuclear transit and port calls. The Australian proposal also was limited to the land area of the parties and their territorial seas—a far cry from the "total nuclear-free zone in the Pacific" that was the formal position of the New Zealand Labor Party.[30]

The new leader of the Labor Party in New Zealand, David Lange, was inclined to sympathize with the Australian proposal. He said that New Zealand could work with its Pacific neighbors and, while the Australian proposal did not go far enough, it was a useful "first step." The Lange government was confronted with the Australian proposal only a month after it had taken office. The public opposition to port calls by nuclear-armed ships remained strong, while an equally large majority of New Zealanders continued to support ANZUS and defense links to Australia. The new government attempted to be more pragmatic in the negotiation leading to the Rarotonga treaty while promptly enacting legislation implementing the domestic part of the New Zealand Labor Party policy, that is, a ban on port calls by nuclear warships. A policy was promptly adopted of not admitting nuclear warships into New Zealand. The government supported ANZUS but restricted its support to conventional defense of the parties.

This led to a major dispute with the United States and to some degree with Australia as well. In February 1985, the New Zealand government refused to accept a visit by the nuclear-capable USS *Buchanan*, and the United States followed with a cancellation of joint ANZUS exercises and certain defense and intelligence cooperation arrangements. The New Zealand position only marginally affected US interests, but it created a precedent that the United States did not want to see repeated in Europe. In August 1986, when further negotiations did not resolve the dispute and the Lange government then proceeded with legislation to implement its policy, the Reagan administration suspended ANZUS security guarantees to New Zealand. Although there was much more the United States could have done—such as impose economic sanctions—US retaliation stopped there largely because of New Zealand's putting aside its more far-reaching proposals for a nuclear-free Pacific and supporting the Australian SPNWFZ proposal. Australia also criticized the New Zealand ship visit and ANZUS policies saying that Australia "could not accept as a permanent arrangement that the ANZUS alliance had a different meaning, and entailed different obligations for different members."[31] Thus it was in this context—criticism by Australia and a major dispute with the United States—that the Lange government was persuaded to give its support to the Australian SPNWFZ proposal rather than the position taken by the 1983 Labor Party Conference for a "total nuclear-free zone in the Pacific."[32]

The Hawke government initiatives had been directed at addressing pressures in Australia and in the region for South Pacific denuclearization while safeguarding ANZUS nuclear policies. The Australian government proposed a limited-scope, limited-domain treaty focused largely on a third-party non-ANZUS nuclear program, and thereby it could maintain control over the regional arms control process and preempt possible moves by a New Zealand Labor government and Melanesian states to initiate more comprehensive SPNWFZ arrangements. The Australian government met with rapid success at the August 1984

South Pacific Forum meeting. The New Zealand Labor government, anxious to limit possible retaliation from its ANZUS partners over its ban on nuclear warship entry, decided to support the Australian SPNWFZ concept rather than seek a more comprehensive agreement. This emerging joint position by Australia and New Zealand made impractical additionally far-reaching efforts by any of the island states. While Australia could have expected—and did in fact receive—US appreciation of an initiative aimed at protecting shared ANZUS nuclear interests, Washington did not elect to sign the protocols to Rarotonga in 1986. The support of France was still paramount, but this did not undermine the success of the treaty. It preempted more comprehensive and potentially damaging measures, and Australia could say, and did, that the treaty in no way depended on US approval of the protocol for its "efficacy." It could also be presented at the United Nations and was as an important arms control step to take its place alongside the Treaty of Tlatelolco.[33]

In 1995, the NPT parties convened at the NPT Review and Extension Conference, at which the treaty's future duration, pursuant to Article X, would be determined. It was strongly the view of the United States, which was shared by a number of states, that the NPT should be given a permanent duration, like all other multilateral arms control and disarmament treaties. But this outcome was not free from uncertainty. At the beginning of the extension process, several years before, a substantial majority of NPT parties held a different view. A more limited extension was favored as a way of pressuring the nuclear weapon states of the NPT to reduce and—reasonably soon—eliminate their nuclear weapons. The vote, pursuant to the treaty, would be decided by a majority of the parties on a one-time basis, voting at the conference without reference to national legislatures. Thus every vote was important, and the South Pacific Forum then had ten voting NPT states, with three other forum members and three associate members with observer status that were also new NPT parties (the Marshall Islands, Micronesia, and Palau brought in to vote at the last minute). The three forum members that did not have a vote at the 1995 conference were Niue and the Cook Islands, which were associated states of New Zealand—not NPT members but considered to be bound by New Zealand's NPT membership—as well as Vanuatu, which joined the NPT several months after the conference. While at the conference, I held a luncheon for the representatives and a few senior staff of the South Pacific Forum states. Speaking on behalf of the US government—without instructions but without any opposition—I promised the ten South Pacific

Forum states that if they all supported permanent, or indefinite, extension of the NPT, the United States would sign and ratify the three protocols to the Rarotonga treaty, a matter that gradually had become an issue of considerable importance to these states. All ten of the South Pacific Forum states that were NPT parties (plus the three forum-associated members that became NPT parties right before the conference) supported indefinite NPT extension. They indicated at the luncheon that they would do so, and they followed through.

Appropriately, the three remaining NPT nuclear states that had not signed the Rarotonga treaty protocols—France, the United Kingdom, and the United States—signed the protocols on March 24, 1996. France terminated its nuclear weapon test program in 1996 and promptly ratified the signature of the protocols. With French ratification of the Comprehensive Nuclear-Test-Ban Treaty in 1997, there is no doubt now that the French test program in the South Pacific is part of history. Britain ratified the protocols in 1997. China and Russia had signed and ratified the protocols in the 1980s. But to its discredit, because the South Pacific Forum states had delivered at the 1995 conference and the United States had benefited, the United States took no step to ratify the protocols. Finally, President Obama in 2010 announced that he would submit the protocols to the Senate for advice and consent to ratification, doing so in 2011. Characteristically, six years later, the Senate had taken no action. This type of an unjustifiable out-of-step behavior does not help US credibility internationally.

The negotiation of the Rarotonga treaty was not complicated. The prohibition on nuclear weapons would be limited to the land territory of the parties and their territorial sea, not the broad Pacific. Only South Pacific Forum members could be parties. The treaty also establishes the SPNWFZ, which is the area south of the equator, north of the northern limit of the Antarctic Treaty, east from the 115th meridian east and west of the 115th meridian west (which is the western limit of the Latin American Nuclear Weapon–Free Zone defined by the Treaty of Tlatelolco). There are three projections of the zone north of the equator to include the territories and territorial seas of Kiribati, Nauru, and Papua New Guinea. Except where otherwise specified, the prohibitions on of the treaty apply only to land area and territorial seas within this zone. The one exception is that the Rarotonga treaty bans the dumping of radioactive wastes and other radioactive matter at sea anywhere in the zone.

The other issues that were decided in advance were port visits and landings by nuclear warships or nuclear-capable aircraft in the territory of a treaty party.

Each party is permitted, but not required, to host such visits. In the language of the treaty, "each party is free to decide for itself" this question, which preserves both the Australian and New Zealand positions described above.

After the more specific Australian proposal of August 1984 was presented to the forum, the treaty was negotiated in a series of four working group meetings held in Suva, Fiji, in November 1984 and in Canberra, Suva, and Wellington in April, May, and June 1985. The actual drafting was done by a legal subcommittee created at the 1984 meeting in Suva. The draft treaty was adopted at a full forum meeting at Rarotonga in August 6, 1985. It was signed by nine of the ten forum members on September 16, 1985, including Australia, Fiji, New Zealand, and Papua New Guinea. Only Vanuatu, breaking the forum's tradition of consensual decisions, did not sign even though it had declared itself nuclear-free. Ten years later, Vanuatu finally acceded to the treaty. On December 11, 1986, Australia became the eighth signatory to ratify the treaty, bringing it into force pursuant to its terms. On August 8, 1986, the forum agreed to the text of the three protocols: (1) that states with territories within the zone place them under the jurisdiction of the treaty; (2) that protocol parties will not use or threaten to use nuclear weapons against parties to the treaty; and (3) that protocol parties will not test any nuclear explosive device anywhere in the zone. Protocols 2 and 3 were open only to NPT nuclear weapon states. As explained above, China and Russia are parties to the second and third protocols, to which they are eligible, and France and Great Britain are parties to all three, as they have jurisdiction over land territory within the zone. The United States is also eligible for all three protocols, has signed all three, but has ratified none. Protocol 3, prohibiting testing, is not limited to land areas within the zone but applies to the high seas area within the zone as well.

The Rarotonga treaty is broadly modeled on the Treaty of Tlatelolco, with a few exceptions. For one, it makes explicit the rights of a party to host nuclear warships and aircraft (indeed, any ship or aircraft a state in the exercise of its sovereignty chooses to admit). It does so by permitting a party in the exercise of its sovereignty to allow visits by foreign ships and aircraft to its ports and airfields and transit of its airspace by foreign aircraft and navigation of its territorial seas by foreign ships where the rights of innocent passage do not apply. It also bans nuclear explosive devices but does not provide for peaceful nuclear explosive devices, as the international consensus at the time was that the former are indistinguishable from weapons. Finally, because the South Pacific is primarily an ocean area as opposed to a landmass, like Latin America, the treaty prohibits the dumping of radioactive waste anywhere in the high seas within the zone. Fear of radioactive contamination of the marine environment was an additional important motivation for the Rarotonga treaty, as there had been widespread reports of waste dumping in the high seas of the South Pacific by states conducting nuclear weapon tests. Verification is carried out through the employment of IAEA safeguards, while the South Pacific Forum, which largely has the responsibility to enforce the treaty, fulfills much of the role that OPANAL performs under the Tlatelolco treaty.

The Rarotonga treaty now has thirteen parties; six of the seven original forum members that negotiated it promptly became parties. Tonga, the seventh, joined the treaty years later. Six other states around the time of the opening for signature of the Rarotonga treaty joined the forum in 1985 and became parties, although the accession by Vanuatu was considerably delayed. The Marshall Islands, Micronesia, and Palau became eligible parties to the treaty when they subsequently became full members of the South Pacific Forum. All three states lie north of the equator. In 1999, the South Pacific Forum became the Pacific Islands Forum, and in 2011 admitted American Samoa, Guam, and the North Marianas as observer states.

With the negotiation and entry into force of the South Pacific Nuclear Weapon–Free Zone, a major step toward the ultimate elimination of nuclear weapons from the face of the earth was taken. The nuclear states had conducted 226 tests of nuclear weapons, including 89 atmospheric tests, in the South Pacific. As a result of the Treaty of Rarotonga and its protocols we can now say, no more.

Chapter 5
The Treaty of Pelindaba

Africa has been the locus of three nuclear weapon programs. First was the French nuclear weapon test program in the Sahara, which was eventually moved to the South Pacific, as described in chapter 4. Second was the serious and relatively advanced nuclear weapon program in South Africa, which produced six 20-kiloton Hiroshima-type weapons and a seventh under construction when the program was terminated. Finally, Libya had a nascent program, derived from purchasing the equipment for a complete production program from A. Q. Khan. The equipment never left the storage facilities.

In 1944, during World War II, Britain asked South African Prime Minister Jan Smuts to assist in the search for material needed in the Allied atomic bomb project. The South African Chamber of Mines was tasked to investigate, and it soon discovered that uranium coexisted with gold in virtually every mine and borehole in the portion of the country known as the Rand. For the next four years, until the establishment of the Atomic Energy Board (AEB) in 1948, uranium production was managed out of the prime minister's office.[1]

While uranium production increased over the next decade, South Africa did not have a nuclear energy program. Starting in 1961, this would change as general research and development began at the Pelindaba Nuclear Research Center near Pretoria. Four years later, ground was broken for the construction on South Africa's first research reactor, Safari. Over 1,300 pounds of 2 percent enriched uranium and 5 metric tons of heavy water, supplied by the United States, allowed Safari to go critical in 1967. By this time, prominent South African officials were already contemplating the merits of a nuclear weapon program. In 1965, Andres Visser, a board member of the AEB, thought that South Africa should build an arsenal for "prestige purposes" and reportedly said, "We should have the bomb to prevent aggression by loud-mouth Afro-Asiatic states." The prime minister at the time, H. F. Verwoerd, proclaimed during the inauguration ceremony of the Safari reactor that it was "the duty of South Africa to consider not only the military uses of the material but also to do all in its power to direct its uses for peaceful purposes," thereby implying that an atomic bomb program was under consideration.[2]

With Safari in operation, South Africa thereby had a training facility for a program designed to produce plutonium. This program was visible, but another program was not. In the mid-1960s a secret program—initially in a warehouse in Pretoria—began to conduct sophisticated experiments aimed at the enrichment of uranium to weapons grade. Soon the site of the experiments was moved to the Pelindaba Research Center, where Safari was located. In early 1969, after reviewing progress in the program, the government authorized the construction of a pilot plant. In July 1970, Prime Minister John Vorster told the South African Parliament that the government had developed a unique method for enriching uranium and announced that a pilot plant (called the Y-Plant) would be built to test the new method. This alleged new method was close to a standard centrifuge, with a few relatively superficial differences. The Y-Plant, would be located at Valindaba, not far from Pelindaba. The facility's location in the Zulu language means "we don't talk about this at all," which probably raised a few suspicions.[3]

South Africa was allegedly developing the capability to manufacture peaceful nuclear explosives for mining. World acceptance of this idea was fast declining because peaceful nuclear explosions were indistinguishable from weapon tests, so the government kept the program secret. In March 1971, the AEB was authorized by the minister of mines to conduct a preliminary investigation into the possibility of producing a nuclear explosive device. At this time, both the minister of defense of South Africa and the chief of the South African Defense Force were publicly predicting that an orchestrated Soviet attack on South Africa was inevitable; thus the restriction to theoretical work did not last long. By 1974, a scale model of a gun-type (Hiroshima-type) nuclear weapon had been successfully tested using non-nuclear material. In the same year, the first part of the Y-Plant nuclear uranium production cascade became operational, and the government of Portugal was overthrown by left-wing military officers. This led the South African government to conclude that the colonial regimes in Mozambique and Angola, which had been in place for four hundred years, would not last much longer. This conclusion substantially raised the level of governmental anxiety and led to Prime Minister Vorster authorizing the construction of a single nuclear gun-type explosive device, referred to as a "peaceful nuclear device." The program remained top secret nevertheless. Additionally, funding was authorized for the acquisition and development of a test site, and the Defense Forces in the Kalahari Desert acquired a location to be carefully guarded and kept secret.[4]

South Africa's nuclear strategy came to be based on three pillars:

> that South Africa should have a credible nuclear deterrent; that it would develop and deploy this deterrent in the most responsible way possible; and finally, that it would limit its nuclear deterrent to a size and shape that would be proportional to the threat and its own scientific and industrial capabilities.[5]

According to those involved, the question of what would be a credible deterrent for South Africa in the minds of the South African policy makers involved two factors. The first factor was what the scientific and industrial base would support, given its size and then current capabilities. This ruled out the possibility of a triad of forces, such as existed in the United States with long-range bombers, a fleet of ballistic missile submarines, and land-based long-range ballistic missiles as delivery vehicles for nuclear weapons. Given their mind-set at the time and their fortress mentality when considering the Soviet threat, however, South African leaders decided not to have air-delivered capability only but also to construct medium-range ballistic missiles. Such a missile capability from the military point of view made little sense, but it did serve to broaden the industrial base. And perhaps this capability could ultimately form the basis for a space program. The approximate number of nuclear weapons that should be built could be debated forever, but the government settled on a decision to build six or seven bombs.[6]

The reasoning was as follows: because the purpose of the South African program was not to wage nuclear war but rather to deter aggression, this small arsenal would be useless unless its existence was known. A debate ensued about how to make its presence known. If demonstrated by exploding a nuclear device, the condemnation of almost the entire world would follow. So this option was discarded. Another option would be to simply announce South Africa's intent to have such a deterrent given the threats that it faced. This alternative would bring the same condemnation, although less brutal and direct. The least problematic option was to quietly inform key government officials in other nations that South Africa would employ its weapons if the circumstances justified it.[7] In the end, South Africa did none of these things.

An intense search for a test site began in 1973. The site needed to be substantially distant from South Africa's borders in case there was an accidental radioactive release, and it needed to have a geology that would permit deep underground placement of a test device. A dummy run (a simulation of all the activities) for a test explosion was planned for August 1977, but at the last moment it was called off after a light plane—heavily camouflaged— unexpectedly flew over the site. Hannes Steyn, Richardt van der Walt, and Jan van Loggerenberg, former officials in the South African nuclear program, reported this event in their 2007 book *Nuclear Armament and Disarmament: South Africa's Nuclear Experience.* As described in the book, despite the precautions taken at the site with a sophisticated camouflage plan, senior officials in Pretoria feared an inspection—one that never materialized. Because of the plane incident, the test was called off.[8]

Richelson in his book reports another story about the incident involving the international community. The US government was aware that in fact two devices had been fabricated. Since insufficient uranium had been produced by mid-1977, a "cold test" (of two devices, not one) was planned. The devices would be fully instrumented but contain depleted uranium—not highly enriched uranium— cores. The devices were based on the gun-type design. Two boreholes were drilled, and, in the hopes of deceiving foreign intelligence services, the process was disguised as the construction of an underground military ammunition depot. The cold test with full simulation activity was planned for August 1977. But the deception did not work; two Soviet satellites photographed the site in late July, allegedly on the tip of a Soviet spy in the South African defense establishment.[9]

On August 6, President Jimmy Carter was delivering a speech in Pretoria, South Africa. At that time, Prime Minister Vorster delivered a message to the president that the US policy of pressuring South Africa to abandon apartheid would lead to "chaos and anarchy." On the same day in Washington, a Soviet embassy official delivered a letter to the president from the Soviet general secretary Leonid Brezhnev. In the letter, Brezhnev said that Soviet intelligence had discovered secret preparations by the South African government to test a nuclear device in the Kalahari Desert. He asked for Carter's help in stopping the test.[10]

Two days later, on August 8, the Soviets made their charges public through the government press agency, TASS. Meanwhile, the US government proceeded, upon receiving the letter, to verify the Soviet claim. A US satellite was reprogrammed to make a pass over the site and a light plane, without filing a flight plan, flew over the site. This was the plane mentioned by the two South African officials. It was not identified by the South Africans, but it belonged to the office of the US military attaché at the embassy and was equipped with appropriate cameras. The photographs plus the satellite imagery were all the evidence that the

United States needed. There followed a serious, in-depth US interagency discussion of the South African government's objectives and the likelihood that South Africa would back away from the test. The US study concluded that South Africa appeared to be intent on acquiring nuclear weapons, but might be flexible as to timing in response to diplomatic threats, although it was unlikely to be deterred in the long run from building nuclear weapons. The study was completed on August 18, but already a heavy diplomatic effort by Britain, France, Germany, the Soviet Union, and the United States was underway. South Africa made a strong public denial of any plans for a nuclear test and at the same time got busy cleaning up the site in case of an inspection. Richelson reports that two days after the over-flight, a senior official at the site was told on a secure line that "You must pack and leave immediately for Pretoria since inspection of the site is imminent. The rest of the AEB team must leave as soon as possible by road!"[11] This account tracks with the account by the three South African officials set forth above.

France threatened to break diplomatic relations and to terminate its assistance in building two nuclear power plants in South Africa. The United States considerably escalated its pressure, as it wanted assurances there would be no test. On August 21, South Africa relented and agreed not to conduct any nuclear tests. On August 23, President Carter announced that South Africa had informed the United States that "they do not have and do not intend to develop nuclear explosive devices for any purpose, either peaceful or as a weapon" and "that the Kalahari test site . . . is not designed for the test of nuclear explosives, and no nuclear explosive test will be taken now or in the future." But the August 18 study had concluded that its drafters did "not see any circumstances" that would cause South Africa to put aside its nuclear weapon program.[12]

The prime minister had lied about the facts in the so-called assurances he gave to President Carter. He followed this up with another lie in October 1977 during an interview in which he stated that he "was not aware of any promise that he had given President Carter." In April 1976, at the prime minister level, South Africa had reached a secret trade agreement with Israel in which South Africa received tritium (vital to a nuclear weapon program) in exchange for 50 tons of uranium from South Africa. In April 1978, Prime Minister Vorster signed a memorandum that approved the acceleration of the program and set out a strategy for South African nuclear weapons. If South African territory were threatened by the Soviets or the Cubans in Angola acting for them, South Africa would reveal its capability to the United States and to other countries. If this had no effect, then there would be a public announcement and perhaps a test. Actual use was not authorized for fear of retaliation.[13]

On September 22, 1979, at 3:00 a.m., a US Vela satellite detected with its bhangmeters (devices designed to record evidence of an atmospheric nuclear explosion) the characteristic double flash of an atmospheric nuclear explosion. The area in view of the satellite was southern Africa, the Indian Ocean, and the South Atlantic down to Antarctica. Hours later, a meeting of senior US government officials, assembled in response to this intelligence, the attendees heard the intelligence community representatives present say that "the odds were at least 90 percent that it had been a nuclear explosion." But everyone realized they were at the beginning of an investigation. A major internal US investigation of this incident began. The objectives of the Carter administration were to determine whether the indications of a nuclear explosive test, the specifics of which the Vela signal suggested was in the 2- to 4-kiloton range, were correct, and if correct, which country was responsible.[14]

Many studies were undertaken, and virtually all concluded that it was a nuclear test. But when it came to assigning blame, for a long time there was considerable uncertainty. South Africa was initially deemed to be the culprit, while others thought Israel might be responsible. The possibility of a joint Israeli–South African test was examined. One scientist suggested France as a possibility, as there were French-owned islands in the South Atlantic once considered as a possible test site. In October 1979, White House science advisor Frank Press established a panel of ten distinguished scientists from across the political spectrum to review both classified and unclassified data to attempt to determine whether the Vela signal had been the result of a nuclear detonation, a "false alarm" malfunction of the satellite, or of natural origin. Dr. Jack Ruina of the Massachusetts Institute of Technology was made chairman.[15]

While the Ruina panel was deliberating, other studies were underway. A study by the Mission Research Corporation of Santa Barbara was completed in December, and studies by Sandia National Laboratory and Los Alamos National Laboratory were issued in May. They all concluded that most probably a nuclear explosion had taken place, the Los Alamos report stating that there was "strong evidence that a nuclear explosion" caused the Vela signal. In addition, a Stanford Research Institute study examining the possibility of meteoroids causing the double flash declared that the possible meteoroid scenario (a collision between two meteors) advanced in the Mission Research Corporation and Stanford studies would likely happen only once in a billion years. Given the limited time for the study, the authors came to no firm conclusion about any other meteor scenario causing the double flash.

The Ruina panel met for a third time in April 1980 and completed its investigation. After reviewing many briefings, reading many reports, and carefully analyzing the Vela signal, the panel concluded that the Vela signal was probably not the result of a nuclear explosion. The panel stated that a meteor impact with the Vela satellite was its best explanation of what happened on September 22, 1979. On the other hand, a report by the Defense Intelligence Agency, completed in June 1980, concluded that the double flash did come from a nuclear explosion, as did a report by the CIA's Nuclear Intelligence Panel, whose chairman asserted, "we had no doubt it was a bomb."[16] Also in June 1980, the Naval Research Laboratory (NRL) completed a three-hundred-page study involving extensive research and analysis, unequivocally concluding that a nuclear device had been detonated on September 22.

Early on, the US government had thought that Prince Edward Island and nearby Marion Island were prime candidates for where a nuclear test might have taken place, if such a test had indeed happened. The islands are South African possessions located between South Africa and Antarctica, far from shipping and commercial routes. One of the NRL scientists noted that if one wanted to conduct a clandestine test, this area was a "splendid place to go." The islands' high mountains were a good place to locate observation sensors, and a barge with a nuclear device could be placed in the shallow water near the islands.[17]

Over the years, official studies declined, but speculation continued. On February 21, 1980, CBS aired a story by correspondent Dan Raviv, who had interviewed two Israeli journalists who had written a novel recounting the Israeli path to nuclear weapons that had been suppressed by the Israeli censor. In the interview, the two journalists told Raviv that the September 22, 1979, incident was a nuclear test conducted by Israel with South African assistance. On December 21 of the same year, Israeli television broadcast a British-produced program alleging that the incident was a test of a new naval warhead developed jointly by Israel and South Africa.

In his 1991 book *The Samson Option*, investigative journalist Seymour Hersh said that the Vela satellite had detected—according to former Israeli government officials, "whose information has been corroborated"—the test of a low-yield nuclear artillery shell and that the test was the third, not the first, test. In April 1997, an article in the Israeli *Ha'aretz* daily newspaper stated that the South

African deputy foreign minister Aziz Pahad confirmed that the double flash had resulted from a test, although he did not assert that Israel was involved. New information in the 1990s suggested that South Africa was not involved, at least by itself, in any test that occurred on September 22, 1979. As of 1995, the US intelligence community had not come to an official consensus about the cause of the double flash, but at least according to one account, based on interviews with US officials (published by Mitchell Reiss in *Bridled Ambition*), "unofficially the widespread view in the US government was that the Vela satellite had detected the test of a low-yield nuclear bomb and that Israel alone was responsible."[18]

Despite all this, as Steyn et al. report, "within a month after coming to power at the end of September 1978, the new South African Prime Minister P. W. Botha set up a cabinet committee to oversee the military aspects of nuclear devices." They further explain the decision of October 31 that ARMSCOR (a South African government-owned defense corporation), the Defense Force, and the AEB would prepare to initiate a nuclear program. The program began to come together in 1979. A three-party committee had begun work on the preparation of this program in early 1979. Several working groups were established, including one tasked to develop a responsible nuclear strategy. During 1980, a facility was created at a high-security ARMSCOR site, and the melting, casting, and machining of enriched uranium and other materials related to an explosive device was transferred from the AEB site. All other mechanical work related to nuclear explosives as well as the development of reliable triggers was likewise transferred. Later, that part of the theoretical physics group working on thermonuclear design was transferred as well. The only work left at the AEB site was in the conversion of uranium from gaseous to metallic form.[19]

In August 1994, accompanied by my deputy Susan Burk, I traveled to South Africa to advocate indefinite extension of the NPT at the conference in New York the next year and to seek the help of the South African government. We spent the first day in discussions at the foreign ministry, and the second day were given a tour of South Africa's former nuclear weapon facilities, including its operating low-enriched uranium plant, its shut-down HEU plant at Pelindaba, and its nuclear weapon assembly and storage facility at nearby Valindaba. Extensive briefings accompanied the tour. At Valindaba, we were told that we were the first Americans to see this facility except for the two IAEA officials on the agency inspection team that came to South Africa to verify the elimination of the nuclear weapon program and therefore determine South Africa's eligibility to join the NPT as a non–nuclear weapon state.

The South African officials conducting the briefings explained that the entire nuclear weapon program produced six nuclear weapons (with an estimated yield of approximately 20 kilotons each), involved a total of only 150 people, was very low budget, involved relatively simple "gun barrel" technology that did not need to be tested, and was completely hidden from view. They also said that they were not far enough along in 1979 to do a test—and that they didn't need one anyway. If we wanted to know which country carried out that test, they affirmed that we should "look to the north."

They took us into the room at ARMSCOR where the weapons were assembled. "Look around, nothing has changed," they said. Susan and I saw nothing there that you wouldn't find in a high school machine shop. They showed us the cases they used to move the weapons around so that we could get an idea of their size. They easily could have been carried in the back of a panel truck. They asserted that we were being shown all this to make the point that to build nuclear weapons, one didn't need a large infrastructure like Iraq had prior to the first Gulf War. Many countries, even substate actors, could do what South Africa had done if they could acquire the fissile material.

With the end of the Cold War, the situation changed in South Africa. The South African nuclear stockpile had been built with the Soviet Union in mind. And by the end of the 1980s, the Cubans were gone from Angola. It all came together over a period of five years: negotiation of independence for Namibia and withdrawal of Cuban forces from Angola; the collapse of the Soviet Union and the end of the Cold War; negotiations within South Africa and the release of Nelson Mandela, which led to the end of the apartheid system; and full disclosure of the South African nuclear weapon program.

F. W. de Klerk's election as state president of South Africa in 1989 helped catalyze some of these changes. He was among those from the ruling National Party who believed that the policy of apartheid should be ended and reconciliation sought while it was still possible. In 1990, he freed Nelson Mandela, went on to end apartheid, and finally laid the groundwork for the 1994 elections, which ended white rule in South Africa. He also decided to end South Africa's nuclear weapon program in 1990, agreed to sign the NPT in 1991, and opened South Africa's nuclear facilities to inspection by the IAEA. He ordered all of South Africa's nuclear weapons destroyed and a full accounting of production and disposition of HEU prepared for the IAEA. Nevertheless, little information about the program had been released to the public.

In March 1993, de Klerk announced that he would address a joint session of parliament on March 24. According to Richelson, there was wild speculation about what he would say in his speech, but none of the guesses "came close to the mark," de Klerk later wrote in his memoirs.[20] In his speech, de Klerk admitted, "at one stage South Africa did indeed have a limited nuclear capability." He explained that the plan was to build an arsenal of seven fission bombs, considered the minimum for testing purposes and a credible deterrent. By the time he took office, six had already been completed. He was aware of the program before he became president, as previously he had been the minister for mines. When de Klerk assumed power as president, in addition to the six bombs there existed the Y-Plant, where the HEU was produced at Pelindaba East, the Pelindaba Nuclear Research Center, and a large windowless building owned by an ARMSCOR subsidiary some 10 miles from Pretoria.[21]

The primary mission of the South African program at the time was the production of HEU and the manufacture of fission devices. It was not until November 1979 (after the 1979 South Atlantic event) that enough HEU had been produced for one gun-type device. The first bomb was constructed shortly thereafter. The second bomb was completed in December 1982. Thereafter, a bomb was produced every eighteen months. There was a review in 1985, which concluded that the program would be limited to seven devices, the seventh of which was under construction when de Klerk took office. Each of the bombs weighed about 1 ton and was about 6 feet long and 25 inches in diameter. They were based on the Little Boy design, which had been detonated over Hiroshima. South Africa's bombs were built on the assumption they would not be tested and thus were packed with twice as much HEU as would normally be used to ensure detonation.[22]

Early in his tenure, President de Klerk decided to end the program, and Y-Plant operations ceased in February 1990. There were two proposals for destroying the bombs: destroying half of each device before destroying the second half, or destroying the arsenal one device at a time. De Klerk brought in a man named Weynand Mouton, a former professor of nuclear physics whom de Klerk had met when he was minister of education and whom he trusted to oversee the weapon destruction process. Mouton recommended the latter process, which de Klerk accepted. Mouton's appointment was an attempt to prevent any possible diversion of nuclear material by dissident conservatives that might plan to resist the end of apartheid.[23]

Mouton and the South African military closely monitored the process. In his final report, Mouton certified that the weight of the nuclear cores approximated the weight of HEU at the end of the disarmament process, but not that he could account for all of South Africa's HEU. Then, on July 10, 1991, South Africa acceded to the NPT and became a non–nuclear weapon state party to it, thereby agreeing that its nuclear activities would be covered by the treaty, with all its materials and facilities covered by international safeguards. In September, South Africa signed a safeguards agreement with the IAEA, and in late October submitted an inventory of nuclear material and facilities under its jurisdiction.[24] That is the end of the South African nuclear weapon story, except to note that the subsequent IAEA inspections added to knowledge of South Africa's program and convinced all that South Africa could not have participated in the 1979 event. Some US officials for some years speculated that there was perhaps a slight possibility that South Africa could have secretly retained enough HEU to have a "bomb in the basement," as it is difficult to prove a negative, but the passage of time has eliminated that possibility.

Libya is another African country that sought nuclear weapons, but, like its longtime leader Muammar Qaddafi, its efforts were quixotic and ultimately fruitless. Libya made numerous attempts between 1970 and 1990 to acquire nuclear weapons capability. At the beginning of this period, Libya had signed—but not yet ratified—the NPT. It was ratified in 1975. In 1970, Qaddafi sent Abdul Jalloud, vice chairman of the Revolutionary Command Council, to ask for President Gamal Abdel Nasser's help in acquiring nuclear weapons from China. Nasser told him such weapons were not for sale, but Jalloud secretly traveled to China anyway on an Egyptian passport through Pakistan. While in China, he met with Zhou Enlai, who declined his request with "perfect Chinese courtesy" while stressing self-reliance.[25]

In 1973, Libya reached a secret agreement with Pakistan Prime Minister Ali Bhutto to finance the Pakistan nuclear weapon program in exchange for full access to the technology. Pakistan took the money but never delivered a nuclear-capable weapon to Libya. Qaddafi tried again to no avail with Pakistan and India in 1978. Jalloud, now prime minister, asked Indian officials, while on a visit to New Delhi, to help Libya obtain "an independent nuclear capability." India refused, and Libya eventually terminated oil shipments to India. This move did not change India's mind.[26]

Eventually, in the mid-1990s, the Libyans approached A. Q. Khan and offered to buy from him the complete capability to develop and construct nuclear weapons. The Khan network reached an agreement with Libya and made initial deliveries in 1997—twenty centrifuges and parts for more—which would permit Libya to begin research. But Libya, having no nuclear infrastructure, never did anything with these devices except to put them in a warehouse. The Khan network went into production in Malaysia to send centrifuges and actual nuclear material to

Libya. By 2002, Tripoli had assembled a few centrifuges and received a design for a nuclear weapon. It was the same design that the Chinese gave to Pakistan in the early 1980s and which was the subject of a 1966 test in China: a 20-kiloton device.

By that time the following year, Libya's nuclear efforts might have culminated. But in 2003 a shipment from Malaysia to Libya was interrupted by Western intelligence. Months earlier, Qaddafi had agreed with the United States and Britain to end his weapons-of-mass-destruction programs—chemical and nuclear—and to allow Western officials into his country to assist in eliminating these programs. This interception accelerated the process, and within a few weeks the entire Libyan nuclear inventory was in the hands of US and UK government officials. Significant parts of it were flown to Oak Ridge, Tennessee.

All of this took place against the backdrop of negotiations to establish a nuclear weapon–free zone in the region. The Organization of African Unity (OAU), at its first regular session held in Cairo in 1964, issued a declaration, motivated by the French nuclear test program in Algeria, stating that all African states were prepared to negotiate and conclude an international treaty under the auspices of the United Nations in which they would undertake not to manufacture or acquire control of nuclear weapons. The declaration asked the nuclear powers to respect and abide by it and asked the UN General Assembly for approval, which it granted the following year.

Nevertheless, challenges to the full acceptance of the Cairo Declaration soon became evident. From the beginning, the nuclear non-proliferation regime has been based on global and regional international agreements as well as on declarations backed by assurances from the IAEA safeguards system. In terms of regional non-proliferation arrangements, the first NWFZ treaty, the Treaty of Tlatelolco, covering all of Latin America, was signed in 1967, as discussed in chapter 3. The second, the Treaty of Rarotonga, covering the South Pacific region, was signed in 1986, as discussed in chapter 4. But during the Cold War, this was as far as the regional nuclear weapon–free zone movement could go. The key countries in the regions where nuclear weapon–free zones were negotiated after the end of the Cold War were themselves in one way or another too caught up in the East-West struggle while the Cold War continued. Thus for many years the objectives of the Cairo Declaration could not be realized.

The prospects for additional NWFZs began to shift in the five years after 1989, as revolutionary changes took place across the globe—changes from which Africa was not excluded. Among the most significant, beyond the end of the Cold War, was the end of apartheid in South Africa and the election of Nelson Mandela as president, along with the decisions of the predecessor de Klerk government to reveal South Africa's secret nuclear weapon program, verifiably destroy the nuclear devices that had been constructed, and become party to the NPT.

This opened the door for Africa to implement the Cairo Declaration, and no time was wasted in commencing the negotiations to do so. Negotiations began with a 1990 UN General Assembly resolution calling for a convening of a group of experts, in cooperation with the OAU, to study the modalities of the implementation of the Cairo Declaration. The first meeting of this group was held at the headquarters of the OAU in Addis Ababa, convened by the UN and the OAU in May 1991. Algeria, Nigeria, Tanzania, Zaire, and Zimbabwe were represented by experts; there were experts from the OAU and the UN and observers from the Tlatelolco and Rarotonga treaties as well as from the IAEA. This group elected Ambassador Oluyemi Adeniji, Nigeria's former representative to the IAEA and representative on the First Committee of the UN General Assembly from 1977 to 1990, as chairman. Two years later, when the negotiations formally began, the UN General Assembly again called on the UN and the OAU to appoint a group of experts to draft an NWFZ treaty for Africa. Ambassador Adeniji was again appointed chairman. He remained a central figure in the negotiations that followed, and his memoir is the definitive work on this negotiation. With his background, Ambassador Adeniji says writing the negotiating history of the Treaty of Pelindaba was an idea that came to him at the conclusion of the negotiations. This idea was reinforced during his attendance at the formal signing of the treaty in Cairo in 1996. Being present at the signing of the Treaty of Pelindaba gave him further incentive to document the process of transformation of the 1964 Cairo Declaration to the 1996 Pelindaba treaty, as he was involved in so much of the long process.[27]

The drafters made clear that the Pelindaba treaty in no way limited—indeed, it supported—peaceful uses of nuclear energy, as was the case of the Tlatelolco and Rarotonga treaties before it. Ambassador Adeniji says on this point, "It is obvious . . . that the only constraint for at least the major African states with relatively greater human and material resources will be the lack of will to take a leap into the nuclear era. Yet by taking that they can also contribute to growth in the less endowed states and thus to continental development."[28]

Ambassador Adeniji had many important comments on the African situation before describing the Pelindaba negotiation process:

By the 1960s when most African countries gained independence, the nuclear era was consolidating itself. . . . France chose Africa as its testing ground. In February 1960 France conducted its first nuclear test in the atmosphere in the Sahara Desert. In the course of the year, it conducted three additional atmospheric tests, all of which resulted in significant radioactive fallout in several African countries, with consequent danger to human and animal lives. The fact that a number of African states had appealed to France not to carry out the tests on their continent, all to no avail, was considered by many as a blatant affront on their newly acquired sovereignty and territorial integrity.[29]

African countries reacted in various ways: Nigeria broke diplomatic relations with France, and Gabon froze French assets in the country. In 1960, several African states introduced a resolution in the United Nations prohibiting nuclear weapon tests in Africa. This resolution in the end was withdrawn for lack of support. But the following year, a larger number of African states introduced a UNGA resolution, which passed.

In May 1963, the Organization of African Unity, the OAU, was founded. By this time, France was no longer conducting atmospheric tests but continued testing underground in the Sahara for several more years before moving the entire program to the South Pacific in 1966. One of the first acts of the new OAU was for its heads of state at the inaugural summit to adopt a resolution opposing all nuclear tests on the continent as well as the manufacture of nuclear weapons. At the first regular assembly of OAU heads of state and government in July 1964 in Cairo, the OAU adopted the Cairo Declaration, the French tests having been the motivation behind a nuclear weapon–free policy in Africa. The French program left Africa in 1966. For the next two decades, it was the South African program that was the obstacle to implementation of the Cairo Declaration. Only after the South African program was terminated in 1990 was the Treaty of Pelindaba possible.

The African view was that, despite Article VII of the NPT calling for NWFZs, prior to 1991 (the end of the Cold War), the reaction of NATO states to any proposal for a nuclear weapon–free zone was dictated by considerations related to the Cold War, not the interest of non-proliferation. Cold War considerations were not as evident in Latin America as they were in the South Pacific and Africa. Africa was convinced that the Western power collaboration with South Africa, supposedly for peaceful purposes, was also extended to assisting the South African nuclear weapon program—denied of course by the West. Ambassador Adeniji cited transcripts from a secret trial of a South African Air Force officer, General Johann Blaauw, which indicated that President de Klerk in his speech to the South African Parliament on March 24, 1993, in which he disclosed South Africa's nuclear weapon program, made at least three important misstatements:

1. South Africa had never acquired nuclear weapons technology or material from another country.

2. South Africa had never provided nuclear material to another country.

3. South Africa had never cooperated with another country in this regard.

The court case revealed extensive collaboration with Israel on nuclear materials, including supplying 50 metric tons of uranium, in yellow cake form, to Israel in exchange for 30 grams of tritium. Tritium helps in significantly increasing the explosive yield of a nuclear weapon—known as boosting—and also in the design of thermonuclear weapons. The tritium was to be flown to South Africa from Israel in 2.5-gram installments over eighteen months. It was reported in the trial record that this amount of tritium was sufficient "for the manufacture of 12 atomic bombs." Given South Africa's intent to build simple gun-type weapons, the tritium was ultimately not used as part of the weapons program. But this fact does not deny the extensive collaboration between Israel and South Africa, of which General Blaauw was a key mediator. There were reports of a second transfer of 50 tons of uranium and a final transfer of 500 tons of uranium yellow cake, which for some unexplained reason was already stored in Israel. As for General Blaauw himself, he was on trial for extortion related to mining concessions and was acquitted of all charges.[30]

Ambassador Adeniji also noted de Klerk's additional assertion that South Africa had never carried out a nuclear weapon test. He cites the 1977 incident in the Kalahari, where boreholes were dug, as an indication that South Africa had planned a test. Upon discovery by a Soviet satellite and heavy diplomatic pressure from Britain, France, Germany, and the United States, the site was closed (although what was planned there were "cold tests," since at that time South Africa did not have enough HEU to carry out a nuclear explosive test). Also mentioned by Ambassador Adeniji in questioning de Klerk's statement was the Vela double-flash incident; Adeniji claimed it was a joint South African–Israeli test. The double-flash incident took place in September 1979, and, as we now know, South Africa did not have enough HEU for a nuclear explosive device at the time either, not reaching this capability until December 1979. Thus it was a joint South African/Israeli test only in the sense that South Africa permitted Israel to use its sovereign territory—the two islands in the South Atlantic—to carry out the test. The Israelis, it appears, were testing a somewhat sophisticated low-yield device, which likely would not provide much, if any, useful technical information for the South African program.

The initial group of experts discussing the modalities and elements for the preparation and implementation of a treaty met first in 1991 in Addis Ababa. Included on their agenda were the necessary political conditions for a nuclear weapon–free zone in Africa, consideration of the geographical area of application, the scope of the prohibitions, verification provisions, obligations of nuclear weapon states, and obligations of outside states that possess territories within the zone. This was much the same agenda as that of the two previous negotiations for an NWFZ treaty in Latin America and the South Pacific.

The conclusions of the group were:

- The 1964 Cairo Declaration should constitute the basic political reference point for the pursuit of the project of the denuclearization of Africa.

- On the geographical extent of the nuclear weapon–free zone to be established by the treaty, the zone should cover the entire continent of Africa and the adjacent islands, as set forth in the relevant OAU resolution. The Convention on the Law of the Sea should be used as a reference point in defining the nautical limits of the zone. It was judged essential for South Africa to be an integral part of the zone and subject to its obligations. And foreign powers exercising responsibilities for territories forming part of the zone should commit themselves legally to accept the obligations of the treaty establishing the zone.

- The responsibilities of the nuclear states for the maintenance of the zone were considered to be of central importance. The NPT nuclear weapon states would be asked to pledge to respect the zone and to agree in a legally binding manner not to use or threaten to use nuclear weapons against any state, territory, or island in the zone, as they did for the first two nuclear weapon–free zone treaties.

- The elements of the prohibition should be comprehensive, covering research, development, production, stockpiling, use, testing, transportation, and dumping. Peaceful nuclear explosives should be examined in light of changes in perception toward them, meaning as in Rarotonga—that nuclear explosive devices should be banned, not just nuclear weapons. There also should be a provision prohibiting an armed attack on peaceful nuclear installations in the zone.

• The issue of the use of nuclear energy for peaceful purposes should constitute an important aspect of the treaty because nuclear energy is a significant resource for Africa.

• There should be an effective mechanism to ensure compliance by the parties.[31]

The report of the experts was submitted to the OAU secretary general and UN secretary general. Among the things suggested by the experts was a second meeting of the UN experts. This meeting took place the following year in April in Lomé, Togo. The group focused on the remaining issues, which were the relationship of the treaty to other international agreements and technical clauses of the treaty, such as ratification and entry into force. One important conclusion was to reemphasize the impact of the Convention on the Law of the Sea on the geographical limit of the zone. In order to attract the maritime states to the treaty, it could not interfere in any way with the freedom of the seas.

Again, the expert group report was submitted to both the OAU and the United Nations. At the June 1992 ministerial meeting in Dakar, it was decided to convene a joint meeting of the OAU Intergovernmental Group of Experts and the United Nations/OAU group to negotiate a draft treaty. Later in the year, the UN General Assembly requested that the secretary general, in consultation with the OAU, enable the UN/OAU joint group to meet in 1993 to negotiate a treaty. Thus the decisive stage began.

The two meetings, in 1991 and 1992, had been conducted without the participation of South Africa. Despite the important changes in South Africa, there was still no all-party government—which the OAU required to deal officially with South Africa—and thus the OAU was reluctant to conduct an official meeting with Pretoria. To solve this problem—and all recognized that it was important for South Africa to participate in this first negotiating meeting—a highly respected nongovernmental organization, the Programme for the Promotion of Non-Proliferation (PPNN), offered to conduct the meeting as part of its own program for non-proliferation.

The meeting was held in Harare, Zimbabwe, in early April 1993. Just the week before, President de Klerk had made his renowned speech to the South African Parliament on the country's nuclear weapon program. PPNN invited the chief executive of the South African Atomic Energy Agency, Dr. Waldo Stumpf, to represent South Africa. According to Adeniji, he emphasized in both oral and written presentations South Africa's determination to be transparent and its acceptance in principle of a nuclear weapon–free zone for the continent. Difficult questions were asked and special clarifications sought, but the participants in this meeting—called a seminar—came away with nascent confidence in contracts between South Africa and the rest of the continent. This confidence was to prove invaluable in the treaty negotiations that followed.[32]

What should have been a negotiating meeting following the seminar with South Africa became—by Adeniji's account—an expert discussion group, in which experts clarified and further refined elements of the treaty. The OAU inter-governmental group of experts did not attend this meeting; the UN/OAU group of experts did attend, though substantially changed in composition; and South Africa was present as an observer, represented by three officials: one from the government, one from the African National Congress, and one from the Pan-Africanist Congress of Azania. Most of the issues that had been discussed in the first two meetings were reopened, and some were vigorously debated. A firm position against peaceful nuclear explosives was agreed. The issue of islands off-shore Africa, where there were disputed claims, was discussed but not resolved. Total transparency was emphasized as well as the need to strike a balance between non-proliferation and the great importance in promoting African expertise in peaceful nuclear technology. Entry into force would require half the membership of the OAU plus one. In general, the essential structure of the treaty developed in the first two meetings was reinforced. There was no time to negotiate many of the articles in the draft treaty, but the report forwarded to the UN secretary general—referred to as the Harare draft—contained extensive discussions of a number of the issues with initial drafts of some of the articles. The group asked the secretary general to convene another meeting so that they could continue.[33]

The UN General Assembly asked that the secretary general, in consultation with the OAU, permit the expert group to meet in Windhoek, Namibia, and Addis Ababa, Ethiopia, in 1994 to finalize the drafting of the treaty. The Windhoek meeting took place in March 1994 and the Addis Ababa meeting in June. An inte-grated report of these two meetings was submitted to the General Assembly later in the year. The report showed that there were still sections of the draft treaty that were not completed, particularly the map showing the geographical limits of the zone. One more meeting was scheduled in May–June 1995 in Johannesburg, South Africa. It was there that the final draft of the treaty was agreed on and named the Treaty of Pelindaba.

Adeniji recounts the article-by-article negotiations of the treaty that began in Windhoek. The definition of the area to be covered by the treaty proved to be the crucial part of the negotiations and its most difficult element. Its text changed almost from one negotiation meeting to another, and as a result the map was not available until the final meeting. The draft of Article 1(a) from the Harare draft defined the zone as follows: "African Nuclear-Weapon-Free Zone means the continent of Africa, and the adjoining islands as described in Annex 1, and as illustrated by the map attached to the Annex." The discussion in Harare had indicated the need for a more inclusive definition, which would include the entire continent of Africa, island-state members of the OAU, and other islands subject to various resolutions of the OAU as belonging to the continent. Thus there was a difficult issue between OAU members and potential parties to the Pelindaba treaty and several European states—namely, Britain, France, and Spain—that administered some of these islands. This issue was extensively discussed at Windhoek and Addis Ababa as well as at the final meeting in Johannesburg in 1995. France, particularly at Windhoek, indicated a desire to know which islands in the Indian Ocean and the Mediterranean the treaty negotiators had in mind to include in the zone. The negotiators then asked France for a list of its island possessions in the Indian Ocean, and the French representative at Windhoek promptly handed over a list of five islands.[34]

With respect to "nuclear explosive device," the drafters of the Pelindaba treaty used an article identical to the comparable article in the Rarotonga treaty. Adeniji's account of negotiations thus places it in the context of other NWFZ treaties. The prohibited nuclear weapon–related activities in the Pelindaba treaty go far beyond the provisions in the Tlatelolco and Rarotonga treaties. In addition to acquisition, possession, and manufacture, the Pelindaba treaty includes research, development, and stockpiling. The Pelindaba treaty added a new definition of "nuclear installation" because, for the first time, a provision was included banning attacks on nuclear installations. The negotiators in Addis Ababa added a provision permitting parties in their exercise of sovereignty to allow port visits and transit of territorial waters by ships and visits and overflights by aircraft not covered by the right of innocent passage. This permits, inter alia, a party to accept if it so chooses port visits and transit by nuclear-powered or nuclear-capable ships. This text was identical to the comparable provisions in Rarotonga. It was modified slightly at the Johannesburg meeting and retained in the final text of the Pelindaba treaty, thus allowing a party to permit port calls and aircraft visits by ships and aircraft that might be carrying or were capable of carrying nuclear weapons. There is also a treaty text provision banning the testing of nuclear weapons implied but not explicitly stated as in Rarotonga. The Tlatelolco provision "Nothing in this treaty shall be interpreted as to prevent the use of nuclear science and technology for peaceful purpose" was utilized. Verification would be by the IAEA. Article II is the prohibition of attack on nuclear facilities by conventional or any other means. A modified implementation and compliance body (called the African Commission on Nuclear Energy, or AFRICONE) was created, which held less power and scope than the implementing body (OPANAL) of the Tlatelolco text, but was more extensive than the authority of the South Pacific Forum as provided in the Rarotonga text. It reviews applications for peaceful nuclear activities, encourages regional programs, brings into effect the treaty's complaint procedure, and meets once a year. The membership of the OAU had increased slightly, so the number of states required to ratify, in order to bring the treaty into force, was changed from twenty-seven to twenty-eight.[35]

From the beginning of the Windhoek negotiations, representatives of France, Great Britain, and the United States attended the negotiation sessions, commenting with some frequency on the issues of paramount importance to them: the area of application and the protocols. Spain was also consulted, as it held territory within the zone of application and also Portugal, briefly. The African negotiating parties showed the utmost interest in drafting the treaty in a way that would permit the NPT nuclear weapon states to adhere to the two protocols open to them. Many believed that the success of the treaty depended on their support. Articles were drafted ensuring that the treaty would be consistent with the rules of the Convention on the Law of the Sea and that parties could permit port visits by nuclear-capable ships and aircraft. Such provisions made the area of application provisions difficult to negotiate: France held territory in the zone, and there was a long-standing dispute over whether Great Britain did as well—in particular, the Chagos Archipelago in the Indian Ocean, where there was also a major US base at Diego Garcia.

When Annex 1—which was to include an attached map of the treaty zone— was negotiated at Windhoek, the negotiators decided to go beyond the minimalist approach of the Harare draft. The Harare draft for Annex 1 referred simply to the continent of Africa and adjoining islands as forming the zone. At Windhoek, the new text of Article 1(a) described the treaty zone as being the continent of Africa, "island states members of the OAU," and "other adjoining islands." France, the United Kingdom, and the United States at Windhoek all made their ultimate support contingent on a satisfactory resolution of the area of application, particularly regarding the "other adjoining islands" part.

This issue was considered at length in Addis Ababa. There, both the United States and Great Britain cautioned against the inclusion of the Chagos Archipelago, otherwise known as the British Indian Ocean Territory, either in Annex 1 or on the attached map. The problem was that Mauritius, to be a treaty party, strongly pressed its claim for the Chagos Archipelago during the negotiations. The solution at Addis Ababa became cemented in the following language: the continent of Africa, island states, members of the OAU, and "all islands considered by the Organization of African Unity in its resolutions to be part of Africa, as well as other islands between those islands and continental Africa. This is illustrated in the attached map."[36] The map could not be completed at Addis Ababa, and the annex, the map, and the closely associated Protocol III were reopened at the joint meeting held to finalize the drafting of the treaty in May/June 1995.

At an early stage, the negotiators decided to draft three protocols to the treaty, as in the Treaty of Rarotonga, rather than two as in the Treaty of Tlatelolco. Protocol I would provide the negative security assurance in which the NPT nuclear weapon states would undertake never to use or threaten to use nuclear weapons against parties to the treaty or any territory within the treaty zone for which a state that has become a party to Protocol III is responsible. Protocol II provided a ban on testing "a nuclear explosive device" anywhere in the treaty zone. And Protocol III provides that each party to the protocol that has international responsibility for any territory within the treaty zone will place that territory under the obligations of the treaty. China France, Russia, the United Kingdom, and the United States were invited to become parties to Protocols I and II, and France and Spain were invited to become parties to Protocol III.

The Harare draft includes the language "never under any circumstances" as a modifier to the negative security assurance provided in Protocol I. France, Great Britain, and the United States strongly objected to this language at Windhoek, and it was dropped at Addis Ababa.

At the final negotiating session in Johannesburg, the Chagos Archipelago issue proved to be the most difficult. The United Kingdom asserted that, unless this issue was satisfactorily resolved, it would be an obstacle to the United Kingdom signing any of the protocols. The United States representative supported the United Kingdom, advising that the treaty should stay away from sovereignty issues. At the time, the Diego Garcia base was an important support facility for US carrier battle groups operating in the Indian Ocean. The representative from Mauritius quickly replied that the Chagos Archipelago had to be in the treaty zone because it was part of the territory of Mauritius.

In front of the negotiators at Johannesburg was the Addis Ababa draft language for Annex 1, which included the phrase "and all islands considered by the

Organization of African Unity in its resolutions to be part of Africa, as well as other islands between those islands and continental Africa." The completed map included, in addition to the continent of Africa and island-state members of the OAU, the Chagos Archipelagos; the French Territories of Réunion, Mayotte, Tromelin, Juan de Nova, and Bossa de India; the Spanish possession of the Canary Islands; and Portugal's territory of Madeira.

France supported the United Kingdom's position on the Chagos Archipelago, but its representative made clear that, in a spirit of cooperation, France would not object to its Indian Ocean territories being included in the treaty zone so long as the treaty clarified that there was no dispute regarding sovereignty over the territories, which were integral parts of France. The representative of Spain reaffirmed Spain's commitment to non-proliferation, including its support for NWFZs under appropriate conditions. He said Spain would undertake a careful legal study of Protocol III and adopt an appropriate final decision. He noted that Spain was in de jure control of the Canary Islands, not merely "internationally responsible for them." Portugal's representative was emphatic in rejecting the inclusion of the Madeira Archipelago, which he contended had been an integral part of Portugal for six hundred years. He also noted that Madeira was farther from Africa than many countries in Europe.

The negotiations then quickly reached consensus on the need to identify on the map all the states, island-states, and territories that would form part of the zone; that there was no basis for including Madeira in the treaty zone, as it was not covered by any OAU resolution; and that some compromise must be found, with respect to the Chagos Archipelago, that would ensure that Mauritius would be a party to the treaty and the United Kingdom would adhere to the protocols. It was proposed that the archipelago be included in a box on the map with a note saying, "without prejudice to [the] question of sovereignty or its future status."[37] This proposal was promptly rejected by both Mauritius and the United Kingdom. It was now widely considered that the comprehensive definition in Article 1(a) was sufficient and that the text of Annex 1 could be deleted, leaving only the map. Annex 1 thus became *only* the map. Furthermore, because the inclusion of Madeira had been rejected, the last phrase in the definition of treaty zone also could be deleted. So, the definition of the treaty zone, the area of application, appears only in Article 1(a), which reads: "'African Nuclear-Weapon-Free Zone' means the territory of the continent of Africa, island-state members of the OAU, and all islands considered by the Organization of African Unity in its resolutions to be part of Africa."[38]

After consideration of IAEA safeguards, the complaints procedure, and the protocols, which were relatively free from controversy, treaty negotiations effectively ended. Adeniji accounts for the treaty's name in this way: at the suggestion of the South African expert, which was enthusiastically accepted, the final draft text was named Pelindaba rather than Johannesburg, which normal practice might have dictated. This was considered appropriate for two reasons: Pelindaba is the location of the headquarters of South African Atomic Energy Corporation—some 30 kilometers from Johannesburg—and symbolized the change of the South African program from being a threat to the rest of Africa to what might become the hub of continental cooperation in the peaceful use of nuclear energy. "Pelindaba" is derived from the Zulu words for "the matter is settled or the discussion is closed."[39]

It followed that the formal adoption of the text took place at Pelindaba. The closing ceremony was on June 2, 1995, in the presence of Dr. J. W. L. de Villiers, chairman of the corporation, and Dr. W. E. Stumpf, the chief executive. The text being formally adopted was sent to the secretary general of the OAU and to the secretary general of the United Nations.

Upon receipt of it by the OAU, the text was scheduled for consideration by the Council of Ministers on June 21-23, 1995. The only part of the treaty that was reopened was Annex 1, the map of the treaty zone. The foreign minister of Mauritius reminded the council that his representative at Johannesburg had expressed reservation about the treatment of the Chagos Archipelago in the map and that the OAU had adopted resolutions supporting the Mauritius claim to the Chagos Archipelago. At the same time, the council noted the flexibility of Mauritius in accepting the terms of the letter it sent to the United Kingdom, that the inclusion of the Archipelago in the zone did not affect the claim of Mauritius or the United Kingdom regarding sovereignty. The council amended the note on the map with respect to the Chagos Archipelago to read simply "without prejudice to the question of sovereignty." The council also endorsed the offer of Egypt to host the signing ceremony, and that of South Africa to host the headquarters of the African Nuclear Energy Commission, the implementing body of the Treaty of Pelindaba. This long and difficult negotiation demonstrated that complicated interstate issues can be overcome in negotiating a nuclear weapon–free zone arrangement, and that the existence of an active nuclear weapon program in a region is not an impediment to the negotiation of such an arrangement.

The Pelindaba treaty was duly signed in Cairo by forty-one OAU member states. Three NPT nuclear weapon states signed Protocols I and II—China, the

United Kingdom, and the United States—while France signed Protocols I and III. Neither Russia nor Spain attended the signing ceremony, but Russia later in the year signed Protocols I and II. Spain has never signed, ratified, nor acceded to Protocol III.

The Pelindaba treaty entered into force on July 15, 2009, when Burundi became the twenty-eighth state to deposit its instrument of ratification or accession with the depository, the Commission of the African Union. The treaty now has thirty-eight parties. It is notable that Libya, which had nuclear weapon ambitions for many years, is a party, along with two other north African states, Algeria and Tunisia.

Protocol I has been ratified by China, France, Russia, and the United Kingdom. The United States sent the protocol to the US Senate for advice and consent to ratification on May 3, 2011. Protocol II has been ratified by China, France (even though it did not initially sign it), Russia, and the United Kingdom. The United States sent Protocol II to the Senate on May 3, 2011. Protocol III has been ratified by France.

Chapter 6
The Treaty of Bangkok

Growing out of a long struggle first against colonialism and then against efforts by outside powers to influence events in Southeast Asia, the states of the region developed their own unique diplomatic and security culture. To some degree, the establishment and subsequent expansion across the region of the Association of Southeast Asian Nations (ASEAN) institutionalized a culture of reducing foreign influence. According to one observer, this diplomatic and security culture differs from the culture in other regions, the basic principles of which include:

1. sovereign equality,

2. nonrecourse to the use of force and the peaceful settlement of conflict,

3. noninterference and nonintervention,

4. the noninvolvement of ASEAN to address unresolved bilateral conflict between members,

5. quiet diplomacy, and

6. mutual respect and tolerance.[1]

These principles have not always been strictly followed, but they have had a strong influence on the region as it developed over time. This culture has been referred to by some as the "ASEAN way," and by the early 1970s it was increasingly respected as a framework for intramural relations. But accommodation and reconciliation still remained in some doubt when ASEAN governments expressed their determination to undertake "necessary efforts to secure the recognition of, and respect for, Southeast Asia as a Zone of Peace, Freedom, and Neutrality, free from any form or manner of interference by outside powers" in the Kuala

Lumpur Declaration of November 1971. This concept has since been referred to as ZOPFAN.[2]

Five Asian nations—Indonesia, Malaysia, the Philippines, Singapore, and Thailand—established ASEAN as an institution on August 8, 1967. The intent was for these nations to establish their own identity, ensure their sovereignty, and develop an interstate culture unique to the region. Brunei joined ASEAN in 1984, Vietnam in 1995, Laos and Myanmar in 1997, and Cambodia in 1999; thus all ten Southeast Asian countries were members by 1999. Nine of the ten had joined by the time of the signing of the Treaty of Bangkok in December 1997, also known as the Southeast Asian Nuclear Weapon–Free Zone Treaty; two of them, Laos and Myanmar, had joined just months before.

ZOPFAN was a compromise attempting to satisfy diverse national and governmental security interests, related to efforts to achieve a position of neutralism in the first part of the Cold War. British forces were drawing down in Malaysia and Singapore, as Malaysia had recently overcome an insurgency with British help. Australia and New Zealand were backing away from the region, and the United States under the Nixon doctrine had indicated that it would fight no more regional land wars on the continent of Asia. Malaysia took the lead in the 1960s in the neutralization effort. The hope was that, by adopting this policy, a neutral Southeast Asia free from big power entanglements could be established. In the Malaysian view, the lesson of Vietnam—particularly the involvement of major powers in the war—made neutralization a necessary step for protecting regional nations and their interests. But Malaysia also made clear that it did not believe that neutralization could be pursued so long as the war in Vietnam continued. Neutralization could only be a successful strategy if individual Southeast Asian governments could restore order in their own houses.

The Malaysian policy contemplated how it could obtain guarantees from major powers for the peace and security for the ASEAN states—guarantees that would underlie the policy of neutrality. Yet no other ASEAN country supported the Malaysian initiative of neutralization. The Thai government believed the root of "foreign interference" in the region was the predatory policies pursued by the government in Hanoi.[3] President Suharto of Indonesia was suspicious of this strategy because he thought that great power guarantees would provoke, rather than inhibit, foreign interference within ASEAN states. Singapore was hesitant about pursuing a policy based on the Malaysian proposal because it questioned Malaysia's intentions. Singapore was concerned that Malaysia proposed this initiative as a way to establish a subregional hegemony for itself. The Philippines also opposed neutralization, but for more domestic reasons. The Philippines benefited greatly from America's naval presence and defense ties with Washington,[4] so the prospect of losing these connections to the United States was troubling.

In the end, Malaysia's neutralization proposal was not completely repudiated, but rather modified so that concerns were assuaged. This happened with the admission of the People's Republic of China to the United Nations and to the UN Security Council in place of the Republic of China, which since 1950 governed only in Taiwan. At the same time, Washington and Beijing announced in July 1971 that President Nixon would soon visit China. ASEAN governments for the most part had hostile views of China, some governments even believing that the People's Republic of China was illegitimate. All ASEAN states feared China's potential power—military, political, and cultural—upon the region. Some ASEAN states, because of the impending US-PRC alignment, were concerned that they might be carved up into spheres of influence. In response, Thailand crafted a revised ZOPFAN declaration that was presented to ASEAN foreign ministers at a special meeting held in Kuala Lumpur. This document declared a "zone of peace, freedom and development" but responded to the objections of Indonesia to great power guarantees for neutrality. It called only for political pledges to support a zone of neutrality. ZOPFAN, in the Kuala Lumpur declaration, presented a two-pronged approach for maintaining regional political order: a legitimate innovative framework to guide future interstate action and the enhancement of national security through practical intraregional cooperation. It was a compromise that revolved around a shared commitment to sovereign equality and noninterference.

The formal meaning of ZOPFAN was agreed to by the ASEAN Senior Officials Committee and made public in July 1972:

> A zone of peace, freedom and neutrality exists where national identity, independence and integrity of the individual States within such a zone can be preserved and maintained, so that they can achieve national development and well-being, and promote regional co-operation and solidarity, in accordance with the ideals and aspirations of their peoples and the purposes and principles of the United Nations Charter, free from any form or manner of interference by outside powers.

> Peace is a condition where the prevalence of harmonious and orderly relations exists between and among States; no reference is hereby made to the internal state of affairs in each of the zonal States. A situation of ideological, political, economic, armed or

other forms of conflict either among the zonal States themselves, between one or more zonal States and outside powers, or between outside powers affecting the region, is not a condition of peace.

Freedom means the freedom of States from control, domination or interference by other States in the conduct of their internal and external affairs. This means the right of zonal States to solve their domestic problems in terms of their own conditions and aspirations, to assume primary responsibility for the security and stability of the region and their regional and international relations on the basis of sovereign equality and mutual benefit.

Neutrality means the maintenance of a state of impartiality in any war between other States as understood in international law and in the light of the United Nations Charter; in the context of the Kuala Lumpur Declaration, however, it means that zonal States shall undertake to maintain their impartiality and shall refrain from involvement directly or indirectly in ideological, political, economic, armed or other forms of conflict, particularly between powers outside the zone, and that outside powers shall not interfere in the domestic or regional affairs of the zonal States.[5]

This definition is in a sense ASEAN's principal document. It is firmly in the tradition of Asian neutralism and nonalignment. In linking freedom and non-interference, the senior officials reflected a sense of grievance experienced by ASEAN leaders owing to their inability to control events affecting their countries. The major powers did not endorse the prospect of a zone of peace, freedom, and neutrality in Southeast Asia, nor did they commit themselves to the principles of sovereign equality, noninterference, and the nonuse of force, as ASEAN urged them to do. Because ZOPFAN could not be supported by major pledges of commitment, attention turned to bringing all of Southeast Asia into ASEAN, so that they might thereby be guided by ZOPFAN. If the external objectives of major power support could not be immediately met, perhaps the internal ones could. This meant focusing on whether ZOPFAN could be made acceptable to Hanoi as the basis for peaceful coexistence.

Neither North nor South Vietnam had been particularly enthusiastic about ZOPFAN. They were warring states and did not have any interest in helping to create and establish "zones of peace" in the region. As Jürgen Haacke narrates in ASEAN's *Diplomatic and Security Cultures: Origins, Developments and Prospects*, ASEAN states had long been suspicious and distrustful of Hanoi, a feeling that the Hanoi government vigorously reciprocated. After the Paris Peace Agreements and the subsequent fall of South Vietnam, however, Hanoi's attitude toward ZOPFAN changed. In 1976, Hanoi seemed significantly more interested in improving its relationship with ASEAN and with ASEAN states. It proposed the establishment of a "zone of peace and friendly cooperation." Although it became clear that this proposition would not be possible after the reunification of Vietnam later in the year, Vietnam began to improve its ties with individual ASEAN states. Unfortunately, this progress faltered after Vietnam invaded Cambodia in 1978. ASEAN states viewed this action by Vietnam as blatantly opposed to the principles embodied in ZOPFAN.

ASEAN members began to reevaluate their defense policies, and when ASEAN diplomacy failed to reverse Vietnam's interventions into Cambodia, some members of ASEAN pressed for further development of ZOPFAN's operational aspects. For example, Indonesia attempted to enforce for itself the Archipelagic Principle, which held that land and waters surrounding Indonesia, regardless of their dimensions, were under the sovereign authority of Jakarta. This principle had not been established internationally, but it was later established when the UN Convention on the Law of the Sea came into force. At the same time, Jakarta urged ASEAN to revive the Association's Working Group on ZOPFAN to study the feasibility of a Southeast Asia Nuclear Weapon–Free Zone (SEANWFZ).[6]

Thus the Treaty of Bangkok, by contrast with the NWFZs established in Latin America, the South Pacific, and Africa, did not come about because of a potential or actual nuclear weapon program; it came to fruition because of the Zone, that is ZOPFAN. Its establishment was not a result of the testing of nuclear weapons by an outside power such as France in Africa and in the South Pacific; a nuclear weapon program indigenous to the zone such as South Africa; nor potential nuclear weapon programs within the zone such as Argentina and Brazil. Rather, SEANWFZ was a natural and logical extension of the ASEAN policy of neutrality and freedom from influence and dominance by major foreign powers that came out of the establishment of the ZOPFAN. Furthermore, by the time the Treaty of Bangkok was signed in 1995, all the ASEAN states were parties to the NPT. The principal purpose of SEANWFZ was not a non-proliferation policy in the zone, but rather a policy to influence the NPT nuclear weapon states and major powers outside the zone.

As a result, SEANWFZ thus far has been to some degree a failure. The nuclear weapon states were expected to sign the single protocol to the Treaty of Bangkok, which is similar in content to the protocols to the Treaties of Tlatelolco, Rarotonga, and Pelindaba. It does not have the provisions for placing territories within the zone under the control of outside states under the obligations of the treaty, as there are no such territories within ASEAN, and it does not ban nuclear weapon testing by outside powers because such tests never occurred in ASEAN territory. But it does contain a provision requiring the protocol parties to respect the obligations of the treaty and a negative security assurance. The negative security assurance is somewhat expanded. Protocol parties are required not to use or threaten to use nuclear weapons against parties to the Treaty of Bangkok, and also not to use nuclear weapons anywhere within the zone. This was one objection to the terms of the protocol by the NPT nuclear weapon states.

The more important objection is the treaty's expansion of the area of obligations of the Treaty of Bangkok to include the waters above the continental shelf and the Exclusive Economic Zone (EEZ)—as defined by the UN Convention on the Law of the Sea—out to 200 nautical miles from the land territory of a state. In effect, this provision adopts the archipelagic rule to all of ASEAN territory, so that it applies to ships and planes of outside powers transiting almost anywhere in the region. The US Navy sees this as a direct threat to its ability to move ships and planes around the world, and it considered this expansion to be contrary to its deterrent posture in that it limited the striking power of carrier-based weapons in the region.

The principal purpose of ASEAN in adopting this position in the Treaty of Bangkok, however, was not to limit the United States—as most ASEAN states see the United States as an essential ally against Chinese expansionism—but rather to contain China's military expansion into the South China Sea and beyond, which is considered a security threat by several ASEAN nations. Even so, none of the NPT nuclear weapon states have thus far signed the protocol, to the profound chagrin of ASEAN states. This position is largely led by the United States. There have been negotiations with individual NPT nuclear weapon states over the years after entry into force of the treaty. Gradually, Britain, China, France, and Russia have come around to a position suggesting they may be prepared to sign the protocol in the near future. But that is not that case for the United States. The United States did join in a statement during an ASEAN summit meeting in 2011 that it expected to sign the protocol in 2012.[7] But this did not happen. So far, none of the NPT nuclear weapon states have signed the protocol, even though over twenty years have passed since the treaty was signed in 1995 and twenty years even since its entry into force. While the Treaty of Bangkok has strengthened NPT obligations in the region and established constraints against the dumping of radioactive waste in the regional waters, it remains in its fundamental purpose an essential failure because it does not regulate the NPT nuclear weapon states in the ASEAN region.

The concept of an SEANWFZ dates to 1971 with the establishment of ASEAN by the five original members. None of the ASEAN members have ever possessed nuclear weapons or had nuclear weapon programs, and most condemned nuclear weapons from the earliest of days. Indonesia's first president, Sukarno, considered initiating such a program in the mid-1960s while announcing, "God willing, Indonesia will shortly produce its own atom bomb." But this never became a reality, and Indonesia joined the NPT in 1970 as a non–nuclear weapon state party.[8] The establishment of an NWFZ was the first initiative of the ZOPFAN that ASEAN pursued. Conflicts in the region and, most importantly, the Vietnamese invasion of Cambodia in 1978 prevented early action, but the concept was successfully raised again by Indonesia and Malaysia in 1984. Within two years, the ASEAN foreign ministers established a working group of ZOPFAN to begin the drafting of an SEANWFZ treaty.

The United States strongly objected to this initiative on the grounds that Hanoi would not join and that consequently such a treaty would not prevent the Soviet Union from stationing nuclear weapons in Vietnam. The United States feared that all other ASEAN states would be disadvantaged by Russia's alliance with Vietnam. Nevertheless, the committee established by the ministers began working on a nuclear weapon–free zone treaty in 1986 for the ASEAN region. Their goal was to prepare a first draft text of such a treaty. In 1991, the Cold War ended and the Peace Agreement on Cambodia was signed. These two major occurrences permitted reconciliation between Vietnam and the other ASEAN states and removed some of the Cold War concerns of the United States. The SEANWFZ idea was once again revived, and by the fall of 1995, the drafting was well into its advanced stages.

In 1993, the ASEAN foreign ministers had met in Singapore to reaffirm their decision to negotiate an NWFZ treaty and their commitment to ZOPFAN. Besides concerns over China's territorial disputes in the South China Sea and its growing nuclear arsenal, there were also concerns about the nuclear weapon program in North Korea and whether that program might push Japan to seek nuclear weapons for defense. The next draft of the SEANWFZ Treaty therefore expanded the reach of the obligations of the draft nuclear weapon–free zone treaty to the continental shelves and the EEZ, which—pursuant to the UN Convention on the Law of the Sea—extends 200 nautical miles off the coast of the parties. It thereby would bring a high percentage of the entire South China Sea under the nuclear weapon–free obligations of the draft treaty. ASEAN argued that the region could better protect against radioactive dumping by expanding the area of the zone, but the real reason, or at least the more important reason, was to better contain China. By the fall of 1995, the treaty draft was virtually complete, with the extension to the continental shelf and the EEZ locked in. This was anathema to two of the NPT nuclear weapon states: China and the United States. The other three P-5 powers—France, Russia, and the United Kingdom—maintained P-5 solidarity with regards to the extension to the continental shelf and the EEZ. China was opposed to it because the provision was specifically aimed at Beijing, while the United States regarded the provision as an infringement on the principle of freedom of the seas and therefore detrimental to US interests.

I pursued an NPT consultation with the government of Ecuador prior to the 1995 conference, and I brought my daughter Eliza with me so that afterward we could take a short vacation in the Galápagos Islands. She returned to Quito to work some months after that first visit. Subsequently, in October 1995, while visiting her there, I received an urgent telephone call from Washington in my room at the Oro Verde Hotel. I was asked if I could lead a delegation to Jakarta. ASEAN was refusing to listen to US concerns on the emerging SEANWFZ Treaty. The United States saw this as contrary to a request of President Clinton in a letter to President Suharto—one I had hand-delivered to Indonesia earlier in the year. The main point of the letter had been to express President Clinton's support for the SEANWFZ Treaty, which was the first time that the United States had expressed support of this measure. It was delivered, in part, with the hope that the Indonesians might come around to the US position on NPT extension at the April–May 1995 conference. They did not. But the United States continued its support for the SEANWFZ Treaty on the assumption—among other conditions—that the principle of the freedom of the seas would not be infringed upon. The United States saw the continental shelf/EEZ provision as doing just that. I was asked to lead a US delegation to join with representatives of the other P-5 states in Jakarta and try to persuade ASEAN to change the text.

The meeting took place in November. The agenda was as follows: each of the P-5 would have a session before the ASEAN states. The United States would have the first day; China and Russia would split the second day; and Britain and France the third. The United States strongly objected to the extension of the obligations of the treaty to the high seas within the EEZ and the waters above the continental shelf. Another concern was the protocol's negative security assurance—appropriate in itself, but in the United States' view, worded incorrectly. Instead of an obligation not to use or threaten to use nuclear weapons against any state party to the treaty, the provision stated that a protocol party could not use nuclear weapons within the zone. This would have the United States giving a negative security assurance to Russian and Chinese ships within the zone. In addition, there was a provision permitting port and aircraft visits as a party so chose, but no provision for a clear right of transit through the zone for vessels carrying nuclear weapons.

We met with the Chinese delegation before the US presentation, and they agreed with all of our concerns. They believed that the EEZ provision was included because of the dispute over the Spratly Islands in the South China Sea. They wanted to be sure that this treaty did not affect any of their territorial claims.

There was another issue of concern to the United States: the protocol, as drafted, was open to any state rather than to just the NPT nuclear weapon states. The Indonesians explained that this was designed to permit India to join. The United States objected to recognition of India as a nuclear weapon state. The Japanese were also worried that they might be forced to join, and that this might compromise their position under the US nuclear umbrella. There were also some minor points at issue, including the right of protocol parties to be notified of changes in the treaty and the right to attend implementing body deliberations.

Seven of the ASEAN states were seated around a horseshoe-shaped table with the podium for the presenter in the middle. I spoke for nearly an hour, after which time there were two hours for questions. The ASEAN states were reminded that without the participation of the NPT nuclear weapon states in the protocol, the NWFZ would not be fully operational. The other P-5 members duly made their presentations as well. On the subject of accession to the protocol, the provision was changed to permit only the NPT nuclear weapon states in the next draft. Corrections were made in the treaty draft; there was some movement on transit rights. But there were no substantive changes to the negative security assurance, and there was no change at all on the EEZ and continental shelf issues. ASEAN promptly proceeded to sign the treaty the following month in Bangkok, and it became known as the Treaty of Bangkok. The protocol was left in draft form so that changes could be made. Malaysia inherited the chair of the ASEAN working group from Indonesia in 1996, and the Philippines took over in 1997, but the central issues were never corrected. [9] And to this day, no NPT nuclear weapon state has signed the protocol despite on-and-off negotiations over the years. The treaty came into force in 1997.

The Treaty of Bangkok is much in line with the NWFZ treaties that came before it: the Treaties of Tlatelolco, Rarotonga, and Pelindaba. It contains a complete prohibition on nuclear explosive devices with respect to all the parties to the treaty. And each party is prohibited from contributing in any way to the stationing or testing of nuclear weapons on its territory by any other state. There are important treaty provisions guaranteeing to the parties the right to nuclear energy. The treaty also urges its parties to adhere to the Convention on Nuclear Accidents, alone among free-zone treaties to do so. It has a commission to oversee verification—which will be performed by the IAEA—and treaty implementation. It prohibits the dumping of radioactive waste anywhere within the zone (which includes the waters over the continental shelf and the EEZ), much like the Treaty of Rarotonga, which extends this provision throughout the ocean waters of the South Pacific. It prohibits the transit of nuclear weapons by a party within the zone, but with respect to transit of foreign ships and aircraft:

- The treaty and its protocol apply to the land territory, the continental shelf, and the EEZ of each party.

- It provides that nothing in the treaty shall prejudice the right of any state under the Law of the Sea Convention, in particular, freedom of the high seas, innocent passage, archipelagic sea-lanes passage, or transit passage consistent with the Charter of the United Nations.

- It provides that each party is free to decide for itself whether to allow visits by foreign ships and aircraft to its ports and airfields, transit of its airspace and navigation by foreign ships through its territorial waters, and overflights of those waters where innocent passage, archipelagic sea-lanes passage, or transit passage does not apply.

By extending the zone to a large area of the high seas within its region (the waters above the continental shelf and the EEZ), none of those innocent passage rights would apply. The question arises: What are the rights of foreign ships and aircraft under the treaty on or above this important part of the high seas? For example, would it prevent the United States from moving its nuclear submarines through this region? It appears that it would, as there often would be no one within a 150-mile radius to determine whether a certain passage is innocent. The NPT nuclear weapon states have considered extension of a nuclear weapon–free zone to a large area of the high seas to be a big problem from the beginning.

On behalf of the US government, I made three subsequent trips in 1996 and 1997 to the ASEAN region, to no avail. I here mention one of the numerous meetings on these three trips. In Kuala Lumpur, Malaysia, in 1996, I met with Deputy Foreign Minister Karim, who at the time was acting foreign minister. After my presentation, he said, among other things, that the Malaysian position on EEZ was inspired by concern about China in the South China Sea and that I should report this concern to Washington.[10]

There have been many attempts over the years to solve the protocol issue. In 1996, President Jacques Chirac said that France would be willing to sign the protocol if some "technical issues were sorted out."[11] According to an Indonesian official in July 1998, China was willing to withdraw its reservation about the inclusion of continental shelves and EEZs in the treaty in view of an agreed "policy statement" claiming that EEZs would not be prejudiced by the treaty.[12] Russia has expressed a positive attitude toward the treaty, but said it needed some clarifications of the geographic scope and regulations on the rights of passage in the treaty zone.[13] China publicly announced its willingness to sign the protocol in 2004.[14] The United Kingdom issued a statement from the foreign secretary that stated, "After over ten years of negotiations, a process for P-5 [China, France, Russia, the United Kingdom, and the United States] signature of the Protocol to the Southeast Asian Nuclear-Weapon-Free-Zone Treaty has been agreed."[15]

The Commission of the SEANWFZ Treaty, the treaty-implementing body composed of the foreign ministers of the parties, held its first meeting in July 1999. The commission and its executive committee over the years have played an important role in the negotiations with the P-5 over the protocol. In May, at the 2010 NPT Review Conference in New York, US Secretary of State Hillary Clinton announced, among other things, that the United States would consult with the parties to the Bangkok treaty in an effort to resolve the impediments to moving forward on the protocol.[16] In August 2011, for the first time in almost ten years, representatives of the five NPT nuclear weapon states met with ASEAN officials to discuss ratification of the protocol. No substantive agreements were reached at this meeting, but it was announced that they would meet again in October to continue talks. At the ASEAN summit meeting in November 2011, member states announced that differences had been resolved, permitting the five NPT nuclear weapon states to adhere to the protocol. At the twentieth ASEAN summit in April 2012, it was announced that ASEAN looked forward to the signing of the SEANWFZ protocol by the five nuclear weapon states in July 2012. The SEANWFZ Commission of ASEAN met at the forty-first ASEAN foreign ministers meeting on July 8, 2012, where it was expected that the protocol would be signed by the P-5; however, four of the NPT nuclear weapon states (France, Russia, the United Kingdom, and the United States) expressed continuing reservations.[17] France had reservations on self-defense, Russia on the rights of foreign ships and aircraft to pass through the treaty zone, and the United Kingdom on new threats and developments. The United States did not disclose its reservations. This meeting had been expected to end with the signing of a memorandum of understanding between ASEAN and China and with P-5 signature of the protocol. ASEAN announced that the NPT nuclear weapon states were not yet prepared to sign the protocol owing to their reservations, so the ASEAN Commission decided to postpone the signing of the memorandum of understanding with China as well.

The main obstacles that remain include the issues related to the continental shelves and the EEZs within the treaty zone. Currently, there is little evidence to suggest that the P-5 will accede to the protocol in the near future.[18] Meanwhile, the disputes between ASEAN and China over the South China Sea continue to grow in intensity, and there are reports that the Philippines is considering reopening the Subic Bay Base to the United States, which withdrew from the base nearly twenty-five years ago.

The protocol situation has posed a serious dilemma for ASEAN. The P-5—in particular, the United States—insists that a key paragraph extending the treaty zone to the continental shelves and EEZs be deleted from the treaty if they are to sign the protocol. If ASEAN were to agree to this contention by the P-5, however, the Bangkok treaty would lose its bite. This simply is not in the interest of ASEAN governments. If, on the other hand, ASEAN does not agree to amend the treaty on this issue, the NPT nuclear weapon states are probably not going to sign the protocol, thereby rendering the treaty ineffective with respect to its central objective.[19]

It is important that this stalemate be overcome. The Treaty of Bangkok applies the nuclear weapon prohibition in areas that are inhabited by hundreds of millions of people, and this treaty's becoming truly effective would make the entire Pacific Ocean region off-limits to nuclear weapons.

Chapter 7
The Treaty of Semipalatinsk and
Mongolia as a Single-State Nuclear Weapon–Free Zone

In 2009, the Central Asian Nuclear Weapon Free–Zone Treaty, also known as the Treaty of Semipalatinsk, came into being. Nearly five hundred nuclear weapon tests were carried out by the Soviet Union at their test range near Semipalatinsk in Kazakhstan. In August 1994, when my diplomatic work included leading US government efforts to permanently extend the NPT, the ambassador from Kazakhstan came to see me in my office. He said that his country would support indefinite extension of the NPT and that the United States could count on Kazakhstan. During our conversation, he mentioned that some 500,000 people in his country were suffering from radiation-related sicknesses as a result of the Soviet tests at Semipalatinsk, which I visited much later in the summer of 2011. Parts of the Semipalatinsk test range, a large area, are still contaminated to this day.[1] What happened at this test range so affected the people of this country that the anniversary of the permanent closure of this nuclear weapon test site has become a national day of remembrance. President Nursultan Nazarbayev formally closed the Semipalatinsk nuclear test site on August 29, 1991. It had been the site of 456 nuclear weapon tests by the Soviet Union between 1949 and 1989. Ever since, August 29 has been Kazakhstan's National Day. This was the real beginning of the Treaty of Semipalatinsk.

In 1991 at the end of the Cold War, Kazakhstan was left in possession of some 1,400 Soviet era nuclear weapons, including 108 SS-18 missiles, the largest intercontinental ballistic missile (ICBM) in the Soviet arsenal. Each such missile was deployed with ten independently targetable nuclear weapons with 500-kiloton warheads. In early 1992, I was part of an arms control delegation dispatched to the major successor states of the former Soviet Union some two weeks after its collapse, following a visit by Secretary of State Jim Baker. We visited the four successor states with nuclear weapons on their territory after the dissolution of the Soviet Union. We went first to Moscow, then to Kiev, then to Minsk in Belarus, and last to Alma-Ata (now called Almaty), Kazakhstan. Our objective was to persuade these new states to sign the START Treaty, the INF Treaty, the Conventional Armed Forces in Europe Treaty (CFE), and the NPT. Kazakhstan was not a problem in this regard. The delegation met with senior foreign ministry officials and the leader of the delegation, Under-Secretary of State Reginald Bartholomew, met with the foreign minister and President Nazarbayev of the two-week-old nation. President Nazarbayev apparently told Bartholomew during the meeting that he had received offers from several Middle East nations to purchase the 500-kiloton warheads of the 108 SS-18s. Nazarbayev said he refused all offers.[2] Eventually, the SS-18s and their warheads were returned to Russia in 1995. In addition, the US-Kazakhstani operation, Project Sapphire, called for Kazakhstan to permit the removal of a large quantity of highly enriched uranium left on its territory by the Russians—by some reports enough material for twenty-five nuclear weapons—to Oak Ridge, Tennessee.

After the dissolution of the Soviet Union, three of the four heirs of the Soviet weapon stockpiles agreed to join the NPT as non-nuclear states—not without some resistance from Ukraine, but the three did join. The Soviet weapons on their territories were returned to Russia, but a legacy of nuclear-related environmental damage, especially at the Soviet test site in Kazakhstan, provided an opening and incentive for advocates of a nuclear weapon–free zone in central Asia. Mongolia took the lead and unilaterally declared itself an NWFZ in 1992 by means of a national law.[3] Mongolia also called for states to establish a regional NWFZ.

President Karimov of Uzbekistan put forward the first formal proposal at the UN General Assembly the following year. This initiative was repeated in 1994, with Kyrgyzstan joining Uzbekistan. The initiative was then supported by the regional states in the Almaty Declaration on February 27, 1997.[4]

The presidents of Kazakhstan, Kyrgyzstan, Tajikistan, Turkmenistan, and Uzbekistan jointly issued the Almaty Declaration, which noted the need for a central Asian NWFZ and a need to "combat the leakage of nuclear technologies and raw materials." The declaration that called for a central Asian nuclear weapon–free zone (CANWFZ) was advocated in connection with a broader call to address the environmental crisis in the Aral Sea basin and acknowledgment of the environmental impact of prior nuclear weapon activities in the region.[5]

Years of discussion followed. At the NPT Preparatory Committee (PrepCom) meeting in the spring of 1997, Kazakhstan, Kyrgyzstan, Tajikistan, Turkmenistan, and Uzbekistan decided to form a working group for the creation of a CANWFZ. In September, worldwide and regional experts, along with experts from other

NWFZs, attended a conference held at Tashkent, Uzbekistan, to discuss the creation of a central Asian nuclear weapon–free zone. They discussed lessons learned in the establishment of other nuclear weapon–free zones (like Pelindaba and Tlatelolco) and what the next logical steps would be in drafting a CANWFZ treaty. The group at the conference also asked the United Nations to establish a group of experts within the specialized UN agencies to assist in the development of the treaty. On December 9, the UN General Assembly adopted a resolution, "The Establishment of a Nuclear-Weapon-Free Zone in Central Asia," to assist the process.

With regional consensus on a way forward, experts from the five central Asian potential treaty parties, the P-5, the United Nations, and the IAEA met in Bishkek, Kyrgyzstan, in July 1998 to consider drafting the basic elements of a central Asian nuclear weapon–free zone treaty.[6] A communiqué was issued after the meeting recognizing that progress had been made in the drafting process. There were further discussions of next steps and a reiteration of continued support and consultation by the P-5 throughout the process. In 1999, expert group meetings took place in Japan to further the process of negotiating and drafting a treaty. The Japanese government at the UN Regional Center hosted these meetings for peace and disarmament in Asia and the Pacific. In 2000, the UN General Assembly passed a second resolution urging negotiation of the CANWFZ Treaty. That same year, the NPT Review Conference in its final document also endorsed the negotiation of a CANWFZ Treaty.

Controversies among the central Asian states emerged during the negotiations related to the delineation of borders between certain states, the legal status of the Caspian Sea, and their close relationship with the Russian Federation. At the end of the meeting in Samarkand, Uzbekistan (September 25-27, 2002), the central Asian states announced that they had reached a preliminary agreement.[7] The regional prospective treaty parties had presented a working paper to the 2002 NPT Preparatory Committee earlier in the year. The paper included a progress report, the latest draft, and a note about the agencies and departments in the United Nations and the entities in the international community that supported the CANWFZ effort. As the first draft of the Treaty of Semipalatinsk was agreed upon in the September 2002 meeting, it was sent to the P-5 states on September 27, 2002, for consideration by the UN-sponsored working group. The P-5 states and the five prospective treaty parties met in New York to discuss the treaty and the protocols under the auspices of the United Nations. The UN General Assembly adopted another resolution on October 25, 2002, which praised the progress that had been made and urged the five Central Asian states to continue working with the P-5 states until full agreement could be reached.

Regional experts continued to meet, with support from the United Nations and the IAEA. On February 8, 2005, the draft was finally fully agreed upon and approved in Tashkent. The treaty was opened for signature on September 8, 2006, in Semipalatinsk near the former Soviet test site. All five central Asian states—Kazakhstan, Kyrgyzstan, Tajikistan, Turkmenistan, and Uzbekistan—signed the treaty. It was to go into force thirty days after the deposit of the fifth ratification. A UN General Assembly resolution of December 6, 2006, welcomed the signing of the treaty and considered the establishment of the zone as "an important step towards strengthening the nuclear non-proliferation regime, promoting cooperation in the peaceful uses of nuclear energy, and in the environmental rehabilitation of territories affected by radioactive contamination, and enhancing international peace and security." The resolution also said that the treaty represented an "effective contribution to combating international terrorism and preventing nuclear materials and technologies from falling into the hands of non-state actors, primarily terrorists."[8] Thus this region of Central Asia, once home to thousands of Soviet nuclear weapons, became an NWFZ.[9]

The CANWFZ Treaty, or the Treaty of Semipalatinsk, obligates its parties not to conduct research on, develop, manufacture, stockpile, or otherwise acquire, possess, or have control over any nuclear weapon or other nuclear explosive device. It obligates parties to prohibit the stationing, storage, or use of any nuclear weapon or other nuclear explosive device in their territories. The treaty also barred the disposal of radioactive wastes of other states in their territories, but defined "radioactive wastes" so as to exclude and therefore permit the import of low- and medium-level nuclear waste. This provision meant that Kazakhstan would have to drop its plan to establish a high-level nuclear waste depository to take waste from other countries and charge considerable fees for this service. It called on all the parties to assist one another with efforts to rehabilitate the environment of territories within the treaty zone that had been contaminated by past nuclear weapon explosive testing. It banned entirely any nuclear explosions for any purpose by adopting language from the Comprehensive Nuclear-Test-Ban Treaty, the CTBT. All five central Asian states were already parties to the CTBT before the CANWFZ Treaty was signed. The transit and transportation of foreign ships and aircraft through the territories of the zone were left to the discretion of each state party.

The treaty raised the verification bar a bit by requiring that CANWFZ Treaty parties conclude an IAEA additional protocol in addition to an NPT safeguards agreement, and to require the same as a condition of supply of exports of nuclear material and equipment to NPT non–nuclear weapon state parties. The treaty provides for a consultative mechanism to review compliance and provide for dispute settlement. A single protocol open only to the NPT nuclear weapon states is included. It provides the essential negative security assurances from the NPT nuclear weapon states to the treaty parties and links the nuclear weapon states to the treaty so as to uphold the integrity of its obligations.[10]

France, the United Kingdom, and the United States presented one of the most difficult questions for the treaty parties. The question concerned Russia's security arrangement with central Asia. The issue at hand was how the new treaty would relate to the Commonwealth of Independent States (CIS) Collective Security Treaty signed by four of the central Asian states (excluding Turkmenistan), along with Armenia, Belarus, and Russia. This CIS treaty was concluded shortly after the collapse of the Soviet Union in 1992 and provided that "in case of an act of aggression committed against any of the States Parties, all the other States Parties will render it necessary assistance, including military." France, the United Kingdom, and the United States were concerned that this provision could be read as granting Russia a right to deploy nuclear weapons within the treaty zone. The three states preferred that the new CANWFZ Treaty take unambiguous precedence over any provisions of previously adopted agreements between Russia and the central Asian states.

The central Asian states differed over how far they were prepared to go in potentially alienating Russia and undermining one of the major collective defense mechanisms in the post-Soviet era. Kazakhstan, Kyrgyzstan, and Tajikistan (countries with closer ties to Russia) argued that the CANWFZ Treaty should specify that it does not affect obligations under previous agreements. Uzbekistan and Turkmenistan were against such language. The parties sought a diplomatic solution. First, the text affirmed that the treaty "does not affect the rights and obligations under international treaties." This was a positive signal to Russia indicating that the Central Asian states wanted to preserve the crucial collective security mechanism in place. At the same time, an additional provision was added that codified an obligation "to take all necessary measures for effective implementation of the purposes and objectives of the Treaty in accordance with the main principles contained therein." The central Asian states wanted this message to be interpreted that the parties to the treaty did not give up on their major collective security arrangement with Russia but would not utilize it in any way contrary to the obligations of the Treaty of Semipalatinsk. The central Asian states believed this was an excellent compromise—France, the United Kingdom, and the United States were less sure—but proceeded to sign the treaty.

One other issue should be mentioned here. Originally, the central Asian states drafted the treaty so that it might be able to expand and to take in immediately neighboring states as new members. The United States strongly opposed this provision because it believed that Iran might become a member. However, it is unclear why that would be considered undesirable, particularly in light of the US policy against a nuclear weapon–capable Iran. As a result of the US opposition, the provision was dropped by the central Asian states.[11]

France, the United Kingdom, and the United States regarded the solution by the negotiators of the CIS Collective Security Treaty as not truly substantive but being simply studied ambiguity and therefore was less than satisfactory. Therefore, when the treaty was signed in September 2006, none of these three states nor Russia or China, the other two P-5 states, signed the protocol.

In 2007, Kyrgyzstan was the first country to deposit its instrument of ratification, followed by Uzbekistan. Turkmenistan ratified in 2008, followed thereafter by Tajikistan in that same year. Finally, Kazakhstan deposited its instrument of ratification in April 2009, and the Treaty of Semipalatinsk came into force on March 21, 2009. At that time, no potential protocol party had signed the protocol. At the 2010 NPT Review and Extension Conference, Secretary of State Clinton said that the United States planned to find a way to sign the protocols to the Treaties of Bangkok and Semipalatinsk, as mentioned in chapter 6. In 2011, President Obama announced that he would be working with treaty parties and also sent the protocols to the Treaties of Rarotonga and Pelindaba to the US Senate. In 2012, Kazakhstan became the chair of the CANWFZ Treaty, giving it the authority to negotiate with the P-5 for the treaty parties. In 2012 and 2013, Kazakhstan held several meetings with P-5 states and also with its treaty partners. This led to a resolution of differences, and on May 6, 2014, the P-5 states jointly signed the protocol to the Treaty of Semipalatinsk on the margins of the NPT Preparatory Committee meeting in New York. The United States sent the protocol to the US Senate on April 27, 2015. France ratified the protocol on November 17, 2014, and the United Kingdom followed suit on January 30, 2015.

Lastly, the definition of a nuclear weapon–free zone adopted by the United Nations contemplated that a valid NWFZ could be limited to a single state. The Mongolian single-state zone, however, does not yet technically qualify as an

NWFZ because the associated legally binding agreements with the P-5 states providing a negative security assurance do not currently exist. But this fact does not diminish its importance. Mongolia has a close geographical and ethno-cultural relationship to central Asia and the CANWFZ Treaty, and it plays a significant role as a peaceful in-between area positively affecting the relationship between China and Russia.

After the collapse of the Soviet Union, the last Soviet troops left Mongolia in 1992. On September 25 of that year, the president of Mongolia—a country with a landmass larger than that of Central Europe and situated between two nuclear weapon states—announced to the UN General Assembly that Mongolia's territory would be an NWFZ. President Punsalmaagiin Ochirbat of Mongolia noted at the time that one out of every four nuclear weapon tests conducted since the beginning of the nuclear age up to that time had occurred in the vicinity of his nation (at Semipalatinsk and in China).

The Mongolian statement was made in the context of its efforts to define and pursue its own interests and priorities while serving as a buffer between two major powers and nuclear weapon states. To an extent, the United States, in subsequent years, became a guarantor of Mongolian independence after it adopted a democratic form of government. Mongolia is a functioning democracy wedged between powerful autocracies and deserves such support. Mongolia's nuclear-free status also has been a strong motivator behind support from Western nations. The Mongolian initiative is unique in the context of the nuclear weapon–free zone movement in that it is not a group of countries comprising a vast geographic area, but rather a single state declaring its sovereign territory to be an NWFZ (even though it does not currently technically qualify as such). The Mongolian example could serve as a model for other nations in a similar situation—such as Nepal—to take a similar action.

On December 4, the UN General Assembly passed a resolution welcoming Mongolia's decision to declare its territory to be an NWFZ. On February 28, 2000, Ambassador Jargalsaikhany Enkhsaikhan, the permanent representative of Mongolia to the United Nations, transmitted to the UN secretary general the text of the Law of Mongolia on its nuclear weapon–free status, adopted by the Parliament of Mongolia on February 3, 2000.

Chapter 8
Where We Are, and Where and How We Must Go

Let's sum up the nuclear weapon–free zone movement at present.

The Latin American continent is entirely free of nuclear weapons up to the border of the United States. All of the Caribbean is covered as well. All thirty-three states of Latin America are parties to the Treaty of Tlatelolco. Should one day all treaty parties—including small island states—conclude their safeguards agreements with the IAEA, then the treaty zone would expand some two hundred miles off the Latin American coast and, in the west, touch the easternmost limit of the South Pacific NWFZ. Those states with territories in the zone—France, Great Britain, the Netherlands, and the United States—have all ratified the relevant protocol placing their territories under the zone, and the P-5 states have ratified the protocol with the negative security assurance and acceptance of the zone. The Latin American zone reaches well into the Northern Hemisphere.

In the Pacific, all the states in the Pacific Ocean below the equator, some thirteen states, are parties to the Treaty of Rarotonga. The treaty prohibits nuclear weapons only in the land areas and territorial seas of the South Pacific, but not the high seas. But the prohibition on radioactive waste dumping applies throughout the zone, even on the high seas. The treaty bans nuclear explosive devices, not just nuclear weapons. The debate about the indistinguishability of nuclear weapons and peaceful nuclear explosives was effectively over by the time of this treaty, which is why this provision is part of the treaty. The Treaty of Tlatelolco addressed only nuclear weapons, although the formula in the treaty to permit peaceful nuclear explosives is impossible to meet, so they were in effect prohibited there as well. In the Treaty of Rarotonga, each party is permitted to decide for itself whether to permit port calls by ships and aircraft landings or overflights by aircraft that are nuclear powered or nuclear capable. Tlatelolco is silent on transit, but there was no objection to an American reservation that permits it. The South Pacific zone's southern limit is the Antarctic Treaty border. Antarctica is nuclear weapon–free pursuant to the Antarctic Treaty. Antarctica is not subject to the claims of national sovereignty and is administered by the Antarctica Treaty parties. The northern limit is the equator, although a portion of land territory north of the equator is included. Three members of the South Pacific Forum— the Marshall Islands, Micronesia, and Palau, which so far have chosen observer status but are eligible to join the treaty—lie entirely north of the equator. The territory of one current treaty party lies partly north of the equator. The western border of the South Pacific lies beyond Australia and Papua New Guinea to the west. States that administer territories in the zone have signed the relevant proto- col placing their territories under the zone. France and Great Britain have ratified this protocol, but the United States has not. The two protocols—one providing the negative security assurance and the provision by which the P-5 states agree to respect the obligations of the treaty, and the other prohibiting nuclear testing in the zone—have been signed and ratified by four of the P-5 states. Only the United States has signed but not ratified, although it did send the three protocols to the Senate in 2011.

The territory of the Treaty of Bangkok lies only partly below the equator; most of it is to the north and includes highly populated areas. All ten ASEAN mem- bers are parties to the treaty. It bans nuclear explosive devices and the dumping of nuclear waste at sea. The treaty permits parties to decide for themselves on visits by nuclear-capable ships and aircraft. But this treaty expands the scope of its nuclear prohibitions to the waters above the continental shelf and the EEZ. Largely because of this provision, the P-5 states still have not signed the proto- col to the treaty. The single treaty protocol obligates the P-5 states to respect the zone and provides a negative security assurance. No outside state has jurisdiction over territory in the treaty zone or has ever tested a nuclear device in the treaty zone. Therefore the protocol for the P-5 states is limited to these first two highly important issues. The failure of the NPT nuclear weapon states thus far to sign the protocol has significantly weakened the Bangkok treaty.

The domain of the Treaty of Semipalatinsk is entirely above the equator. It bans nuclear explosive devices and the dumping of high-level nuclear waste in the treaty zone. Each party is free to decide for itself about visits by aircraft or ships. All five central Asian states are members. The protocol providing a negative secu- rity assurance and P-5 recognition of the treaty zone was signed by all five P-5 states in New York at UN headquarters on May 6, 2014. Four of the five P-5 states have ratified; the United States sent the protocol to the Senate in 2015. In addition, Mongolia has declared itself to be a nuclear weapon–free area.

Finally, the Treaty of Pelindaba established all the nuclear weapon prohibitions of the other free-zone treaties: prohibition of nuclear explosive devices, bans on the dumping of nuclear waste at sea, freedom to grant ship and aircraft visits, and protocols for outside countries that have jurisdiction over territory in the treaty zone, as well as a ban on nuclear tests, the negative security assurance, and a commitment to respect the treaty zone. Not all African states have joined, however. Although thirty-eight of the eligible treaty parties have joined the treaty, sixteen have not. Egypt considers itself more a part of the Middle East rather than Africa, but the other states do not have that excuse; Libya, after all, is a party to the treaty. Also, of the three protocols—(1) placing dependent territory under the treaty, (2) establishing the negative security assurance and respect for the zone, and (3) instituting the ban on testing—the latter two protocols have been signed by the P-5 and have also been ratified, except by the United States. The Obama administration sent the two protocols for P-5 states to the Senate in 2011. With respect to the protocol, which places territories controlled by outside states under the treaty zone, three states are eligible to join—France, Great Britain, and Spain. Britain and France have signed and ratified. Spain has not even signed. The Canary Islands is the Spanish territory in question, and Spain does not consider it to be part of Africa, even though the Organization of African States has claimed that it is. For Britain, the Chagos Archipelago, south of India, where the former large US base of Diego Garcia was located, is the relevant territory; Britain agreed to include this territory in the zone as an adjacent African island, but with a caveat written in the treaty annex that this inclusion has no effect on sovereignty. Otherwise, the bans on nuclear explosive devices and nuclear testing cover the entire African continent and its adjacent islands, including the territorial seas, but not farther out to the high seas. But, again, of the fifty-four members of the Organization of African States eligible to be part of the treaty, only thirty-eight are. Work remains to be done to fully implement the Treaty of Pelindaba. And, finally, all the nuclear weapon–free zone treaties strongly support the peaceful use of nuclear energy, as does the NPT itself.

In short, all the land area of the Southern Hemisphere is legally free of nuclear weapons (except for fifteen or sixteen states of Africa), and some of the high seas areas have appropriate related constraints. The situation with the protocol to the Treaty of Bangkok remains to be positively resolved as well. Generally, however, nuclear weapons have been largely eliminated from the Southern Hemisphere. Also, significant areas of the Northern Hemisphere are nuclear weapon–free thanks to the Treaties of Tlatelolco, Bangkok, and Semipalatinsk and to a small degree the Treaty of Rarotonga.

Next, the NWFZ movement must turn to areas in which it is truly difficult to make progress; these areas include the Middle East, northeast Asia, and South Asia. If after many years a NWFZ could be negotiated and established in these areas, then the five NPT nuclear weapon states that remain would indeed call to mind Garcia Robles's isolated contaminated islands theory and would represent the last step toward eliminating nuclear weapons from the face of the earth.

To accomplish this would be a truly Herculean task and one in which the US government would need to reorganize itself if it aspires to be a leader in any such effort. The United States might need to reassess how it approaches arms control and disarmament altogether, and look to organizations from the past to better shape its future. The US government once had an organization dedicated to arms control and disarmament, the US Arms Control and Disarmament Agency (ACDA). This organization negotiated for the United States almost all the significant international arms control limitations that exist. It was founded by President John F. Kennedy in 1961 and eliminated at the end of the Clinton administration in 1999, almost forty years later, under pressure from Republican senators. Its remnants in the US State Department were cut back during the George W. Bush administration, and much of its valued expertise was lost—including those officials who had worked with the NWFZ efforts around the world—and its direct access to the president was eliminated. This agency was the model for the world, and its elimination was a grave mistake. Something like the ACDA should be revived if the nuclear weapon–free movement is to move ahead.

In an article I wrote for the *Foreign Service Journal* at the time of the passing of the Arms Control and Disarmament Agency, I noted that on April 1, 1999, the US Arms Control and Disarmament Agency went out of business. As part of a reorganization of foreign affairs agencies, the main functions of ACDA became incorporated into the State Department. I then asked whether this was a wise decision. Did America and the world become safer with the US arms control portfolio integrated into the vast range of foreign policy concerns occupying the Department of State, rather than constituting the sole responsibility of a specialized agency?[1] To this day, I continue to believe that this was not the case.

Beginning in 1992, when the first pressures to eliminate ACDA and submerge the government's arms control effort began to appear, much effort went into formulating a strategy for ACDA's survival. But in late 1996, when ACDA independence no longer appeared to be a viable objective, my colleagues in ACDA and I negotiated the best deal we could for the preservation of the arms control mission. Nevertheless, over the years, this attempt to preserve what was essential about an independent agency for arms control can only be said to have been met with failure. Commitments made were not honored, and this valuable asset—an independent government role for arms control—was lost.

"When President John F. Kennedy signed the legislation creating the Arms Control and Disarmament Agency in September 1961, the time was ripe for the establishment of such a body. John J. McCloy, the Administration's sponsor of the legislation, said in his Senate testimony, in effect, that arms control and disarmament is too important a subject to be 'buried in the State Department.'" Instead, a new agency should be created with a director who would have direct access to the president.

Previously, in the Eisenhower administration, the responsibility for arms control had been placed in the White House under former governor and frequent presidential candidate Harold Stassen, but this had not worked well. There were serious conflicts with the State Department and Secretary of State John Foster Dulles.

By 1961, arms control had become a major national security issue for the United States. In the 1950s, the Soviet Union had developed its nuclear weapons and nuclear weapon delivery systems to such a degree that a nuclear arms race was in full swing. During the 1960 presidential campaign, John F. Kennedy had warned of a possible "missile gap." Because of these developments, Kennedy decided to establish a separate executive branch agency for arms control and disarmament.

Kennedy's secretary of state, Dean Rusk, supported the draft legislation. Rusk testified, "Disarmament is a unique problem in the field of foreign affairs. It entails not only a complex of political issues, but involves a wealth of technical, scientific, and military problems which in many respects are outside the [State] Department's normal concerns and, in many instances, reach beyond the operational functions the Department is designed to handle."[2] The legislation received strong support from foreign policy leaders in both the Senate and the House. They understood the argument that arms control is just one of the tools of national security policy but nevertheless a separate and distinct arena. It is not an end in itself, but it represents one of several alternative paths toward solution of national security problems.[3]

The fundamental rationale for not subordinating the agency within the State Department was that the pursuit of arms control and disarmament goals would often conflict with the department's primary mission, which is to foster good relations with other countries. For example, to press Pakistan on nuclear non-proliferation issues or criticize Russia for perceived arms control treaty violations can be contrary to pursuing improved relations with those countries and will often be opposed by the regional State Department bureau responsible for relations with the country in question. Most often, in the competition of ideas within the State Department, interests of improved bilateral relations will prevail over arms control, disarmament, and non-proliferation interests.

The early years of the agency in the 1960s were prosperous and successful, as Secretary Rusk believed in and supported the role of ACDA. ACDA was effectively led by Director William Foster, a former deputy secretary of defense; Deputy Director Adrian Fisher, a former State Department legal advisor; and General Counsel George Bunn, the drafter of the Arms Control and Disarmament Act.

Over strong opposition by the State Department—which was pressing for the establishment of a multilateral nuclear force with our NATO allies in Europe— ACDA successfully argued for the Nuclear Non-Proliferation Treaty, which is now considered a centerpiece of international security. ACDA almost single-handedly advocated this proposal within the US executive branch and went on to play the leading US role in the complex multiparty negotiations in Geneva. If it had not been for an independent ACDA, this important agreement might never have come into being.[4]

Over the years that followed, the post of ACDA director was filled by a series of distinguished public servants, and the agency had several significant accomplishments. Among the highlights: negotiation of the SALT I and SALT II agreements as well as START, the negotiation of the Chemical Weapons Convention (CWC), the long-term continuation of the nuclear weapon test moratorium in 1993 (initially and for several months advocated by ACDA alone), the indefinite extension of the NPT, and the negotiation of the CTBT. These successes and others all depended to an important degree on the existence of an independent arms control agency, with a director who could take controversial issues directly to the president and the national security advisor.

But there was always another side to this history. ACDA was controversial because its responsibility was to negotiate the limitation of national armaments— an emotional and difficult subject in any society. But those members of Congress who supported arms limitation remained strong champions of an independent ACDA. Senator Henry Jackson, a Democrat from Washington, was a strong opponent of arms control over the years, but there were always senators willing to contend with him. I remember one powerful liberal senator saying that in domestic policy and some aspects of foreign policy, Senator Jackson was one of the best members of the Senate, maybe one of the best ever, but when it came to arms limitation he was "a menace."

He was succeeded in opposition by Senator Jesse Helms of North Carolina and Senator Jon Kyl of Arizona, both Republicans. The entire Republican Party shifted to the right on this subject after the 1994 elections. This was the party that produced Senator Richard Lugar, who along with Senator San Nunn of Georgia, a Democrat, were the leaders of sound practical arms limitations policy in the US Congress for many years. Fortunately for ACDA, while congressional support waned somewhat over the years before the 1994 elections, many supporters remained. Also, the other agencies of the national security establishment, except for the State Department, remained steadfast in their support. This enabled ACDA to successfully oppose the first attempt of the State Department to eliminate ACDA in 1993. But after 1994, this support largely faded.

In 1996, the CWC entered the equation and further contributed to the demise of ACDA. The United States had a strong desire to achieve CWC ratification by early 1997. This was necessary, as the United States needed to be an original party to the convention to have maximum influence in shaping the treaty's verification regime. In early 1997, the CWC was on the verge of having enough ratifications by signatories to come into force, which would close the door on original parties. The situation gave Senator Helms, then the chairman of the Senate Foreign Relations Committee and therefore in control of the schedule of the committee, significant bargaining power. He could hold the CWC in committee if he wished. Part of his price to send the convention to the Senate floor for a vote was the elimination of ACDA. The agency no longer had the inherent political strength to resist—if the White House did not oppose Helms, which it did not because it wanted the CWC—and was forced to negotiate.

In December 1996, the ACDA director learned from the White House that the ACDA "independent box" had to disappear. In the absence of former allies and in a weak bureaucratic position, ACDA had little choice but to try to negotiate the best outcome possible. The idea was to try to negotiate something like an independent ACDA located within the Department of State.

These negotiations lasted over a year. I participated along with other senior officials from ACDA (including the director, John Holum), the State Department, and the National Security Council (NSC). The most important attributes of an independent arms control agency were as follows: the existence of a senior US government official responsible for arms control, who by right attended all NSC meetings related to arms control and who had the authority to communicate

directly with the president on these matters; the acquisition and long-term retention of a highly qualified technical staff to support arms limitation policy and
negotiation; and the development and long-term retention of an expert staff on
verification capable of playing a special role within the government on this issue.
To achieve this in the State Department was a difficult objective, as no one in the
State Department except the secretary ever had had the right to communicate
directly with the president on any subject. But this right to direct communication
with the president was extremely important; it was the idea of an "independent
advocacy role" separate from the requirements of State Department "country"
issues and a Defense Department weapon program that was the primary reason
that President Kennedy had wanted to create ACDA in the first place. He wanted
the president and the NSC staff to at least understand directly the arms control
issues no matter what the final decision on a particular issue might be. Expert
staff to support arms control and non-proliferation policy and negotiations generally as well as a special view on verification were also important. In its heyday,
ACDA probably had the finest staff of experts in these two fields that existed not
only within the US government but also in any other government. But retention
of long-term specialists and experts was contrary to the State Department gen-
eralist culture and its policy of rotating an officer out of one position and into
another every three years or so.

There was a compromise on the independent advocacy matter, where it was
agreed that the undersecretary of state responsible for arms control would have
the right to communicate directly with the president on arms control issues but
only through the secretary of state, who must forward to the president the under-
secretary's views but could append his own. There was also strong language developed to support expert technical staff. This all found its way into a Presidential
Decision Directive (PDD), which ultimately led to an official State Department
Reorganization Plan and Report that, pursuant to the law passed by Congress to
authorize the ACDA merger into the State Department, set forth guidelines for
the new office within the State Department that would replace ACDA:

- "The head of the Office, a new undersecretary will have an 'unique' role 'reflecting
  authorities transferred from ACDA.'"

- "The new structure within the State Department is to 'ensure that unique arms control and non-proliferation perspectives will continue to be available at the highest
  levels of the U.S government, including the President.'"

- "An entity will provide 'independent arms control and non-proliferation verification and compliance assessments.'"

- "The new undersecretary will 'provide oversight for State's new interagency leadership in non-proliferation.'"[5]

This report, implementing the law that authorized the elimination of ACDA and its merger into the State Department, is authoritative and cannot be modified without further legislation. Combined with the PDD, it sets forth as US government policy that the independence of the arms control and non-proliferation process is to be strengthened and preserved. The arms control alternative in policy debates on national security issues would continue to be made available at the highest levels of the US government, including the president, as was the case when there was an independent ACDA director.

If this arrangement had been implemented properly, it is possible that the arms control, non-proliferation, and disarmament process would have emerged stronger and more effective than before. But I thought at the time and articulated the hope in the abovementioned article that, should the result be otherwise, some future president or Congress should reenact something like the original Arms Control and Disarmament Act and thereby reestablish an independent arms control agency similar to the independent ACDA.

So, how has arms control fared as a policy after its merger into the State Department? Have the pledges made by the Clinton White House designed to preserve the institutional strength of arms control after the merger of ACDA into the State Department been observed? Also, when ACDA was merged into the State Department in 1999, three separate bureaus within the State Department were created to house the pieces of ACDA being absorbed: the Non-Proliferation Bureau, the Arms Control Bureau, and the Verification Bureau—how have these three bureaus fared in the culture of the State Department? Again, the two pledges made by the Clinton White House were as follows:

> First, that the independent advocacy role of ACDA [which permitted an independent voice for arms control at the top of the government] would be retained under the new structure. The Under Secretary of State for Arms Control and International Security—the successor position to the position of ACDA Director—would also serve as the Senior Advisor to the President and Secretary of State on arms control, non-proliferation, and disarmament matters. . . . [and, by right, would] attend and participate in meetings of the NSC on matters pertaining to arms control. . . . The Under Secretary of

State for Arms Control and International Security would have the right to "communicate with the President through the Secretary of State. . . .

Second, that the State Department would retain ACDA's function as a repository of technical expertise on arms control and non-proliferation matters [as well as verification issues].[6]

Thus the ACDA independent voice would be preserved—by law—within the State Department. Historically, most ACDA directors met alone with the president only a few times, except for Gerard Smith (1969-73), who met over forty times with President Nixon, but the separate vote in the NSC was used more frequently.

The following three epigraphs—contained in an outstanding paper on the effect of ACDA's elimination, written by Leon Ratz and published at the John F. Kennedy School of Government at Harvard University in 2013—give a partial answer to the questions raised above:

- In the absence of the agency [ACDA], neither I nor a future President could count on receiving independent arms control advice, unfiltered by other considerations. A President would thus at times have to make the most consequential national security decisions without the benefit of vigorous advocacy of the arms control point of view. —President Bill Clinton, Letter to Congressional Leaders, July 13, 1995

- [The] new Under Secretary . . . will not only have a reporting relationship to the Secretary of State, but the ability to speak directly through the Secretary to the President of the United States on matters of arms control advocacy. And what was very important to the Vice President in putting this [the merger] together is that there be that independent advocacy role of ACDA preserved in the State Department. —Elaine Kamarck, White House Press Briefing, April 18, 1997

- There was never any opportunity or expectation that the Under Secretary of State for Arms Control would express a view to the President different than the view of the Secretary of State. That would not have been considered kosher. That would not have been appropriate. —Gary Samore, White House Coordinator for Arms Control and WMD issues (2009-13), interview with author, March 13, 2013[7]

In 2005, the Bush administration abolished the Arms Control Bureau, tipping the scale entirely against arms control. And when the Obama administration revived the Arms Control Bureau in 2009, it combined it with the Verification

Bureau, effectively erasing the institutional divide between arms control and verification that had existed for decades.[8]

With respect to preventing the erosion of arms control technical capability, the State Department has unquestionably failed. In 1999, shortly before the merger, ACDA director John Holum said, "In the State Department's own interests, our experts, and those in other functional areas, too, need to be first-class citizens in a culture that has operated differently in the past." Fourteen years later, he said, "In contrast to the solemn promises made during the reorganization, the State Department has flopped on this."[9]

In 2008, former senator Sam Nunn, chairman of the Nuclear Threat Initiative, when asked about the challenges facing arms control, pointed to the absence at the highest levels of government of an actor that could be held accountable for arms control: "What is missing is an organization in the United States, Russia, and other countries that is held accountable for real execution and performance. Most of the efforts disappear at third and fourth levels in the bureaucracies without people at the top paying a lot of attention."[10]

The elimination of an independent ACDA and its merger into the State Department was a huge mistake and has been a complete policy failure. None of the pledges that were made at the time of the merger have been observed. There has been an almost complete absence of arms control progress and non-proliferation success since the merger. The principal exceptions in fourteen years have been the new START and nuclear agreement with Iran. These are highly important agreements, but when put alongside the abundance of the forty-year record of ACDA, they do not measure up. There would have been no NPT if it had not been for ACDA. And probably there would have been no CWC, no SALT agreements, no START agreements, no INF Treaty, no CFE, and no CTBT. The State Department culture, based on the central objective—a good one, of course—of improving relations with other countries, is antithetical to arms control. Arms control interests in the United States are buried in the third and fourth levels referred to by Senator Nunn.

If there is to be an effort one day to expand the NWFZ movement, to undertake the negotiation of the extremely difficult regional nuclear weapon–free zone agreements mentioned above in advancing the cause of the worldwide elimination of nuclear weapons, a new organization in the US government, like ACDA, with real expertise and real staying power, will need to be established or reestablished.

Chapter 9
The Middle East

The Middle East has been called the cradle of civilization, but it is also home to thousands of years of conflict and war. One of its best-known cities, Jerusalem, is an example of and model for this history of violence. Jerusalem has been destroyed twice, besieged twenty-three times, attacked fifty-two times, and captured and recaptured forty-four times. In 70 AD, at the time of the Jewish revolt, the Romans destroyed the city and renamed it Aelia Capitolina, which was its name until the Arabs took it from the Byzantines in the seventh century. To the region came many conquerors, rulers, and occupiers. Among them were the Egyptians, Assyrians, Babylonians, Persians, and Greeks. Then followed the Romans, Byzantines, Arabs, Ottoman Turks, Western imperialist states (primarily Britain and France), and finally—in the twentieth century—the Zionist movement pursuant to the Balfour Declaration of 1917, in which Britain formally recognized Palestine as a Jewish national home, leading to the independence of Israel but not of the Palestinians.[1]

In the First World War, Britain and France defeated the Ottoman Empire and took away from it all except its base location of Turkey. In April 1920, the San Remo Conference confirmed the League of Nations mandate allocations of the London Conference of February 1920. The provisional independence of Syria and Iraq from the Ottoman Empire, or Turkey, as the successor to what was left of the empire after the war was also recognized. France and Britain received League of Nations mandates for the administration of these regions until they were ready for full independence. Neither had been an independent state for over two thousand years. At the time, Lebanon was considered part of Syria. Britain also received the mandate for Palestine pursuant to the Balfour Declaration. Under its mandate, Britain was to establish a national home for Jews without prejudice to the civil and religious rights of historically non-Jewish communities—principally Palestinian Arabs who had been there since the seventh century. This mandate followed Lawrence of Arabia's successful efforts to bring Arabia to the side of the Allies in World War I against the Ottomans. While trying to convince them, he also promised these areas to the Arabs, including Palestine. The Balfour Declaration's promise to give Palestine to the Jews was a World War I wartime measure to keep Jewish industrialists in Great Britain vigorously committed to the war effort. Meanwhile, Britain and France secretly negotiated the Sykes-Picot Treaty in 1916, in which Britain and France divided up the Middle East. This meant that the Arabs would not control any of these areas after joining the Allies. These areas had been wrested from a Sunni Muslim empire with the help of the Arabs, who had held these regions for over a thousand years. This land would be under Western Christian military occupation under the Sykes-Picot Treaty. And the Jews, who had not been in control of Jerusalem or Palestine for nearly two thousand years, would be encouraged to return gradually and to establish a larger presence in the area, ultimately leading to the establishment of their national home. The aim was to bring Jews back to Israel, achieving their national home in Palestine, but under British military occupation. This arrangement was not the objective of the Zionist movements, whose followers were beginning to flock into Palestine and create conflicts with the people already residing there.

A strong case can be made that placing Western expeditionary forces in the Middle East and Christian armies of occupation in Muslim lands, lands that had been ruled by Muslims for nearly 1,500 years, was probably never a good idea. Despite its past, the Middle East, by comparison with Europe, was a relatively quiet place before World War I and had been so for several hundred years. Jerusalem was still an important place, being sacred to the three great monotheistic religions, but in the nineteenth century, it was a town of fewer than ten thousand people, where Arab Jews coexisted with Muslims and Christians.

In the settlement after World War I, however, Britain and France elected to destroy the Ottoman Empire and in the process carved it up, distributing among themselves the spoils of war. They did so in a way that allowed them to claim former Ottoman territories such as Iraq and Syria and then occupy these lands with their armies. In addition, Britain had been in control of Egypt for over fifty years. This carving up of the Middle East created the modern borders and the related issues that we have been dealing with ever since.

Many of these nations have developed, or have attempted to develop, nuclear weapon programs as one symptom of the violent phase they have been in for so many decades. There is hope that the era of violence and conflict that has plagued these nations will gradually come to an end in the next decade or so. But with the failed Arab Spring, the unspeakable six-year civil war in Syria, and the rise of ISIS, the situation does not look immediately promising. If the nuclear agreement with Iran can develop from simply an agreement among governments and become an agreement among peoples; if the Syrian civil war can be ended and the refugee crisis managed; and, lastly, if ISIS can be contained, then perhaps Western armies can leave the Middle East, a Palestine settlement somehow be found, and a reduction of violence and chaos everywhere achieved. A nuclear weapon–free zone in this war-torn region would help a lot with these goals. Then, over time, a fruitful, positive, and lasting relationship between the West and the Middle East, between the Muslim East and the Christian West, could perhaps finally be achieved. Such a development would restore something important that has been missing from world affairs for the past thousand years.

Given the violent history of the Middle East and the region's recent chaotic conditions, it should not be surprising that the region has been replete with attempts—one successful—at nuclear arming. There have been several candidates: Iran, Iraq, Israel, Libya, Syria, and some say Saudi Arabia through its ally Pakistan.

ISRAEL

There is one Middle Eastern state that succeeded in its attempt to acquire a nuclear stockpile: Israel. Israel decided to acquire nuclear weapons only a few years after it was founded. The first prime minister of the newly independent Israel, David Ben-Gurion, had strong opinions about a nuclearized Israel. After the Holocaust, he believed that Israel, the newly established home for the Jews, must always rely on its own strength—and *only* its own strength—to ensure its survival. Arab statements about the "destruction of the Zionist enemy" and "pushing Israel into the sea" defined Israel's worst-case scenario and were reminiscent of the Holocaust.[2] Avner Cohen in his well-known book *Israel and the Bomb* writes that, to Ben-Gurion, this meant among other things that the bomb—as the ultimate weapon—was necessary to ensure the continued existence and safety of Israel. The bomb would keep Israel secure and ensure that there would be no more Holocausts. The fear of destruction was and has remained the strongest incentive for Israel to maintain its nuclear program. There was also a secondary reason of real importance. It has been said that "the strategic objective of the nuclear weapon option was not to deter the Arabs, but to maintain a bargaining chip vis-à-vis the United States" as well as a last-resort weapon.[3] To this end, Ben-Gurion established the Israeli Atomic Energy Commission in 1952.[4] It was decided that the next step for Israel would be to acquire a small research reactor from the United States. But soon a much better opportunity came their way. In July 1956, President Gamal Abdel Nasser of Egypt decided to nationalize the Suez Canal, which had been owned by Britain and France since the construction of the Canal in the early 1880s, when Britain ruled Egypt. France had been concerned about Soviet influence in Egypt since the large Soviet-Egyptian arms deal of the previous year. Britain and France decided upon military seizure as a response to Nasser's nationalization of the canal. France approached Israel about joining the military offensive against Egypt. Israel decided to join the expedition, in part hoping to get a better deal on a nuclear reactor from France than from the United States.

Before starting the operation against Egypt, France agreed to sell a research reactor to Israel. The military action was a complete failure both militarily and politically; Britain and France made little headway in their landings in Egypt, and the United States and the Soviet Union both denounced the expedition. An angry President Eisenhower, who was not informed in advance of the action, forced Britain and France to withdraw. Israel, on the other hand, had seized the entire Sinai Peninsula from Egypt.

After the collapse of the expedition, Israel asked France for an upgraded sale. In particular, Israel asked France for a reactor similar to the 40-megawatt reactor at Marcoule, France, which produced a significant amount of plutonium every year. France agreed to supply such a plutonium-producing reactor, to be built at Dimona in the Negev Desert. Dimona became the center of Israel's nuclear weapon program and has remained such ever since. Israel also requested that Saint Gobain Nucleaire build an underground plant attached to the reactor that would include a reprocessing facility to extract plutonium from the spent fuel from the Dimona reactor. France agreed, and a sales contract was signed in mid-1957. The reactor was to be used for "peaceful purposes." The sales agreement made no reference to the reprocessing plant; this was covered by a separate contract. Not long after that, France provided Israel with important information on the design and manufacture of nuclear weapons.[5] The heavy water required for the reactor was purchased in early 1959 in a third deal, this time with Norway, and Israel again promised to use the material for peaceful purposes only.[6] All these purchases were made for "peaceful purposes," but, in reality, Israel had acquired a nuclear weapon program from France.

By the time the heavy water was purchased from Norway, construction of the nuclear facility was underway. Later, in 1959, excavation work on the reprocessing plant began. The nuclear reactor at Dimona was complete in the early 1960s, and the reprocessing plant was complete by 1965. The first plutonium from the reactor was separated in 1965, and the following year the physical infrastructure of the project was complete or near completion.[7] By the 1967 Six-Day War, Israel had two or three nuclear devices in its possession.[8] In 1963, Israel signed an agreement with the French company Dassault to develop surface-to-surface ballistic missiles.[9]

The US Central Intelligence Agency became aware of this project not long after France began construction of the nuclear complex for Israel at Dimona. By the late 1950s, the US intelligence community was convinced that Israel was engaged in a secret nuclear weapon program. The CIA learned of Norway's heavy-water sale to Israel, and there were reports that Israeli observers were present at France's first nuclear weapon tests. Through surveillance by U-2 aircraft, imagery of the construction project became available in 1958. By 1960, the US government considered Dimona to be a "probable" nuclear weapon development site. In late 1960, Secretary of State Christian A. Herter of the outgoing Eisenhower administration met the Israeli ambassador in Washington and presented him with the US intelligence community's consensus that Israel was building a facility at Dimona that could not be intended solely for peaceful purposes and could be intended for the production of nuclear weapons. The ambassador pleaded ignorance and said that he would seek instructions.[10]

On December 20, 1960, the ambassador replied to Herter that what was being built at Dimona was a small research reactor that would be used solely for peaceful purposes. The US government was not convinced. In December 1960, newly elected President John F. Kennedy asked Herter which countries he believed would likely be the next to acquire nuclear weapons. Herter told him, "India and Israel."[11] President Kennedy was persuaded that there was a reasonable prospect that nuclear weapons would spread all over the world, to the enormous detriment of the United States and world security. In this regard, he considered Israel to be the greatest short-term threat. If, in the end, the United States could not effectively say no to its ally Israel, how could it say no to Germany? And should Germany acquire nuclear weapons, the Soviet Union would likely convert the Cold War into a "hot" war. Accordingly, he tried hard to stop the Israeli nuclear weapon program but failed. Upon assuming office, President Kennedy pressed for inspections and, within a few months, the Israeli government allowed one at Dimona, with occasional inspections continuing until 1969. During these inspections, Israeli officials successfully deceived American inspectors and concealed the true purpose at Dimona. The US inspectors were persuaded that the reactor at Dimona was a small research reactor, rather than the large plutonium producer it actually was; the reprocessing plant was never found. Even so, officials at the CIA and the State Department remained skeptical.

By 1964, Israel had achieved the necessary technological steps and by 1967 had two or three workable nuclear devices. During the 1973 war between Egypt and Israel, the so-called Yom Kippur War, Israel had several crude nuclear weapons in its possession. Prime Minister Golda Meir briefly contemplated using them when the war was going badly for Israel in the first days.[12] After August 9, 1945, until the present, this was probably the closest any nation has come to actually using nuclear weapons in a deliberate battlefield plan. Over the years, the Israeli arsenal improved and expanded. Israel likely conducted one or more nuclear weapon tests on a remote South African island group in the South Atlantic, as discussed in chapter 5. In 1986, a disaffected employee at Dimona resigned after secretly photographing all levels of the vast underground complex. He subsequently gave the photos to the *London Times* and it became clear that Israel possessed a large nuclear weapon arsenal. Their arsenal consisted of as many as two hundred nuclear weapons, including some high-yield weapons and even thermonuclear weapons, a stockpile similar to that possessed by France. Although the US intelligence community gave US policy makers early warning of an Israeli nuclear weapon program in the late 1950s, by the 1980s the estimate had slowly increased in size, but only to the level of twenty to thirty nuclear weapons. The warnings of the program had been timely, but the size of the program was ultimately vastly underestimated.[13]

The Israeli arsenal has only continued to improve, and its weapons are capable of being delivered throughout the Middle East by means of the Jericho ballistic missile and its follow ons. In 1994, when I went to Egypt seeking its vote for indefinite NPT extension, the Egyptian foreign minister told me, in effect: I live next door to a country that can destroy the entire Middle East in fifteen minutes, why should I be interested in the Nuclear Non-Proliferation Treaty?

President Johnson was entirely committed to the NPT but much less interested in pursuing inspections in Israel. In 1969, Prime Minister Golda Meir met with President Nixon and National Security Advisor Henry Kissinger in Washington. In the meeting, she admitted that "Israel already had nuclear weapons but pledged to keep them invisible, that is untested, and undeclared. In return Nixon agreed to end the United States annual visits to Dimona and agreed not to pressure Israel to sign the NPT."[14]

The effort to stop Israel from becoming a nuclear weapon state formally ended in 1969 with this secret agreement that Israel could be an exception to the US non-proliferation policy so long as its program remained a "bomb in the basement." Thereafter, Israel never mentioned its program publicly or privately; it was considered unmentionable even by Israeli private citizens who did not work for the government. This policy remained intact even after the whole world knew the extent of the Israeli program as a result of the 1986 disclosures. The Israeli government would consistently repeat that it would not be the "first" to "introduce" nuclear weapons into the Middle East. And all of this would culminate in the remarkable spectacle of an Israeli prime minister in possession of a sophisticated, large nuclear weapon arsenal deliverable by ballistic missile everywhere in the Middle East. The centerpiece of the government's national security policy under this prime minister was a declaration that Israel faced an "existential threat" from a nation—Iran—that was hostile and had nuclear ambitions but as of yet had no nuclear weapons, while Israel, by far, possessed the strongest conventional armed force in the Middle East, in addition to its modern nuclear weapon arsenal.

IRAN

With the assistance of France, Germany, and South Africa—and without opposition from the United States—Iran began building a large nuclear power infrastructure in the 1970s under the former shah, Mohamed Reza Shah Pahlevi. Two large 1,000-megawatt reactors were under construction by Siemen's of Germany at Bushehr on the Persian Gulf not far from Baghdad. The probable goal was perhaps twenty reactors or even more, making Iran a major player in the world nuclear power industry; in 2004, a former foreign minister confirmed that Iran's nuclear program under the Shah had a dual purpose: to provide power and to give Iran the nuclear option.[15]

After the Islamic Revolution, Ayatollah Khomeini initially declared that nuclear weapons were un-Islamic. The reactor program was not pursued, with the reactors left unfinished. Khomeini changed his mind during the Iran-Iraq War, but Iran's program did not truly begin again until after Khomeini's death in the late 1980s. Efforts were undertaken to contract with Russia to rebuild one of the two Bushehr reactors, both of which were badly damaged during the war. Also, Iran made a secret agreement with A. Q. Khan, the rogue Pakistani nuclear proliferator, to supply centrifuge machines for producing enriched uranium and possibly the design of a Chinese nuclear weapon (which Khan also supplied to

Libya during more or less the same time frame). In 2000, Iran began the construction of a large underground facility at Natanz, capable of housing a pilot plant of around a thousand centrifuges plus a much larger chamber that could hold up to fifty thousand centrifuges. The larger chamber had the potential to give Iran the ability to construct nuclear weapons on an industrial scale, in the range of up to twenty per year. Iran also began building a heavy-water plutonium production reactor at Arak, modeled on the North Korean reactor at Yongbyon, which was the foundation of the nuclear weapon program in that country.

In 2002 at the National Press Club, the People's Mujahedin, known as the MEK, a former terrorist organization in Iran and at the time a wholly owned subsidiary of Saddam Hussein (later referred to as an Iranian dissident organization) publicly revealed the existence of the construction at Natanz and Arak. In 2003, Iran admitted that, in failing to report the transactions with A. Q. Khan, it had violated its NPT safeguards agreement with the International Atomic Energy Agency and promised to never do that again. The United States had the opportunity to turn the Iranian program in 1997, 2001, and 2003 but failed to follow through on any of these opportunities. The Clinton effort to improve relations with Iran featured the lifting of trade sanctions, and a speech by US Secretary of State Madeline Albright, apologizing for the US-engineered overthrow of Iranian Prime Minister Mossadegh in 1953, was too little, too late, and too limited to have any real effect. In 2001, Iran took steps to distance itself from al-Qaeda and the attacks on New York and Washington. The mayor of Tehran sent his condolences. When the United States was preparing its assault on the Taliban government in Afghanistan, Iran indicated that it would return any US pilots downed in the fighting. It also pressed its allies in the Northern Alliance in Afghanistan to work with the Americans and permitted the United States to transport food by truck across its territory to Afghanistan. After the Taliban government was overthrown, Iran played a helpful role in the creation of the Karzai government in the Bonn negotiations of December 2001. Also, in January 2002, at the meeting of donor nations in Tokyo, Iran pledged $350 million for rebuilding Afghanistan.

Senior Iranian leaders began making statements that a limited rapprochement was possible. The president of Iran, Mohammed Khatami, made a public plea for foreign investment, and former president Rafsanjani said that Iran had never opposed "economic, technological, and scientific relations with America." Supreme Leader Ayatollah Ali Khamenei also stated, "We and the U.S. have many differences. But that does not mean that we cannot adopt a regular policy in view of our national interests."[16] Iran's reward for all this cooperation was inclusion as a member of the "Axis of Evil," along with Iraq and North Korea, in President George W. Bush's State of the Union speech in January 2002. In this speech, President Bush said that he "would not permit the world's most dangerous regimes to threaten us with the world's most dangerous weapons."[17] In the context of September 11th and the subsequent retaliatory invasions of Afghanistan, this characterization could only be considered by Iran as a direct threat. It made any negotiations on Iran's nuclear program impossible—with one brief exception in 2003—until the election of President Hassan Rouhani in Iran in 2013.

In the spring of 2003, the Iranians considered themselves to be vulnerable after US forces rapidly destroyed the Iraqi Army in three weeks, something Iran had been unable to do in eight years. It was decided at the highest level in Tehran to put everything on the table and propose a grand bargain on all outstanding issues between the United States and Iran. With respect to the nuclear program, it would be completely open to inspection to alleviate any fears of weaponization, and Iran would permit extensive US involvement in its nuclear program. It included other provisions, such as ending support of Hamas and Islamic Jihad, the disarming of Hezbollah, recognition of Israel, and acceptance of the Saudi peace plan for Palestine. It was sent directly to the White House with copies to the State Department and the Defense Department. Secretary of State Colin Powell wanted to accept this proposal as the basis for negotiations, but Vice President Dick Cheney and Secretary of Defense Donald Rumsfeld prevented any internal consideration by the US government. Their objective was to overthrow the Iranian government after they were finished with Iraq, so they had no reason to negotiate with Iran, as negotiations could get in the way. US policy, in the famous words of Ambassador John Bolton, was to go to Baghdad and "turn right." The Bush administration never responded to this proposal but instead sent a message to Iran through the Swiss government that it would not be seriously considered.[18]

The Iranian nuclear program became a national program. In 2003, the EU-3 (Britain, France, and Germany), later joined by the United States, began negotiations with Iran. Over the years, the United States—as did the EU-3—insisted that Iran agree to forswear enrichment before serious negotiations could begin. Iran consistently refused, and over the years went from 164 operating centrifuges to thousands by 2008, when these negotiations were discontinued. By 2015, the number of centrifuge machines in Iran was 19,000.

Since 2010, the United States ramped up sanctions on Iran with the cooperation of China, the European Union, and Russia. Severe sanctions were placed on banking, oil, shipping, gold, and so on, with the goal of achieving a diplomatic solution. Also in 2009, France, the United Kingdom, and the United States publicly revealed that Iran was building a second enrichment site deep inside a mountain near the holy city of Qom. The West claimed that Iran's failure to report this new site was a second safeguards violation, even though this claim was somewhat controversial. The IAEA had previously required notification upon completion of construction, but while the Qom site (known as Fordow) was being built, the notification requirement was changed to commencement of construction. In 2013, President Rouhani was elected in Iran on a platform of improving relations with the West and negotiations between the P-5+1 (China, France, Russia, the United Kingdom, and the United States plus Germany) with Iran, which had begun some months earlier, were intensified. Rouhani on entering these more intense negotiations had Supreme Leader Khamenei's support. Finally, after years of negotiations on July 18, 2015, a nuclear agreement—the Joint Comprehensive Plan of Action (JCPOA)—was concluded between Iran and the P5+1, or, as some call it, the EU-3+3 (France, Germany, and the United Kingdom plus China, Russia, and the United States).

It was, in actuality, an agreement between the UN Security Council, represented by the P5+1, with Iran as to what Iran must do to restore itself as a compliant party to the NPT and to return to being a full-fledged member of the world community. It was approved by a 15 to 0 vote in the UNSC shortly after its signature, and it came into full force ninety days later, on October 18, 2015. The debate in the United States concerned whether Congress should pass a resolution of disapproval on the agreement, which would have prevented the president from carrying out US obligations under the JCPOA—the lifting of sanctions—thereby forcing the United States to drop out of the agreement. But international sanctions on Iran related to its nuclear program would have been lifted regardless of what the United States did; they would have been removed either gradually, over ten years as set forth in the JCPOA, or immediately, because the agreement fell apart after US withdrawal. In the end, powerful efforts to block the agreement failed, and Congress did not pass the resolution of disapproval. Some weeks later, the Iranian Parliament approved the agreement, and it became operational as scheduled on October 18. But the question as to why Iran would want nuclear weapons is important to consider.

First, the Islamic Republic shares with the government of the Shah a sense of national prestige. Since the earliest days of the Cold War, at least among major states, what distinguished Great Powers from lesser states was the possession of nuclear weapons. Second, nuclear weapons in the eyes of the Iranian government would give Iran more influence in the region. Third, Iran is surrounded by nuclear weapon states: Israel to the west, Russia to the north, Pakistan to the east, and US carrier-based weapons to the south. Fourth, Pakistan is a Sunni state, and Iran is the principal Shia state. If the Pakistani Taliban ever took power in Islamabad, Iran could reasonably fear nuclear attack. One only has to recall the continuing violence between Sunni and Shia in Iraq and Syria to believe in the plausibility of such an attack. President Rafsanjani of Iran publicly expressed this concern at the time of the Pakistani tests in 1998.

In 2015, Iran could have built a nuclear weapon in a few weeks given its scientific expertise and the amount of low-enriched uranium that it had. Why did Iran choose to negotiate? First, there was a major demographic issue. At the beginning of the Islamic Republic, women were encouraged to have as many children as possible. Then, when the government saw how rapidly the Iranian population was increasing, it changed that policy and urged its citizens to have smaller families, resulting in a huge population bulge of people in their twenties—many currently jobless. Second, sanctions have wrecked the economy, particularly in the oil and banking sector. Third, the Iranian people—the most Internet-connected country in the Middle East—are tired of being isolated, and the government doesn't want another Green Revolution. Fourth, Iran is fearful that if it creates a nuclear weapon stockpile, Saudi Arabia would promptly acquire weapons from Pakistan—as the financier of their nuclear program—and deploy them on their missiles, which are easily capable of reaching Tehran. This would be a worse threat than the one from Israel, based on the Sunni versus Shia rivalry and competition over regional hegemony.

Below is a brief overview of the JCPOA:

ENRICHMENT

Iran must reduce its number of deployed centrifuge machines by two-thirds. Iran may keep only 6,140 active centrifuges, only 5,060 operating for enrichment purposes at Natanz, with the remainder at Fordow but not operating. The excess centrifuges will be dismantled and placed in IAEA-monitored storage. There will be enrichment at Natanz only and exclusively with older types of centrifuges. These requirements will last for ten years.

Iran may enrich only to 3.67 percent. It must reduce its current stockpile of enriched uranium from 10,000 kilos to 300 kilos of 3.67 percent enriched uranium. No new enrichment plant may be built. These requirements will last for fifteen years.

Fordow will be made into a science center, with no enrichment there for fifteen years.

Arak reactor: It will be converted into a new type altogether and will produce almost no plutonium.

Thus Iran must eliminate 98 percent of the enriched uranium it possesses, including all of the 20 percent enriched; two-thirds of its centrifuges will be dismantled and stored under IAEA monitoring; the Arak reactor will be disabled and converted; and enrichment at Fordow will be terminated. These are the requirements for initial implementation.

VERIFICATION AND ENFORCEMENT

There will be intrusive countrywide IAEA inspections on an almost continuous basis as well as a robust dispute resolution process with snapback sanctions if there is judged to be a violation.

SANCTIONS

Some Iran nuclear sanctions will be lifted, upon initial implementation as described above. Some of the major sanctions will be lifted after the passage of eight years, and a declaration by the IAEA that Iran's program is transparent and peaceful and the remainder after ten years as the UNSC declares the completion of its supervision of the issue.

PROCUREMENT

There will be strict limits on research and development of the Iran program for ten years. The phasing in of modern centrifuges at Natanz can begin after ten years. Iran's borders will be monitored and its uranium mining will be subject to be verification measures for twenty-five years.

The period of time in which Iran could break out of the agreement and build a nuclear weapon has been increased from the present few weeks to ten to twelve months. One of the preambular paragraphs in the agreement reads, "Iran reaffirms that under no circumstances will Iran ever seek, develop, or acquire nuclear weapons." No other country in the world has made such an unequivocal and unconditional commitment.

What are the benefits of the agreement? First, it reaffirms American world leadership. Second, the JCPOA places well-defined time limits on Iran's nuclear program of ten to fifteen years, immeasurably enhancing confidence during the agreement's term that Iran will not seek or acquire a nuclear weapon. Third, it provides the basis for transparency of procurement and verification of nuclear activities so that the IAEA can determine whether Iran's program is exclusively peaceful.

On August 6, 2015, the deputy ambassadors in Washington of the other P5+1 members briefed twenty-five Democrat senators. These five diplomats said that if the president is prevented by Congress from lifting sanctions as required under the JCPOA, thereby rejecting the agreement, then:

1. International sanctions would collapse.

2. Iran would ramp up its nuclear program—probably to the 190,000 centrifuges of which the Supreme Leader has spoken.

3. There would be no possibility of getting Iran back to the negotiating table—Iran might promptly become a nuclear power or near-nuclear power.

4. China, Europe, and Russia would see rich trading profits in Iran and would want to begin trading right away. A German trade delegation of a hundred prominent business leaders had already been to Tehran, followed shortly thereafter by a seventy- to eighty-person delegation of French businessmen. The 1996 US attempt to enact third-country sanctions—meaning that any third party that trades with Iran cannot trade with the United States—failed because the European Union adopted legislation prohibiting any European company from cooperating with this US legislation and threatened to take a complaint against the United States to the World Trade Organization dispute process.

And military action is no solution. The American people do not want such a war—one far larger than the Iraq War. Robert Gates, the former US defense secretary, has said a military attack on Iran by the United States could: (1) bring together a divided nation, one that is determined to get the bomb, and (2) cause the Iran nuclear weapon program to become more covert. And Iran would get the bomb.[19] Therefore diplomacy and economic pressure are the best course, because every other path is a journey to likely something worse. No real alternative to the agreement exists, but now we must look at the prospects for success of the agreement.

This highly complex agreement, designed to prevent Iran from acquiring a nuclear weapon—which Iran easily could have done—came into operational status as planned on October 18, 2015. It is testimony to its restrictive nature that, while the negotiations were ongoing, Saudi Arabia firmly stated publicly that it wanted the same deal that Iran got; once the agreement was concluded, Saudi

Arabia appeared to have no interest in the restrictions of the agreement. It was approved 15 to 0 by the UN Security Council, with the United States voting in the affirmative, which was all that was required to bring it into force. But two nations opted to submit their participation in the agreement to a vote in their national legislatures. In the United States, this led to an intense and prolonged political struggle. In the end, the US Congress did not take action to prevent the president from lifting sanctions related to Iran's program pursuant to the agreement; therefore the United States will participate. The Iranian Parliament subsequently voted to approve the agreement.

What will this agreement bring? Will Iran remain in compliance? Will this agreement have an effect in other areas? Will it lead to improved business and cultural relations with Iran? What will be the effect on nuclear power? Will it be a cold peace, like the Israel-Egypt Treaty, or will it lead to more than that? Will it remain an agreement among governments only, or over time will it become an agreement among peoples? Answers to these questions may not be known for years.

As to compliance, only time will tell. If the Iranians do not abide by the agreement, the sanctions will return. Any violation would be promptly and widely known, given the unprecedented, comprehensive verification system that will be in place under the agreement. The Iranians, for their part, would appear to have little motivation to breach the agreement. Their primary objective is to rebuild their economy, which has been devastated by sanctions. Over time, this agreement removes the sanctions prompted by the Iranian nuclear program, and they will only return if there is a violation of the agreement. And, to be realistic, there never was any real alternative to this agreement.

The JCPOA is an impressive collection of restrictions, restraints, and monitoring provisions applicable to the Iranian nuclear program. Under this deal, Iran's path to a nuclear weapon using declared facilities is effectively closed for at least ten years, for fifteen years with respect to some important provisions, and for twenty-five years for others. There will be a comprehensive, pervasive, and constant presence by the IAEA. Tehran could attempt to produce nuclear weapon material using the declared nuclear program. But this would risk almost immediate detection and response. This situation is created by a combination of measures that constrain Iran's capabilities and ensure their monitoring.

Although media and public attention has often focused on the known nuclear program, experts generally agree that it is the possibility of a covert program that causes the most concern. At a fundamental level, proving that there is no covert program is difficult. It is not easy to prove the absence of something, particularly in a country as large as Iran. But the subtle effectiveness of the agreement may be most pronounced in the provisions dealing with potential covert activities. It is geared to ensure that no covert program can exist. To have a covert nuclear weapons program, Iran would have to address three needs: access to nuclear materials, access to equipment, and time. But there are extremely strict controls on nuclear materials. Under the JCPOA, uranium acquisitions, through both mining and importing, will be subject to monitoring by the IAEA pursuant to "agreed measures that will include containment and surveillance measures, for 25 years, [covering] all uranium ore concentrate produced in Iran or obtained from any other sources." All possible entry points will be monitored in some way, to verify legal imports and to prevent illegal ones. So, a secret stockpile of uranium would simply not be possible. A covert enrichment path by Iran would require replicating its entire current enrichment program—a costly, complicated, and detectable enterprise. And there are similarly tight restrictions on equipment acquisition. The agreement's provisions will deter any attempt at violation, making any violation a virtually impossible task. So, the possibility of continued Iranian compliance is high. Unfortunately, even if Iran in good conscience strictly adheres to the JCPOA, there will be charges and countercharges over the years. One observer has stated that this agreement, because of continued opposition to it, risks becoming the Obamacare of international agreements, in that it could become subject to frequent attempts at overturning. The international community must be prepared for this possibility.

As to international relations, China, Europe, and Russia all see rich trading potential in Iran and want to start doing business as soon as possible. German and French businesses have already been there. American business in Iran has been quite slow, and that largely remains the case two years later. American goods are reportedly in demand in Iran. The JCPOA could improve Iran's role in international economic partnerships.

Regarding cultural relations, approximately two million Iranians who live in the United States and many more in other countries will want to visit Iran and vice versa. The agreement could create a boom in tourism, which likely would support full-scale and widespread business participation. Iranians possess a rich culture going back thousands of years. Persia has long been one of the world's great cultures, and a medieval Iranian poet, Rumi, has been among the most popular poets in the United States for many years. Iran also has a significant movie industry. Thus there is much in Iran for tourists to see, and Persian culture has much to share with the world community if allowed to do so.

Although the nuclear program in Iran has been a national one for some years, the JCPOA puts important constraints on the development of a full-scale program. Iran can build nuclear power reactors, subject to rigorous inspection and the provisions of the agreement. The parties to the JCPOA are authorized to engage in mutually determined civil nuclear cooperation pursuant to Annex III of the agreement. And the agreement strictly limits fuel cycle activity in Iran. For example, for the next fifteen years, Iran cannot enrich uranium beyond 3.67 percent, and it cannot have a stockpile greater than 300 kilograms of uranium enriched to this level during that period. All spent fuel will be shipped out of the country. Thus it does not appear, even though Iran has said many times that it is committed to a nuclear energy program, that Iran will be a significant participant in the nuclear power industry for some years.

But will the JCPOA add to or detract from stability in the Middle East region? This will be determined by the degree to which Iran is a good partner under the agreement and the extent to which the agreement helps Iran moderate its behavior and become a constructive international player. But there is more to it than that. Will Iran limit its cooperation with the world community largely to the subjects covered by the agreement and perhaps increased world trade, or will it become more of a contributing national player in many fields? No one knows the answer to this question. The Iranian leaders themselves may not know.

On September 18, 2015, the *New York Times* partially addressed the uncertainties in Iran with regard to the JCPOA. It quoted Supreme Leader Ayatollah Ali Khamenei, "We have announced that we will not negotiate with the Americans on any issue other than the nuclear case." By contrast, President Rouhani had said a few days earlier that the nuclear agreement was "not the end of the way" but "a beginning for creating an atmosphere of friendship and cooperation with various countries." To some extent, there appears to be a reassessment of America as scapegoat for all that is evil in the world. "Our Great Satan without sanctions is just not the same anymore," said a prominent economist and supporter of President Rouhani, "Perhaps we should use 'lesser Satan' now or something like that."[20]

Outside Iran, there is a wide divergence of opinions about future prospects; one expert notes that some members of the Iranian foreign policy and security establishment insist that the resolution of the nuclear standoff strengthens Iran's position, gradually opening the way for diplomatic progress on difficult issues like Syria. But critics inside Iran object to the agreement's inspection regime because they say it violates Iran's sovereignty and puts too much trust in the United States. Others object to the mere idea of compromise with the United States.

Another Iran specialist in the journalism field comments that, because the negotiations focused solely on Iran's nuclear program, many are wondering what this might mean generally for the Middle East. This analyst believes that a richer Iran is likely to do things such as double down on its support for President Basher al-Assad in Syria. Iran, with Russia, is Assad's main supporter and ally. Europe, the Gulf States, and the United States are Assad's main opponents. The civil war in Syria has already killed more than 500,000 people and is without question one of the greatest humanitarian crises since the Second World War, with half of the prewar population of 22 million people displaced from their homes and a quarter of the population in exile. Huge numbers of desperate Syrian migrants are seeking new homes in Europe.

In theory, the nuclear deal could lead to more open discussions among the many countries that have a stake in Syria, but this is far from certain. Assad has called the nuclear agreement a "victory." But Iran's hegemony in Syria is not assured even though it has poured billions into the regime's survival. The journalist makes this assertion because Iran's influence in Syria relies far more on money than natural affinity. Thus a richer Iran will be more likely to considerably increase its support for the Syrian regime, rather than promote a reasonable negotiated settlement and behave in a similar fashion in other areas.

In the past, Iran has done many things that the United States and its friends and allies strongly opposed. And many of the Iranian officials in the past are still in the government. But the operative word is the past. There is hope that the future will be better, although the West must remain cautious. As President Ronald Reagan famously said, "trust but verify." And Iran is pragmatic. In the past, Iranian officials have indicated that they are not wedded to Assad. Therefore continuing to work with Tehran while verification is in place could lead to positive results. The legislative election in February 2016, which resulted in some victories for moderates in Iran, was encouraging. And President Rouhani was decisively reelected in May 2017.

Now we turn to the regional implications of the agreement, which are not so straightforward. The six member states of the Gulf Cooperation Council (GCC) share a consensus on the nuclear agreement signed by the six major powers with Iran. Their common position was set forth in the joint statement issued by GCC foreign ministers and the US secretary of state on August 3 in Qatar. The statement endorses the nuclear agreement, partially because Gulf states hope that the accord could eventually reduce regional tensions. At the same time, GCC countries, especially Saudi Arabia, are wary that the deal could (1) bring about Iran-US rapprochement and reduce their strategic value vis-à-vis the United States, and (2) empower Iran (financially and with newfound confidence) to activate Shia factions within these states (particularly in Saudi Arabia, where the Shia populations are mainly located in oil-producing areas and Bahrain, which has a relatively large Shia minority). Activation of these factions could encourage instability and present problems for the regimes. Therefore, although these countries have publicly supported the deal, they have been privately lobbying for increased US security assurances (mainly weapons sales and ballistic missile defense).

What will be the effect of the agreement on peace and stability? Iranians are fully aware of what is going on in the rest of the world, and they no longer want to be isolated and thereby unable to truly participate in international affairs. If the nuclear agreement gradually evolves into an agreement among peoples, meaning an agreement among the peoples of Iran and the six other powers, then the prospects will greatly improve in the long run in terms of peace and stability. At present, however, the JCPOA is an agreement between governments. It affects only what governments do among themselves, which may or may not add to stability in the long run, although it certainly does in the short term.

In conclusion, will this agreement do what it is supposed to do and prevent an Iranian nuclear weapon for fifteen years or more? The odds seem good. But will this lead to other things, such as improved business and cultural relations? The Iranian government appears to say no to all such things; the supreme leader in public statements has been explicit on this point. The US government is not positive either. But there are some encouraging signs: President Rouhani's desire to improve Iran's relations with other countries is one of them. In the long run, might this desire lead to improved political relations? That is much less clear, but if the above areas become and remain positive, improved political relations cannot be ruled out.

IRAQ

Saddam Hussein personally drove Iraq's pursuit of nuclear weapons. In 1959, the Iraqi Atomic Energy Commission was established. By the 1960s, the Nuclear Research Center at Tuwaitha, near Baghdad, began operating a small research reactor acquired from the Soviet Union. By 1968, when he was in his late thirties, Saddam rose to prominence following a coup. This coup was the third in ten years and the last as Saddam became in 1969 vice chairman of the Baath party's all-powerful Regional Command Council. He would remain, at least on paper, the second most powerful man in Iraq until July 16, 1979, when the president and chairman of the council, Saddam's cousin, Ahmed Hassan al-Bakr, retired. Saddam was then in a position to eliminate his Baath party colleagues and take full power for himself.

But even before becoming the official ruler of Iraq, Saddam was taking steps to acquire a nuclear capability for the country. In 1974, French Prime Minister Jacques Chirac visited Iraq, and his visit led to an agreement two years later between the Iraq and French nuclear industries to acquire a nuclear reactor. Under this contract, Iraq was to receive a 70-megawatt research reactor similar to the Osiris reactor at the French nuclear research center at Saclay. Accordingly, the French called it the Osiraq reactor, combining the words "Osiris" and "Iraq." Saddam Hussein named the reactor the Tammuz I or the July 1 reactor, thereby commemorating the month of the coup of 1963 that brought the Baath party to power. In return, France received a large interest in the Iraqi oil industry.

The reactor that France sold to Iraq was later modified to be a 40-megawatt light-water nuclear materials testing reactor (MTR). Although Iraq claimed that it only wanted this reactor for peaceful applications, it was an unusual choice. The MTR is particularly valuable to countries with established reactor programs, but it is not especially useful for a country like Iraq, which had no established nuclear reactor program, unless the purpose of the acquisition was to produce plutonium for a nuclear weapon program. The operational date for the Osiraq reactor was set for late 1981. All along, the Iraqis had insisted on using HEU, which was the standard for an MTR reactor, but under pressure from the Israelis, the French had offered the Iraqis low-enriched uranium (LEU) fuel. Along with plutonium, HEU is one of the two fuels needed to make a nuclear weapon. The spent fuel from this large research reactor could be reprocessed to extract plutonium to make nuclear weapons, just as the Israelis had done with their reactor at Dimona, which had also been sold to them by the French. Israel's concern continued to grow while the French were constructing the Iraqi reactor. Saddam Hussein announced that the construction of the Osiraq (or Tammuz I) reactor was part of the first Arab attempt to build nuclear weapons, and this announcement did not help ease Israeli concerns. In 1980, the Iran-Iraq War broke out, and on September 30, 1980, Iran attacked the Osiraq reactor with two F-4 Phantom fighter-bombers, slightly damaging it. Then came the big blow on June 7, 1981, when, just days before Osiraq would become operational, Israel attacked the reactor in an air assault using six F-14s and six F-15s and destroyed it.

In Israel, the opposition strongly criticized the attack, but the government asserted that it was important to carry out the strike before the reactor became operational so as to eliminate the possibility of radioactive fallout.[21] The attack was carried out not long before the incumbent Prime Minister Menachem Begin sought and achieved reelection. Egypt had ratified the NPT a few months before the attack, and Egyptian leaders asserted for many years thereafter that they never would have joined the NPT had the Israeli raid on Osiraq been carried out before they became an NPT party.

The UN Security Council condemned this action by the Israelis; the United States voted to label the act as a violation of international law. The Israeli opposition leader at the time, Shimon Peres, was critical of the attack for years, asserting that it had driven Iraq to enhance its program and take it underground. Moreover, because Iraq was an NPT party, Osiraq would have been under IAEA safeguards, so diversion to a weapons program would not have been a simple undertaking or one that could go unnoticed.

In the aftermath of the raid, Baghdad continued its pursuit of nuclear weapons, but by a different clandestine route—via uranium enrichment. Within a few years of the Osiraq attack, at least six secret weapon laboratories had been established at Tuwaitha, and by 1988, shortly before the First Gulf War, Iraq was prepared for a major expansion of its nuclear weapon program, despite its use of calutrons (an outmoded uranium separation technology used during World War II as part of the program to construct the Hiroshima bomb).

Not long after the end of the eight-year-long war between Iran and Iraq in 1988 came Saddam Hussein's invasion of Kuwait in 1990 and Iraq's seizure of the Kuwait oil fields. This was followed by the defeat of Iraq in the four-day First Gulf War and its expulsion from Kuwait. Iraqi forces had been defeated by the United Nations coalition led by the United States. The central objective of the United States, along with most members of the international community, was to keep the Iraqis from advancing toward the Saudi Arabian oil fields while at the same time driving them out of Kuwait. But a secondary objective also motivated the United States and others of the coalition; they wanted to eliminate Iraq's nuclear weapon program. The US intelligence community had believed that this program existed, despite the failure of the IAEA to find anything significant during NPT safeguards inspections over the years. Neither the United States nor the IAEA (and presumably the Mossad in Israel) had successfully detected the significant extent of this program until UN inspections began after the First Gulf War.[22]

Four days after it began, the First Gulf War ended. The Iraqi Army was decimated, and the international community decided to take the opportunity to make a clean sweep of Saddam Hussein's programs to produce weapons of mass destruction (WMDs). In March 1991, the UN Security Council passed ten resolutions directed at Iraq. These resolutions, unlike the negotiations with Iran that led to the 2015 agreement on the Iran nuclear program, were not negotiations; instead, they were mandates issued to a defeated enemy by the world community. In the second of these resolutions, which consisted of thirty-four points, Iraq was required, among other things, to "unconditionally accept the destruction, removal or rendering harmless, under international supervision, of all chemical and biological weapons and all stocks of agents" and related subsystems; to destroy all ballistic missiles of a range greater than 150 kilometers; not to obtain or develop any nuclear or any nuclear weapon–usable material or any related subsystems; and to submit a declaration of all nuclear weapon facilities. Hans Blix, the director general of IAEA, was instructed to immediately conduct on-site inspections of all nuclear facilities and to develop a plan for the destruction or removal of all nuclear facilities and material in Iraq within forty-five days. The Security Council also created a UN Special Committee (UNSCOM), to be led by Swedish diplomat Rolf Ekeus, which received the same assignment for Iraq's chemical and biological weapon programs.[23]

The IAEA inspections in Iraq began shortly after the adoption of the resolutions. The inspection teams were immediately met with Iraqi deception and obstructions. Nevertheless, they persevered and by the sixth inspection, some five months later, had a good idea of the extent of the programs. The facility at Tuwaitha was much larger and more extensive than imagined; it was clear that Iraq had been engaged in a significant and comprehensive effort to acquire nuclear weapons and likely would have been able to construct a nuclear weapon in two or three years. After a huge effort, the IAEA believed by 1996 that it had completely destroyed the entire Iraqi nuclear infrastructure as well as all related equipment and material, despite the many obstacles that the Iraqi government had placed in its path. Furthermore, also by 1996, UNSCOM believed that all the Iraqi stocks of chemical and biological weapons had been eliminated.

Because of continued Iraqi obstructionism, the United States and the United Kingdom decided to carry out an extensive bombing campaign against Iraq in December 1998. The bombing campaign lasted for four days, prior to which the new UNSCOM director, Australian diplomat Richard Butler, ordered all UNSCOM inspectors out of Iraq (the IAEA had already completed its task). After the bombing, Saddam Hussein refused to allow the inspectors to return. Inspections did not continue, but Iraqi imports remained under tight supervision and there was constantly increasing surveillance from satellites. Furthermore, the probability that Iraq would ever be able to reconstitute anything of significance from its destroyed WMD programs was extremely low.

Nevertheless, when President George W. Bush assumed office, his administration's top two national security objectives were the invasion of Iraq and the expansion of missile defense. Everything else, including defense against international terrorism, was secondary. The real reasons for the invasion of Iraq were different, the elimination of the supposed WMDs serving as a convenient public excuse.

On the eve of the US invasion of Iraq in the spring of 2003, the US government was still insisting that Iraq possessed extensive stocks of weapons of mass destruction. On November 8, 2002, the UN Security Council passed Resolution 1441, which among other things provided that UN inspectors could return to Iraq with a new mandate utilizing the successor to UNSCOM, the UN Monitoring Verification and Inspection Commission (UNMOVIC) headed by Hans Blix, having completed his term at the IAEA. The IAEA also returned under Blix's successor, Mohamed ElBaradei. Iraq, under powerful military threat from the United States, had to allow the inspectors to return, and UNMOVIC and IAEA resumed inspections in Iraq on November 27, 2002. As early as January 8, 2003, however, Blix's doubts about Iraq's possession of WMDs were increasing. The intelligence services of several countries, including the United States, had given UNMOVIC "a good number of sites for possible inspection," and UNMOVIC had not found any prohibited activity at any of these sites, even though this was supposedly the best intelligence that various intelligence agencies could provide. Blix wondered how there could be "100-percent certainty about the existence of weapons of mass destruction but zero-percent knowledge about their location."[24] He also noted that all members of the Security Council shared the view that the nuclear weapons case against Iraq had effectively been closed by 1998. This view was also held by the US military. On February 24, 2001, Secretary of State Colin Powell, the former chairman of the US Joint Chiefs of Staff, stated that Saddam Hussein did not have "any significant capability with respect to weapons of mass destruction."[25]

The Bush administration's invasion of Iraq went ahead anyway in March 2003 without authorization from the Security Council and with no justifiable basis for a claim of self-defense. This invasion was a violation of international law. And after US troops had quickly conquered Iraq and US inspectors had thoroughly searched the country, no WMDs of any kind were ever found. Saddam's nuclear weapon program had ended in 1991, the chemical weapon stockpile destroyed the same year. The last biological agent was destroyed in 1996. The British government shared this information, which was obtained from the chief of the Iraqi intelligence service in a series of meetings by one of the senior agents of MI6, the British intelligence service. Sir Richard Dearlove, the chief of MI6, came to Washington in February 2003 to brief US decision makers on this information in person, but his presentation was dismissed as misinformation.[26] After all, the invasion of Iraq was never about nuclear weapons, WMDs, or al-Qaeda, for that matter. It was about making the Middle East safe for Israel, Iraqi oil, and most importantly a demonstration of American power for its own sake.

SYRIA

The Syrian civil war is one of the greatest humanitarian disasters since the Second World War. More than 500,000 people have been killed. From a prewar population of 22 million, 11 million have been displaced from their homes, with 4 million having become refugees in other countries. The government of Bashir al-Assad has repeatedly demonstrated its viciousness and cruelty. It has conducted deplorable military operations, like the use of so-called barrel bombs, against its own people. These are attacks on innocent civilians who have not committed any crime but have had the misfortune of living in Syria, while some citizens try to establish basic civil rights for the Syrian people against the express wishes of the current regime. The Syrian government has even used sarin gas, a deadly nerve agent, perhaps the deadliest of poison gases, against its own civilian population. This led to international pressure from Russia, the United States, and other UN members that successfully forced Syria to destroy its chemical weapon stockpile and join the CWC. Although events in April 2017 indicated that it was not all destroyed, as the Syrian government has pledged.

Earlier in 2007, this same terrible government made its way onto the public's radar as another country attempting to develop nuclear weapon capabilities. On September 6, 2007, Israel—implementing a unilateral government decision (as it had with respect to Iraq in 1981) to use military force to halt suspected nuclear proliferation—conducted an air raid on a facility named Al Kibar in northern Syria, not far from the border with Iraq.

Satellite imagery indicated that the destroyed facility, the construction of which was almost completed, was similar in design to the 5-megawatt gas-cooled, graphite-moderated reactor that had been the centerpiece of the North Korean nuclear weapon program, producing enough plutonium for one nuclear weapon per year.[27]

The Bush administration had reportedly been skeptical prior to the Israeli raid that the facility at Al Kibar—which had been under US satellite observance since 2001—was in fact a nuclear reactor supplied by North Korea. But in late April 2008, the CIA reportedly testified in a secret session to Congress on what it believed to be the facts about the facility bombed by Israel. According to unconfirmed reports, the testimony asserted that the facility had a structure similar to those used to house gas-graphite reactors. Also, a video taken clandestinely prior to the Israeli raid revealed that the Syrian reactor's core design was the same as that of the North Korean reactor at Yongbyon. The video apparently showed alleged North Koreans inside the unfinished reactor structure, which convinced the Israelis to destroy it. There was no explanation as to how the individuals were identified as North Koreans. They weren't South Koreans, which left only the North Koreans, some might argue.[28]

In his first public comment on the issue, then CIA director Michael Hayden stated that the plutonium reactor was within weeks or months of completion, that it was similar in size and technology to North Korea's Yongbyon reactor, and that it could produce enough plutonium for one or two bombs per year.[29] There was no identifiable plutonium reprocessing facility located in the region of Al Kibar,[30] but there was evidence of multiple visits to Syria by senior North Korean nuclear officials and a suspected cargo transfer in 2006.[31] Also, the reactor being built in Syria with North Korean assistance was even more questionable than the Iraqi Osiraq reactor that France had supplied and Israel destroyed. The Osiraq reactor was openly purchased from France, declared, and made subject to IAEA monitoring. By contrast, the undeclared Syrian reactor was being secretly built and deliberately concealed. Additionally, it was based on a model designed specifically to produce plutonium for nuclear weapons.

There was a counter-narrative promoted by British and French intelligence that this was a three-party effort, which included Iran, with the reactor designated to supply plutonium to Tehran.[32] But the United States and Israel held to their view that this was a Syrian–North Korean exercise only. This time, no one—not even Syria—denounced Israel for its action.

LIBYA

Between 1970 and 1990, Libya made numerous attempts to acquire nuclear weapons. In 1970, Muammar Qaddafi sent a senior official to China to buy one or
more nuclear weapns. He was politely rebuffed. In 1973, Libya reached a secret
agreement with Prime Minister Ali Bhutto to help finance the Pakistan nuclear
weapon program in exchange for full access to the technology. Bhutto took the
money but never delivered the technology. Qaddafi tried to buy a research reactor from the United States, but that attempt was also rebuffed. After those two
failed attempts, he was able to purchase a research reactor from the Soviet Union
in 1975. The reactor became operational in 1981. Libya repeatedly pressed India
and Pakistan for nuclear weapons to no avail.[33]

Libya continued to pursue the development of a nuclear weapon, or the acquisition of one in a desultory fashion, but after many years Qaddafi had nothing to
show for his efforts. He decided to approach the principal trader of nuclear weapons, the great proliferator himself, A. Q. Khan. Khan made a major agreement
with Libya to first supply it with twenty centrifuges plus parts to begin research
and eventually realize a complete nuclear weapon production capacity. The first
shipment was made, and then the Khan network was expanded to carry out this
deal, establishing facilities in Malaysia and elsewhere, reaching a final agreement
in 2000.[34] Khan sent further enrichment and actual nuclear material to Libya. By
2002, Libya had assembled a few centrifuges and been supplied with the design
of a nuclear weapon.

Finally, in 2003, with intelligence coming in from the CIA and MI6 to
Washington and London, it was clear that something had to be done. Dealing with
the Khan network was a subject of intensive debate in Washington and London
during this time. Meanwhile, Qaddafi had decided to try improving relations
with the West as early as 1999, and negotiations to this effect began in the spring
of 2003. Qaddafi's chemical, biological, and nuclear weapons programs were
subjects of these discussions. Libya had long retained a robust chemical weapons stockpile. Negotiations dragged on through the summer. But in September,
Western intelligence received a tip that a ship named the BBC *China* was on its
way to Libya from Malaysia carrying key technology—largely centrifuges—for
the Libyan nuclear weapon program. The German-owned ship was stopped and
searched in Italy. It was believed that crates on board contained equipment necessary for a nuclear weapon program. When the crates were opened, officials
were able to confirm that they contained centrifuge components. It was clear to

Libyan officials that British and American intelligence knew exactly what they were doing. The game was up for Libya. An NPT party in good standing has the right to acquire components of the fuel cycle such as centrifuges, but not secretly; such acquisitions must be reported to the IAEA. Libya's violation was the same violation that Iran had committed. Within two weeks, Libya admitted the first Western inspectors to their WMD sites.[35] With respect to the nuclear weapon program, the inspectors found centrifuges in warehouses and the nuclear weapon design in a desk drawer. Little had been done because Libya had no infrastructure. All the equipment and any associated material were removed to Oak Ridge National Laboratory in the United States.

SAUDI ARABIA

Saudi Arabia invested heavily in the Pakistani nuclear weapon program. Some are of the view that Saudi Arabia believes, as the principal financier, that it can obtain nuclear weapons from Pakistan should they ever become necessary. A NATO official told a BBC reporter in 2015 that nuclear weapons made in Pakistan on behalf of Saudi Arabia are now sitting ready for delivery. In October of that year, Amos Yadlin, a former head of Israeli military intelligence, told attendees at a conference in Sweden that if Iran got the bomb, "the Saudis would not wait one month. They already paid for the bomb; they will go to Pakistan and bring what they need."[36] Gary Saymore, who was President Barack Obama's counter-proliferation advisor until March 2013, commented to the same BBC reporter, "I do think that the Saudis believe that they have some understanding with Pakistan that, in extremis, they would have claim to acquire nuclear weapons from Pakistan."[37]

In the late 1980s, Saudi Arabia secretly bought dozens of CSS-2 ballistic missiles from China, and they were deployed a few years later. A new CSS-2 base with missile launch rails aligned with Israel and Iran was reportedly completed in the summer of 2015. The nuclear weapon design acquired by Pakistan from China and sold to Libya is for a device engineered to be delivered on a CSS-2 ballistic missile. The Saudi officials denied the accusation of an arrangement with Pakistan and noted that their country was an NPT party. They then called for a nuclear weapon–free Middle East and pointed to the existence of an advanced nuclear weapon arsenal in Israel. Because of circumstantial evidence, allegations of a secret Saudi-Pakistani deal began to circulate as early as the 1990s.

A senior Pakistani official, speaking on background terms, confirmed the broad nature of the probably unwritten deal his country has reached with the kingdom and asked rhetorically, "What did we think the Saudi's were giving us all that money for? It wasn't charity."[38] With the removal of Saddam Hussein from power to check the Iranians, Saudi statements about the need for Saudi weapons, should Iran ever acquire them, have grown stronger over the years. And the gradual improvement of Western relations with Iran during the negotiation of the nuclear agreement with Iran of July 2015 only increased that sentiment. Amos Yadlin has said, "Unlike other potential regional threats, the Saudi one is very credible and imminent." Even if this view is accurate, however, there are many legitimate and beneficial reasons for Saudi Arabia to leave its nuclear warheads in Pakistan for the time being. Doing so allows the kingdom to deny that there are any nuclear weapons in its territory, it remains in compliance with the NPT, and it avoids challenging Iran to cross the nuclear threshold in response.[39] Whether this is a true nuclear weapons program or political bluster cannot be determined. Perhaps it is both. But like all the other programs in the Middle East, this one must also be considered when determining the prospects for an eventual NWFZ in the Middle East. There have been other possible nuclear weapon programs in the Middle East, or at least ones that have been suspected for a time.

ALGERIA

Today, Algeria does not possess nuclear weapons or a nuclear weapon capability. It is not suspected of pursuing or considering the pursuit of such a capability. Between 1960 and 1966, France carried out seventeen nuclear weapon tests in the Algerian Sahara: four atmospheric and thirteen conducted underground. The long-term effects of these tests remain a point of contention between France and Algeria.

Algeria ratified the NPT in 1995 and soon thereafter became one the first countries to sign the Treaty of Pelindaba. Algeria possesses a small civil nuclear research program and currently operates two research reactors under its Atomic Energy Commission. Both are under IAEA safeguards.

This was not always the case. Following the signing of a nuclear cooperation agreement with China in 1983, construction of Algeria's second nuclear research reactor began in 1988. The first was constructed in 1987-89 time frame by the INVAP Company of Argentina. The second, the Chinese-built research reactor named Es Salam, is a 15-megawatt heavy-water-moderated reactor located about 140 kilometers south of Algiers in the Sahara Desert. It is fueled by 3 percent enriched uranium.

In 1991, the secretive construction of the Es Salam reactor raised concerns among intelligence analysts about the reactor site's purpose and the possibility of an Algerian nuclear weapon program. Some analysts argued that the unusually large cooling towers were too big for the reactor's declared power output. The deployment of Russian-made SA-5 air defense batteries at this site created additional doubts about its civilian purpose. In April 1991, an article in the *Washington Times* accused China of helping Algeria to obtain nuclear weapons. Algerian officials responded by asserting that the reactor was designed for civil purposes, such as making medical radioisotopes. They also said that the reactor's design was not suitable for plutonium production.

The IAEA inspected the reactor in January 1992, and the following month Algeria signed a facility-specific safeguards agreement with the IAEA. After acceding to the NPT in 1995, Algeria also signed a full-scope safeguards agreement with the IAEA. Algeria is planning a nuclear power program with two reactors coming online in the late 2020s.[40]

EGYPT

Although suspected of harboring nuclear weapon ambitions at various points in its history (especially under President Gamal Abdel Nasser), modern-day Egypt is a member in good standing under the NPT and has been the leading proponent of a weapons-of-mass-destruction-free zone in the Middle East. Today, Egypt seems to perceive the development of nuclear weapons as contrary to its national interests. It also harbors an extremely negative view of the Israeli nuclear weapon program, regarding it as contrary to the national interests of Egypt and of peace in the Middle East and beyond.

Egypt operates two small research reactors and has attempted, so far unsuccessfully, to acquire nuclear power reactors. Egypt has not acquired or pursued enrichment or reprocessing technology. Today, most experts agree that it is unlikely that Egypt will in the future seek a nuclear weapon capability.

But in the past, there were times when the outlook wasn't so positive. In 1958, in a deal with the Soviet Union, Egypt acquired a small two-megawatt light-water research reactor. But during the 1960-67 time frame, statements by senior Egyptian government officials, after the disclosure by Israeli Prime Minister David Ben-Gurion of the construction of the Dimona reactor, caused scholars to conclude that Egypt was also actively interested in acquiring nuclear weapons. During this period, the Egyptian government significantly increased its investment in nuclear technologies. And there were persistent attempts to acquire a sizable nuclear power heavy-water reactor that was fueled by natural uranium—a better plutonium producer than light-water reactors.

There were promising discussions with Siemens of Germany about acquiring such a reactor, but these negotiations ultimately fell apart. Nasser never developed a dedicated budget for nuclear weapons. In any case, the 1967 war with Israel crippled the Egyptian nuclear program. The Egyptian economy was devastated by the 1967 war, and there was no money for things related to acquiring a nuclear program. Soon after, in 1968, Egypt signed the NPT and, with Anwar Sadat's assumption of the presidency after Nasser's death in 1970, Egypt's rhetoric concerning nuclear weapons suddenly changed. In 1974, Sadat attempted to negotiate a large power reactor deal with the United States, but the prospective agreement was not achieved because of conditions that the Americans proposed. In the eyes of the Egyptians, these conditions were unacceptable. In December 1980, Egypt decided to ratify the NPT, which the Egyptian legislature authorized in February 1981. Ratification occurred not long before the Israeli raid on Osiraq, which could have severely complicated the Egyptian decision to ratify. Egypt was now subject to international safeguards and full IAEA transparency.[41] Egypt in 2016 expressed an interest in acquiring nuclear power reactors, but this interest has not come to fruition.

Egypt has pressed for the negotiation of a weapons-of-mass-destruction-free zone (WMDFZ) in the Middle East for many years. It has also often criticized the lack of universality of the NPT, particularly the lack of adherence by Israel. Egypt was opposed to supporting the indefinite extension of the NPT in 1995 without—at least in Foreign Minister Amr Musa's words—a "concrete step" on Israel's part in the direction of eventually becoming a party to the NPT. (The minister never specified what such a step would be: some suggested an agreement to negotiate a nuclear weapon–free zone through the Arms Control and Regional Security Group, or ACRS, others something at Dimona.) Egypt's concern about nuclear Israel was one of the most difficult problems that the United States had to address in pursuing a permanent NPT at the 1995 conference. Eventually, reluctantly, Egypt settled for a resolution at the conference calling on all states in the Middle East not yet party to the NPT to join the treaty and for the negotiation of a WMDFZ in the region. This resolution enabled the NPT to be extended by consensus at the 1995 conference but led to severe trouble down the road, particularly at the 2010 and 2015 NPT Review Conferences.

My first discussion of the subject of NPT universality and extension with Foreign Minister Musa is a good example of the Egyptian view. I went to Cairo in the spring of 1994, accompanied by my deputy for NPT extension, Ms. (later Ambassador) Susan Burk. Our purpose was to discuss NPT extension with the foreign minister and ask him to at least consider indefinite or permanent NPT extension. We were met in the outer office of the minister by Nabil Fahmy, the special assistant to the foreign minister, later for many years Egypt's ambassador to the United States and foreign minister himself in 2013-14. As we were waiting, Nabil said to Susan, "Susan, what you are proposing for the NPT is Catholic marriage!" Susan, a devout Catholic, replied, "And what is wrong with Catholic marriage?"

Soon we were ushered into the minister's office. I sat in a chair next to his desk. Susan and Nabil sat about fifteen feet away in chairs along the opposite wall in front of the desk. Then began a lengthy diatribe by the minister along the following lines: "Why should Egypt be interested in the NPT? We live right next to a country that can destroy the entire Middle East in fifteen minutes. What good is the NPT to Egypt? Our relations with the current government in Israel are good. But what guarantee can you [pointing at me] give me that some crazy Likudist like that Major that killed twenty-nine worshipers in a mosque a few months ago, will not come to power in Israel someday?" Several times I said, "But you don't want Libya to have nuclear weapons," but the minister waved this question aside. The discussion went on for what seemed like a long time. Finally, it ended and I took my leave. As I was walking out the door with Susan, Nabil said, "Tom, you should not think of your meeting with the minister as a failure." "What other word should I use?" I replied.

This was the first of seven meetings with Foreign Minister Musa regarding the NPT extension process. The sessions improved significantly in tone and to some extent in substance. And the foreign minister in 1996 was a great help in bringing the CTBT negotiations to a close in Geneva.

A brief mention of the status of peaceful nuclear power in the Middle East is warranted here. Turkey has attempted to initiate a nuclear power program for many years without success. Turkey currently has a contract with Russia to build four nuclear power plants, but the project seems to be moving slowly. The United Arab Emirates (UAE) has initiated the first new nuclear power program in the world in over thirty years, since the beginning of the Chinese program. Four identical 1,400-megawatt reactors are being built by Korea, with construction spaced exactly one year apart. When the fourth is online in 2020, they will provide a significant percentage of the electrical power of the country. Other countries in the region, such as Saudi Arabia and Jordan, may follow their lead.

For many years, an NWFZ or a WMDFZ for the Middle East has been on the international agenda. The Middle East is home to a full-fledged nuclear weapon state, Israel; a near–nuclear weapon state, Iran; a might-have-been nuclear weapon state, Iraq; a potentially instant nuclear weapon state, Saudi Arabia; and various thoughts and attempts in Algeria, Egypt, Libya, and Syria. Is an NWFZ possible or even conceivable in such a region? Fundamentally, to achieve such a zone, the problems of the P-5-like nuclear weapon arsenal in Israel would have to be resolved to the satisfaction of all parties. But before that can happen, Israel's security would have to be guaranteed to the satisfaction of the Israelis. That is reality.

Israel, of course, understands that its conventional forces are far stronger than any combination of forces that could be arrayed against them. But they must be absolutely assured against a nuclear weapon attack. In 1999, I was part of a nongovernmental discussion involving delegations approved by the Egyptian, Israeli, and Jordanian governments and a group of former senior US government officials. One of the officials who addressed us during our meeting in Israel was the deputy defense minister. (The prime minister then was Ehud Barak.) During the question period, I asked him whether Israel would ever consider negotiating away its nuclear arsenal. His answer was a strong negative. But what if Israel could be absolutely guaranteed against nuclear weapon capability anywhere in the region by means of Israeli inspectors on the ground in every Middle Eastern country? "That would be a different situation," he replied. But that was then.

In December 1994, I was once again traveling in the Middle East in search of support for indefinite NPT extension. Susan Burk and a US State Department official accompanied me. First, we stopped in Cairo for another session with Foreign Minister Musa. The substance was the same, but this time the atmosphere much better. We then went to Israel in search of a "concrete step" but had little success. Officials at the State Department had told me that if I went to Israel and brought up the NPT, I had better have a ticket on the next flight out. The event proved otherwise. There was a lecture at Tel Aviv University that was politely received at which many good questions were asked. Discussions at the Defense Ministry and the Foreign Ministry were to the effect that: "we recognize the importance of the NPT and we will consider doing something someday, but for now, we are just not in a position to do anything." The bottom line was that Israelis were not prepared to take the step that the Egyptians wanted, and they never did.

We then traveled across the Jordan Valley to Amman, where we were scheduled to meet with the special assistant to the crown prince, the senior arms control official in the Jordanian government, Abdullah Toukan. During our discussion, he said, "The Egyptians have it wrong. One day the Israelis will join the
NPT, but only after a long process during which their security is assured."

The UN General Assembly first endorsed the concept of a Middle East nuclear
weapon–free zone (MENWFZ) in a resolution in December 1974, following a
proposal by Iran and Egypt. Every year, beginning in 1980, the resolution on a
MENWFZ has passed by consensus without a vote in the UN General Assembly.
This proposal has also been incorporated in several UN Security Council resolutions. From 1991 on, the IAEA General Conference has adopted every year, on a
without-objection basis, a resolution calling for the adoption of full-scope safeguards on all nuclear facilities throughout the Middle East region "as a necessary
step for the establishment of the NWFZ."[42]

At the suggestion of Egypt in 1988, the UN secretary general undertook a study
on effective and verifiable measures that would facilitate the negotiation of an
NWFZ in the Middle East. This study suggested numerous measures, including
confidence-building agreements. Following the 1988 study, a technical study in
1989 considered various alternatives for applying safeguards on nuclear facilities
in the Middle East. The technical study also took up the geographical delimita-
tion of a MENWFZ. The conclusion of the study was that the appropriate area for
such a zone would be bordered by Libya on the west, Iran on the east, Syria on the
north, and Yemen on the south. Suggestions to include Afghanistan and Pakistan
on the east and Turkey to the north have not gained any significant traction.[43]
The UN secretary general publicly released his study in 1991. Also in 1991, UN
Security Council Resolution 687 explicitly endorsed the goal of a WMDFZ in the
Middle East, with strong encouragement from Egypt. This proposal was put forward by President Mubarak of Egypt in 1990 and was simultaneously introduced
into the Conference of Disarmament in Geneva.

In 1992, discussion of regional arms control issues began in the ACRS process, a multilateral regional body established pursuant to the Madrid Middle
East peace process of 1991. The idea was that, among other things, ACRS could
discuss the prospects of a future WMDFZ in the Middle East. Although only
one state in the Middle East, then and now, is in possession of a nuclear arsenal,
several states had chemical and biological weapon programs. Today, only Egypt
and Israel have chemical weapon programs, although the Syrian government
has demonstrated, in recent acts in the Syrian civil war, even after joining the

Chemical Weapons Convention under pressure from Russia and the United States, that it has illegally retained an extremely dangerous nerve-gas capability. The ACRS discussions included thirteen Arab states, Pakistani representatives, and Israel. Israel was very much a part of the ACRS process, but Iran and Iraq (then under heavy UN sanctions as a result of the First Gulf War) did not participate. Following disagreements with Israel over the agenda for discussing WMDFZ issues and the decision in May 1995 to extend the NPT indefinitely without a concrete step by Israel, Egypt placed these discussions on hold in the latter half of 1995.[44]

The document "Principles and Objectives for Arms Control and Disarmament" stated that there should be additional NWFZs negotiated, "particularly in the Middle East." This document was adopted by consensus by the NPT parties in May 1995 and was a part of the extension package, which also included the resolution on strengthening the NPT review process and the indefinite extension resolution. In addition, a fourth resolution was adopted by consensus at the same time as the extension package on the Middle East, which called for "the establishment of an effectively verifiable Middle East zone free of weapons of mass destruction, nuclear, chemical, and biological, and their delivery systems." Importantly, the resolution also affirmed "the importance of the early realization of universal adherence" to the NPT and called "upon all States of the Middle East that have not yet done so [here the Arab states had insisted on naming the relevant states: Djibouti, Israel, Oman, and the UAE], without exception, to accede to the Treaty as soon as possible and to place their nuclear facilities under full-scope International Atomic Energy safeguards."

The resolution came at the end of a long process to enable Egypt to accept NPT indefinite extension by consensus. Egypt had wanted a commitment from Israel toward eventual NPT adherence, which had not been forthcoming. The Egyptian position was supported by Saudi Arabia and Syria, but the Saudis faded from the scene before the end of the process. And the Arab League never supported Egypt on this issue during the many months of discussion leading to the NPT Review and Extension Conference. Some have said that the resolution on the Middle East was carefully drafted, but this was not so. It was put together at the last minute, to some extent as an act of desperation, like so many other things in history ultimately important to peace and security. In the months after the spring of 1994, there were many meetings on the question of Egypt and its desire for a "concrete step" from Israel, which would justify their support of NPT extension. There were meetings in Cairo, in Israel, and in Washington. Many officials were involved, including presidents, foreign ministers, the US secretary of state, and ambassadors. Many ideas were put forth, but nothing that Egypt would accept or that Israel would ever do under existing conditions. Egypt never really wavered from its initial position—likely it became too public a stance to compromise. By the time of the conference, with no Israeli action forthcoming, some other solution had to be found. So, a last attempt to solve this problem began in the basement of the United Nations headquarters at 4:00 p.m., the day before adoption of the resolution on indefinite extension and the companion resolutions on principles and objectives and on enhanced review. An effort to finally find a resolution that Egypt would find acceptable was underway. No proposed text existed, only a few ideas.

Egypt and Syria were present, represented by their ambassadors. For the United States, it was UN Ambassador Albright, Bob Einhorn from the State Department, and myself. Presiding over this small group was the conference president, Ambassador Jayantha Dhanapala. There was a general understanding in the room that the resolution would call for the negotiation of a WMDFZ in the Middle East and would urge all states in the Middle East that had not yet become a party to the NPT (Israel, Djibouti, Oman, and the UAE) to join the treaty as soon as possible. The principal outstanding issue was whether the four states that had not yet become parties—who would be urged to join—would be listed by name. Egypt, supported by Syria, strongly wanted them to be named; Israel objected. Formulations for the provisions were discussed, the Israeli mission was telephoned every half hour or so and kept informed on what was going on. Several hours of stalemate ensued as the US delegation argued against states being named. Then representatives of Djibouti, Oman, and the UAE appeared and said that they didn't want to be named, either.

Thus there was no solution for this issue other than a general exhortation for all non-NPT parties in the Middle East to join. Egypt and Syria were so disgusted that they refused to sponsor the resolution. Ambassador Dhanapala firmly declined and turned to me, asking if the NPT depositaries would agree to co-sponsor (Russia, the United Kingdom, and the United States; it was customary during the Cold War for multilateral security treaties to have three depositories—for ratification documents—instead of one: one for Western states, one for Eastern states, and one for neutrals), even though we did not yet have a written text. I replied in the affirmative for the United States, but said I would have to check with the United Kingdom and Russia. I told Dhanapala that I would let him know in the morning.

The Russian and British ambassadors along with the ambassadors from France and Germany were at a dinner in a nice restaurant, where I was supposed to be as well, had I not been waylaid by the meeting in the UN basement. I called the restaurant and was connected to the room where the dinner was located. Sir Michael Weston, the UK ambassador, came to the telephone first and promptly agreed. Sergey Kislyak, the Russian ambassador, said that he thought it would be possible, but he would have to ask Moscow. I then went over to the dinner myself. At 7:30 the next morning, Sergey called me in my hotel room and said that Moscow had informed him that he could co-sponsor. There was a condition, however. "What is that?" I asked. "Moscow says I have to read it first," Sergey replied.

The resolution was printed that morning, and Ambassador Kislyak had his opportunity to read the resolution that he was going to co-sponsor before the proceedings began later that morning. The extension package introduced by the conference president was promptly passed by consensus, and then conference president Dhanapala brought up a resolution on the Middle East introduced by the three depositaries—it sounded a bit odd, but there it was. It also passed by consensus after a two-hour wrangle on the floor with Iran over a positive reference to the Palestinian peace process. So, the conclusion of the NPT extension process committed all NPT parties to "take practical steps . . . aimed at making progress towards . . . the establishment of an effectively verifiable Middle East zone free of weapons of mass destruction."

Of course, no such progress has been made. In the final document of the 2000 NPT Review Conference, the NPT parties reaffirmed "the importance of the Resolution on the Middle East adopted by the 1995 Review and Extension Conference" and noted that it "is an essential element of the outcome of the 1995 Conference and of the basis on which . . . [the NPT] was indefinitely extended without a vote in 1995." The final document also invited "all states, especially states of the Middle East, to reaffirm or declare their support for the objective of establishing an effectively verifiable Middle East zone free of nuclear weapons, as well as other weapons of mass destruction . . . and to take practical steps toward that objective."

Nothing happened at the 2005 NPT Review Conference, as it was a complete failure in every respect. By the time of the 2010 NPT Review Conference, fifteen years had passed without any tangible progress toward the establishment of a Middle East zone free of WMDs.

The stalled process seemed to have been overturned at the 2010 NPT Review Conference, but only momentarily. In view of the limited progress since 1995,

Arab states pushed for tangible steps toward the establishment of the WMDFZ with Egypt indicating that they would block consensus approval of a final document if this were not achieved. Another failed review conference was something that the United States wanted to avoid. The result was a provision in the conference final document calling for a discussion on the establishment of a Middle East WMDFZ to be attended by all states of the region.

Negotiating this Middle East solution was difficult. Egypt wanted a negotiating conference, while the United States would only support a conference that did not have a negotiating mandate. Several months of negotiations ensued. During this time, I was scheduled to make a presentation to the Council on Foreign Relations in Cairo, an entity composed of former senior ambassadors. The National Security Council staff, on learning I was going to do this presentation, asked whether I could include a pitch for a nonnegotiating conference. I did so, and one of the former ambassadors asserted during the discussion that the only reason Cairo was pushing for the negotiating mandate was to ensure that Israel would come and actually say something. Some delegates at the review conference believed that the United States had indicated it could deliver Israel if the conference did not have a negotiating mandate.

As part of the final document, the three NPT depository states committed to work together with the UN Secretary General to convene a regional conference in 2012 to discuss, but not negotiate on, implementation of the 1995 NPT Review and Extension Conference's Middle East resolution. Finland was designated as the host for the 2012 conference, and a facilitator was appointed to help make sure the conference happened. The conference was scheduled for December 2012 in Helsinki, and Finland's Under-Secretary of State Jaakko Laajava was named as the facilitator.

But it wasn't long before Israel began backing away. In March 2012, an Israeli official said that Israel would attend something like the planned conference, but only after there was comprehensive peace in the Middle East region. Israel had also expressed a desire that the conference must not be convened as part of an NPT process, of which it is not a party. Once it appeared that Israel would not attend, Iran joined Arab nations in indicating that it did plan to come to the December conference, leaving Israel as the only holdout.[45] Citing "present conditions in the Middle East" and the lack of agreement by participating states on "acceptable conditions," the United States issued a statement postponing the December 2012 conference. The conference was not rescheduled, and agreement on this front seems elusive for the near future. Although some progress has been made with respect to chemical weapons in the region (only Egypt and Israel remain nonparties to the CWC), no progress has been made with respect to a zone free of nuclear weapons.

On April 29, 2013, Egypt walked out of the NPT Preparatory Meeting in Geneva in protest over the postponement of the December 2012 conference. Between October 2013 and June 2014, facilitator Laajava held five consultations with regional states in an effort to agree on an agenda for the postponed conference. The Arab League and Israel attended all five meetings, Iran only the first, although it was regularly briefed. No consensus was found, however.

From an Arab point of view, Israeli insistence that the Helsinki agenda include regional security and confidence-building measures deliberately diverted attention from regional attempts to control WMDs. Egyptian leaders claim that when they attempted a "security first" process in the ACRS forum, the Israelis arrived "empty-handed" and did not deliver on nuclear disarmament. For Israel, however, an incremental approach that involves confidence building and political transformation leading to further discussions on a WMDFZ may be the only way forward.[46]

During the 2015 NPT Review Conference, Egypt led the Arab League in presenting a rather uncompromising new proposal. The UN Secretary General would be the sole convener, and the facilitator and would be charged with holding the new conference within 180 days of the end of the review conference. There would be two working groups: one for basic provisions such as scope, prohibitions, and interim measures, and the other for verification and implementation. It would be a negotiating conference. A modified version of this proposal was in the draft final document, and it charged the UN Secretary General to convene the conference by March 1, 2016, with the objective of "launching a continuous process of negotiating and concluding a legally binding treaty" that establishes a WMD-free zone in the Middle East. The secretary general was to appoint a facilitator by July 1, 2015, to work with the secretary general and the NPT depositary states and to consult with regional states in attempting to establish an agenda for the conference. Canada, the United Kingdom, and the United States decided not to support the draft final document for the NPT review conference because of the language on the proposed conference in the final document to negotiate a Middle East WMD-free zone. The United States, speaking at the review conference, said it objected because the plan to set an agenda and hold a conference was not based on "consensus and equality" and that the document proposed "unworkable conditions" and "arbitrary deadlines."[47] Israel attended the 2015 Review Conference as an observer and presented its own ideas toward a regional dialogue in the Middle East.

As a result, there was no agreed final document, and the 2015 NPT Review Conference failed. The failure also brought into some disrepute the successful 2010 NPT Review Conference, as its success was dependent on the agreed conference, which did not happen. The lack of a process to achieve an MENWFZ or WMD-free zone is now a threat to the viability of the NPT.

The inability of the world community to even organize a dialogue on the governmental level on the subject of a Middle East nuclear weapon–free zone or WMD-free zone has become a major international issue because of its effect on the NPT and on world order generally. It began, in large part, as a concern expressed by Arab states about the large and highly modern nuclear weapon stockpile present in the region and the accompanying vulnerability of the entire Arab world. When Susan Burk and I visited Riyadh in 1994 to discuss NPT extension with Saudi officials, we also met with representatives of the Gulf Cooperation Council (an organization of Persian Gulf states that is always chaired by a Saudi official). The chairman of the group said the following calmly but firmly. The Israeli program created real political problems for Arab states; it would help, he said, if occasionally the United States would denounce the Israeli program, "even if you don't mean it."

As discussed above, the WMD-free zone issue became perhaps the most difficult among many serious issues in the 1995 NPT extension effort. And it was settled with an uneasy compromise that resulted in the passage of a resolution that called on all states in the Middle East that had not joined the NPT to promptly join the treaty and also obligated all NPT parties to support and pursue a WMD-free zone in the Middle East.

Years passed with little action on the resolution. The remaining states not party to the NPT in 1995 other than Israel—Djibouti, Oman, and the UAE—joined the treaty before the next review conference in 2000. The resolution was mentioned as an important undertaking in the 2000 final document. Yet little progress has been achieved ever since.

By 2010, the Egyptians were seeking action on the resolution. A lengthy negotiation between Egypt and the United States ensued, with the Egyptians pressing for a Middle East conference on the resolution, which could begin negotiations on a WMD-free zone. The United States was willing to agree only to a conference without negotiating power. It was recognized that this was an important issue, and probably essential, to a successful conference and an agreed final document.

The issue was compromised by an agreement to a nonnegotiating conference in Finland in 2012. All Middle East states were to attend including Israel and Iran. Some believed that the United States was really saying that a nonnegotiating conference would enable it to deliver Israel.

In the end, Israel refused to come, and the conference did not happen. In 2015, the Arabs were no longer interested in compromise; in the draft final document, they inserted a proposal for a negotiating conference on a WMD-free zone in the Middle East to be convened by the secretary general of the United Nations by March 1, 2016. This provoked Canada, the United Kingdom, and the United States to block the final document to protect nonparty Israel, and the 2015 NPT Review Conference failed. This issue will likely come up again at the 2020 NPT Review Conference. Without an agreement to at least meet to consider the negotiation of a WMDFZ in the Middle East, the NPT could face a major crisis.

The problem with respect to the active pursuit and establishment of a Middle East nuclear weapon–free zone or WMD-free zone is Israel. This is so even though the conventional armaments of the Israeli Defense Forces are more powerful than the rest of the Middle East combined. Israel says it will only discuss such a concept after a comprehensive peace in the region has been secured. Only a solution of the Palestinian-Israeli conflict would permit that. But how likely is such an achievement in today's world?

In the eyes of the well-known *New Yorker* journalist and Middle East expert Dexter Filkins:

> However slim the chances for a comprehensive peace agreement were in the nineteen-nineties, today they are effectively zero. . . . It's possible that the course of events in Israel and Palestine might be altered by some extraordinary act of leadership—by some Rabin we haven't met, or by some crisis we have not foreseen. But, for now, nothing like that seems remotely possible. Tolstoy posited that history is not made by individuals, that it is, rather, the continuously unfolding consequence of innumerable interconnected events. But, if the story of Yitzhak Rabin [the Israeli Prime Minister in the 1990s who came close to peace] and Yigal Amir [the man who assassinated Rabin] has anything to teach, it's that individuals matter. Rabin was the right man at the right time, and so, in his perverse way, was Yigal Amir. The opportunity that Rabin was trying to seize—however small—was there for a moment, and it may never come again.[48]

We must hope that the opportunity will come again and that there will be another Rabin.

Chapter 10
Northeast Asia

Unlike the Middle East, northeast Asia has only one nuclear weapon program threatening the security of the region: that of North Korea. Nonetheless, two of the five nuclear states in the NPT, China and Russia, have territory in the region, and two other states have significant nuclear weapon breakout capability. These other states once had potential plans to develop nuclear weapons but somewhere along the line abandoned them.

During World War II, Japan attempted to build nuclear weapons, but among other setbacks, basic resources such as uranium were lacking.[1] Their program never came close to fruition, even though the physics and the engineering required were well understood.

The leading figure in the Japanese program was Yoshio Nishima, a close associate of Niels Bohr and a contemporary of Albert Einstein. In 1931, he established his own nuclear laboratory, the Institute for Physical and Chemical Research, known as the RIKEN Institute. By 1939, after the experiments of Lise Meitner and Otto Frisch in Germany, he recognized the military potential for nuclear fission. He was worried that the Americans were working on a nuclear weapon that could be used against Japan. Not long after, of course, preliminary American investigations developed into the vast Manhattan Project, which culminated in the 1945 attacks on Hiroshima and Nagasaki.

In 1940, Nishima attempted to interest the military in pursuing a nuclear weapon. After serious consideration in 1943, the Japanese Navy concluded that its development was not feasible. However, the army was interested and passed the authority to pursue development of a nuclear weapon down the chain of command to the RIKEN Institute. During the war, the RIKEN Institute investigated various methods to separate U-235 using the cyclotrons that had been built. No attempt was made to build a uranium pile, and heavy water was unavailable. The army and navy did conduct searches for uranium in several locations and finally succeeded in persuading their German allies to ship 500 kilograms of unprocessed uranium oxide to Japan aboard a submarine in April 1945. But the submarine surrendered to US forces in the Atlantic after Germany's capitulation.

In 1943, a separate naval command began a nuclear research program known as the F-Go Project at Imperial University in Kyoto under Bunsaku Arakatsu, Japan's most distinguished nuclear physicist. Arakatsu had studied under Ernest Rutherford at Cambridge and Albert Einstein at Berlin University. The navy's Chemical Section had requested that Arakatsu work on the separation of U-235. To this effect, Arakatsu included Hideki Yukawa on his team, a man who, in 1949, became the first Japanese physicist to win the Nobel Prize. By the end of the war, the design of an ultracentrifuge had been completed, but the program did not proceed beyond the design of ultracentrifuge machinery before Japan's surrender.

Shortly after Japan's surrender, the Manhattan Project's Atomic Bomb Mission, which arrived in Japan in September 1945, learned that the F-Go Project had obtained a small amount of heavy water each month from electrolyte ammonia plants in occupied Korea and Kyushu. Despite the availability of heavy water obtained in this manner, Japan did not explore the possibility of using heavy water as a moderator for a nuclear reactor, which could produce plutonium. One historian alleged that, shortly before the end of the war, US intelligence had learned that Japan planned to carry out a test of a nuclear weapon. This test was to take place on August 12, 1945, near Konan (now known as Hungnam), where the Korean Hydro Electric Company—the site of the ammonia plant—was located. But nothing further could be learned about this plan, as the Red Army overran Hungnam a few days later. In 1946, a reporter who had been stationed in Korea as a US Army investigator after the war published a story in the *Atlanta Constitution* asserting that Japan had successfully tested a nuclear weapon near Hungnam before the Soviet Army captured the town. US officials publicly dismissed the report.

In October 1945, Nishima sought permission from US occupation forces to use the two cyclotrons at the RIKEN Institute for biological and medical research. The initial response was positive, but in early November, the US secretary of war ordered that the cyclotrons at the RIKEN Institute, Kyoto University, and Osaka University be destroyed. In late November the cyclotrons were dismantled and thrown into Tokyo Bay.[2]

Ever since the bombing of Hiroshima and Nagasaki and the end of World War II, Japan has been an upholder of its nuclear weapon–free status and, since the 1970s, the NPT. Its postwar constitution, formulated during the period of the US occupation, forbids the establishment of offensive military forces. In 1967, Japan adopted the well-known Three Non-Nuclear Principles, which prohibit: the introduction of nuclear weapons into Japan, their indigenous production, and their possession. Japanese Prime Minister Eisaku Satō said, however, to President Lyndon Johnson in January 1965, shortly after China's first nuclear weapon test, that if the Chinese communists had nuclear weapons, then the Japanese also should have them. Because of this assertion, the United States became sufficiently anxious about Japan's nuclear interests to make securing Japan's membership in the NPT—signed in 1968—one of its top priorities. But the Sato government continued to discuss the nuclear option. One suggestion was that tactical nuclear weapons could be defined as defensive and therefore consistent with Japan's constitution. A white paper was released stating that possessing small-yield, purely defensive nuclear weapons would not violate the constitution. It was at this point that the Three Non-Nuclear Principles were announced to reassure the Japanese public. Although they were adopted by the Diet, they are not law. Nevertheless, they have remained the basis of Japan's nuclear policy ever since.

Prime Minister Sato, concerned after making the Three Non-Nuclear Principles declaration and fearing it would be too constraining, clarified the declaration in an early 1968 speech to the Diet. In this speech, Sato announced the so-called Four Pillars Nuclear Policy: promotion of peaceful nuclear energy, efforts toward global nuclear disarmament, reliance on extended US nuclear deterrence, and support for the Three Non-Nuclear Principles, where Japan's national security is guaranteed by the other three policies. One could derive from this policy that if American assurance was ever removed or became unreliable, Japan might have to build nuclear weapons. So, even though Japan was a worldwide champion of global nuclear disarmament, it kept the nuclear option available. Japan finally signed the NPT in 1970 and ratified it in 1976, but only after West Germany became a party and the United States promised not to interfere with plutonium reprocessing capabilities related to Japan's civilian nuclear power program. Notwithstanding this outcome, an earlier 1969 Japanese Foreign Ministry policy-planning study concluded that, even if Japan became an NPT party, it should retain the economic and technical capability to develop and produce nuclear weapons, should that ever become necessary.[3]

Over the years, interest in the nuclear option remained, and in 1998, two events strengthened the hand of those who argued that Japan should at least reconsider, if not reverse, its non-nuclear policy.

The first was the occasion of nuclear weapon tests by India and Pakistan and their announcements that they were now nuclear weapon states. About this time, a senior official in the Japanese Foreign Ministry told me at a private dinner, "When we signed up for the NPT we expected five nuclear weapon states, not seven [forgetting about Israel] and if there is an eighth, named North Korea, there surely will be a ninth, named Japan." The Japanese government was troubled by the reluctance of the international community to condemn India and Pakistan for the tests. When Japan had decided to join the NPT, it expected that there would be severe penalties for any state that would defy the international consensus that the NPT represented. In addition to lack of severe penalties for India and Pakistan, Japan feared the possibility of a nuclear arms race between India and China and the effect of such a development on Japan.

The second event was the August 1998 launch of a North Korean Taepodong-1 missile over Japan into the Pacific, supposedly a space rocket sending a satellite into orbit. The launch caused major public outcry. Some quarters called for remilitarization or the development of nuclear weapons in Japan. The head of the Japanese Defense Agency, Fukushiro Nukaga, said his government would be justified in carrying out missile strikes against North Korean missile bases. Prime Minister Keizo Obuchi hastily reiterated Japan's non-nuclear weapon principles, asserting that Japan would not build a nuclear arsenal, and that this matter was not worthy of discussion.

While there are no known plans for Japan to produce nuclear weapons, it is widely believed that Japan has the technology, raw material, and capital to build nuclear weapons if it so chooses, within a year or perhaps more quickly. As a result, some analysts refer to Japan as a de facto nuclear weapon state.

Significant amounts of reactor-grade plutonium have been produced by Japan through the reprocessing of commercial nuclear power plant waste. In 2012, reports suggested that Japan possessed 9 tons of reactor-grade plutonium—enough for around one thousand nuclear weapons. It has an additional 35 tons stored in Europe. As of 2014, Japan had 1,200 to 1,400 kilograms of HEU supplied by the United States and the United Kingdom for research reactors and fast neutron reactor programs as well as its own uranium enrichment plant. Japan has a large three-stage solid-fuel rocket similar to the US Peacekeeper ICBM and a simpler-to-launch second-generation solid-fuel rocket, named Epsilon. Japan also has investments in reentry technology.

So long as Japan retains a "nuclear-ready" status, it will have no reason to produce nuclear weapons. By remaining below the threshold, but with the capability to cross it quickly and by retaining US support, Japan can present itself as an equal to China and Russia.[4]

South Korea, or the Republic of Korea (ROK), has also seriously considered nuclear weapons, given the ongoing aggressive nuclear weapon program in North Korea. According to a poll taken in February 2013 in the wake of North Korea's third nuclear weapon test, large majorities in the ROK support the concept of a nuclear weapon deterrent for the country. A second poll, conducted later in 2013, produced a similar result. There are doubts about the reliability of the US nuclear weapon extended deterrence guarantee, with somewhat less than half of the public expressing confidence that the United States would in fact come to the aid of the ROK in the case of an attack by North Korea.[5]

This public anxiety is a recent development. The South Korean public formerly had little or no reaction to North Korean threats and provocations. North Korea conducted its first nuclear weapon test in 2006. Largely a failure, its 4-kiloton expected yield came in at less than half a kiloton. The second test was in 2009 in the range of 6 kilotons, and the third in February 2013, in the range of 6–10 kilotons, was slightly more successful. Increasing success and North Korean hostility toward its southern neighbor ignited public anxiety in South Korea. In 2010, North Korea attacked an ROK battleship, killing more than forty sailors, and then shelled a South Korean island later that year.

Public calls for a nuclear deterrent appeared soon afterward. In September 2013, conservative commentator and political analyst Kim Dae-jung argued in a column of the newspaper *Chosun Ilbo* that South Korea should develop and deploy nuclear weapons. Although conservative politicians and columnists had long called for South Korea to respond in kind to North Korean threats with a "South Korean bomb,"[6] such calls had gone largely unheeded, with only a tiny fraction of the public supporting nuclear weapons for South Korea. Not anymore. In the last ten years, attitudes have profoundly changed; two-thirds of the public now support the policy recommendation mentioned in the 2013 column.

South Korea has the raw materials to build nuclear weapons, but it has not done so. The United States has constantly reassured the ROK that the US nuclear arsenal will suffice to protect its national security. But in recent years, the South Korean public has become skeptical and now supports an independent ROK nuclear weapon deterrent by a two-thirds margin. It has been estimated that South Korea could break out and construct nuclear weapons in one to three years.[7] In a 1983 study, South Korea was on the list of "potential members of the nuclear club" and credited with possessing at least 3,000 tons of uranium reserves. At the time, according to one study, it would take South Korea four to six years to acquire nuclear weapons.[8]

South Korea contemplated the development of its own nuclear weapons for the first time when the United States informed South Korea of its intent to withdraw the 7th Infantry Division from Korea in 1970. After the 26,000 US troops were withdrawn in 1971, an entity called the Weapons Exploitation Committee began exploring the possibility of acquiring plutonium-reprocessing facilities. After the fall of South Vietnam in 1975, ROK President Park Chung-hee first mentioned South Korean interest in acquiring a nuclear weapon deterrent at a press conference in June 1975. In a National Security Council memorandum of March 3, 1975, American officials concluded that South Korea was in the first stages of developing a nuclear weapon program.[9] The US government concluded that it was necessary to approach South Korea directly, particularly with respect to the reprocessing plant it was negotiating to buy from the French. In August 1975, there were several conversations among US Secretary of Defense James R. Schlesinger, President Park Chung-hee, and other senior South Korean officials. There were also approaches by the US embassy in Seoul. But as late as the end of October, South Korea was still pressing ahead with its plans to purchase a nuclear reprocessing plant.[10] By the end of the year, the United States was successful in persuading France not to sell the reprocessing plant to South Korea.

Throughout this period, while South Korea was contemplating a nuclear weapon stockpile and had an active nuclear weapon research program, Washington kept pressing South Korea to make good on its signature of the NPT by ratifying it and becoming a party. On April 23, 1975, South Korea did ratify the NPT, thereby legally committing itself to not acquiring nuclear weapons. To a degree, the ROK nuclear weapons research program ended as a result,[11] but interest in such weapons did not abate, the Ford administration believed that President Park still hoped to have a secret or "latent" nuclear weapon program of some sort despite joining the NPT. South Korea's pursuit of the purchase of a plutonium reprocessing plant from France was seen as evidence of this. Seoul remained interested in at least the option to build nuclear weapons one day if necessary.[12]

South Korea ratified the NPT under pressure: the United States reportedly threatened to withdraw its security guarantees if Seoul did not halt its weapon development plans.[13] South Korea complied but continued its efforts to acquire the reprocessing plant from France, thus placing South Korea's continued interest in the nuclear option on the public record. But the campaign to acquire the plant ended with the French decision before the end of 1975. An NPT party is permitted to have reprocessing technology if the facility is under IAEA safeguards—which South Korea's plant would have been, as it had signed a safeguard agreement with the IAEA—and if the intended use is not for weapons. This second condition is questionable given President Park's interest in nuclear weapons.

A few years later, President Jimmy Carter announced that the United States planned to withdraw its remaining troops from the Korean Peninsula, and President Park promptly revived the ROK's efforts to acquire reprocessing capabilities from France. This effort was blocked by President Carter's personal intervention and the contemporaneous decision to cancel the troop withdrawal plans.[14] South Korea became a party to the IAEA additional protocol in 2004 after having strongly supported the indefinite extension of the NPT in 1995. When the ROK submitted its initial declaration under the additional protocol, however, it disclosed a series of previously undeclared laboratory-scale experiments by scientists at the Korea Atomic Energy Research Institute. The experiments were related to uranium enrichment and conversion and plutonium separation pursuant to reprocessing. The experiments produced small amounts of nuclear material and did not appear to be part of a nuclear weapons program. Nevertheless, the activities involved technical skills that would be useful in a weapons program. The IAEA determined this capability to be a matter of serious concern. South Korea subsequently informed the IAEA that these experiments were conducted without the knowledge of the government and were carried out solely to satisfy the scientific interest of the scientists involved. In May 2008, the IAEA concluded its investigation and stated that all questions concerning these past undeclared experiments involving uranium enrichment, conversion, and plutonium separation had been resolved.[15]

Although South Korea is and has been a strong supporter of the NPT and of non-proliferation norms and is under the US umbrella, it could break away and try to develop its own nuclear weapons given a sufficiently severe provocation from North Korea. The technical capabilities exist, with the ROK currently possessing ballistic missiles that are nuclear capable and can reach anywhere in North Korea.[16] Public support for such action is certainly indicated; after the third weapon test by North Korea, less than half of the public fully trust the US nuclear guarantee, and two-thirds favor an independent nuclear deterrent.

Like Japan, the Republic of Korea has the technology and materials to easily build nuclear weapons if it believes they are necessary. The ROK, like Japan, would face a considerable diplomatic cost, given its many international treaty commitments—as is the case with Japan—were it to do so. But the South Korean government, like the Japanese government, presently sees no reason to do so, given the protection of the American nuclear arsenal. However, if a conflict with

North Korea should break out, South Korea—once more, like Japan—could rather quickly evolve into a nuclear-armed state even with the continuing support of the United States.[17] Thus the key to nuclear peace and the possibility of one day achieving a nuclear weapon–free zone in northeast Asia is heavily dependent on outcomes in North Korea.

The nuclear weapon program in North Korea began many years ago. In 1964, the North Korean dictator installed by the Soviets, Kim Il-sung, traveled to China seeking nuclear weapon technology. North Korea, also known as the Democratic People's Republic of Korea (DPRK), had invaded South Korea in 1950. After a three-year war, Kim's forces were crushed by the United Nations coalition led by the United States. His country was devastated by three years of aerial bombardment and only survived because of the intervention of massive Chinese forces. An uneasy truce has succeeded the Korean War in the region of the 38th Parallel, near the original border between North and South established at the end of World War II.

When China successfully tested its first nuclear weapon in 1964, it became a new member of the nuclear club and, as it turned out, the fifth and last nuclear weapon state recognized by the NPT. France, the Soviet Union, the United Kingdom, and the United States were existing members of the club. Serious non-proliferation efforts were already underway in the world community. The UN General Assembly unanimously adopted the Irish resolution calling for a nuclear non-proliferation treaty in 1961, and the commencement of the NPT negotiations followed only a few years later. Under these circumstances, with a brand-new nuclear deterrent, China was not interested in being labeled a nuclear weapon proliferator. China therefore politely declined Kim's request. As described in chapter 9, Libya's Muammar Qaddafi also tried unsuccessfully to obtain nuclear weapon technology from China. And in 1974, at a time when South Korea was considering the nuclear weapon option, Kim Il-sung made another request. China again responded in the negative. As a result, in the late 1970s, Kim ordered DPRK government officials to begin an independent program of seeking nuclear weapons.[18]

The Soviet Union had sold a small 2- to 4-megawatt research reactor to North Korea in the 1960s. This reactor was sited near Yongbyon in North Korea, and Soviet scientists established a research center there. Later, in the early 1980s, North Korea began work on a larger research reactor in the 20- to 30-megawatt (thermal) range, which would provide approximately 5 megawatts in electric power.[19] Subsequently, this reactor was usually described as a 5-megawatt research reactor.

It was designed for the dual purposes of producing both heat and electricity as well as plutonium. It could produce approximately enough plutonium to fuel one nuclear weapon per year. This reactor began operating in 1986. By 1991, North Korea had expanded its uranium-mining program and nuclear weapon research, and had begun construction of two much larger plutonium-producing reactors.

With all this nuclear activity, the DPRK came under heavy pressure from the Soviet Union to accede to the NPT. North Korea finally did so in 1986, the same year that the Yongbyon 5-megawatt reactor became operational. North Korea initially declined to sign a safeguards agreement with the IAEA as required by the treaty, but after facing significant additional international pressure—not the least from the Soviet Union—the DPRK at last signed an agreement in early 1992. At the end of 1991, the two Koreas signed an agreement on the denuclearization of the peninsula, but the agreement gave only a short respite from tension and was effectively a dead letter after a few months.

Several IAEA inspections followed the signing of the safeguards agreement, led by Director General Hans Blix. The inspections focused on the 5-megawatt reactor and the two larger reactors under construction. Early in the process, an IAEA inspection identified discrepancies in the North Korean inspection declaration. What North Korea had declared to be a radioisotope laboratory (supposedly capable only of research) was in fact an undeclared reprocessing plant capable of separating plutonium from reactor spent fuel. The US government later concluded that North Korea had shut down its 5-megawatt reactor for three months in 1989, perhaps long enough to withdraw sufficient spent fuel to reprocess adequate plutonium to fuel one or two nuclear weapons.[20] The inspectors in this context became suspicious of two areas that might be undeclared waste storage sites. Inspectors had analyzed sufficient nuclear waste samples to conclude that North Korea had processed more plutonium than the 90 grams that they admitted to having produced. The IAEA inspectors requested an inspection of the two sites. The request was denied.

In late February 1993, the IAEA board approved a strongly worded resolution requesting a "special inspection" of the two sites. Based on satellite imagery supplied by the United States, the board was persuaded that an inspection would reveal evidence of undeclared plutonium production. The board gave North Korea thirty days to permit the inspectors access to the site and thereby to comply with the resolution, but they did not have to wait nearly that long for an answer. North Korea rejected the inspection request contained in the resolution the next day. And on March 12, the DPRK gave the required three-month notice of withdrawal from the NPT and halted all further IAEA inspections. This was a shock to the international community; no state had ever exercised the right to withdraw from the NPT or from any other international arms control or non-proliferation agreement. But this decision to withdraw did not end the matter.

A few weeks later, near the end of March, the IAEA approved and sent a resolution to the UN Security Council stating that it could no longer certify that nuclear material had not been illegally diverted from peaceful activities to a weapons program in North Korea and that it was forwarding the North Korea case to the council for consideration of sanctions.[21]

Even though it was by no means certain that China, a permanent member of the Security Council with the right of veto, would support international sanctions on already destitute North Korea, messages soon arrived from North Korea indicating its willingness to negotiate. By early spring, the United States and Kim Il-sung's "Hermit Kingdom" agreed to negotiate directly on the nuclear issue. In June, on the eighty-ninth day of the ninety-day notice period, North Korea "suspended" its withdrawal from the treaty. (Whether it was truly a suspension or a cancellation of plans to withdraw was debated for years thereafter. In other words, did North Korea now have a notice period of one day, or the standard ninety days?)

The negotiations began and proceeded slowly. In the spring of 1994, the two parties came close to war over the North Korean nuclear program. North Korea suddenly decided to pull the fuel rods out of its 5-megawatt reactor without permitting IAEA inspection, raising the risk of reprocessing the spent fuel, which was believed to contain enough plutonium for five to six nuclear weapons. The United States informed the North Koreans that, if the reprocessing of spent fuel began, it would destroy the reprocessing plant with cruise missiles. The North Koreans replied that if the United States did that, they would turn Seoul into a "sea of fire."[22] The Clinton administration began to make preliminary war plans. There was a real possibility of a second Korean war.

At that point, former president Jimmy Carter ended the impasse by responding to an invitation from the North Korean government to visit the country. Grudgingly, the White House agreed and authorized the US negotiator, Ambassador Robert Galucci, to brief President Carter. He then departed for Pyongyang. Carter met at length with Kim Il-sung and developed some level of understanding with him. Kim Il-sung died of a heart attack not long after his meeting with President Carter, but his son and successor Kim Jong-il carried out his policies. The negotiations were back on track. They concluded at the end of

1994, with an executive agreement—not a treaty—called the Agreed Framework. Pursuant to the agreement, the North Korean program, including the 5-megawatt reactor at Yongbyon, was shut down. The Agreed Framework remained in force for eight years until terminated by the Bush administration in 2002. Because the 5-megawatt reactor could make enough plutonium for one nuclear weapon per year, North Korea did not get the eight bombs it might otherwise have had. Under the agreement, the withdrawn fuel rods remained in the spent-fuel pond under the watchful eyes of the IAEA inspectors.

Thus the agreed framework during its eight years of existence prevented the North Koreans from acquiring the plutonium for an estimated eight nuclear weapons. But the other parts of the agreement did not work out well. Beyond freezing development of nuclear weapons, the agreement was supposed to lead to broader, better relations between the two countries. Such rapprochement, however, did not happen. Instead, the expanding DPRK ballistic missile program was increasingly seen as a real threat. North Korea developed a highly successful regional ballistic missile program and the beginnings of an ICBM program capable of delivering nuclear weapons against North America.

Another threat that only became clear later was the secret agreement between the North Korean government and A. Q. Khan. Khan was essentially representing the Pakistani government in exchanging uranium enrichment technology for North Korea's medium-range ballistic missile known as the No-Dong, renamed the Ghauri in Pakistan. At the same time that North Korea was negotiating the Agreed Framework with the United States, it was secretly negotiating an alternative route with A. Q. Khan. The deal with Khan was agreed on the margins of a state visit to North Korea by Pakistani Prime Minister Benazir Bhutto in 1993. Khan then made perhaps a dozen subsequent visits to North Korea, always in Pakistani Air Force planes, delivering components, plans, and centrifuge machines in exchange for components and designs of the No-Dong missile to Pakistan. The Ghauri missile would become Pakistan's first long-range ballistic missile with delivery capability for Pakistani nuclear weapons. For their part, the North Koreans did little with the uranium-enrichment technology until the Bush administration abandoned the Agreed Framework in 2002.

North Korea is a dangerous state with a long history of being willing to sell anything to anyone for its own benefit. It also has a significant record of state terrorism. Nuclear weapons in the hands of this government pose a double danger: it could sell nuclear weapons or technology to a terrorist organization or to another state clandestinely seeking nuclear weapons and at the same time threaten northeast Asia with nuclear attack using its formidable medium-range ballistic missiles as delivery vehicles. At the same time, Pyongyang's track record included a certain realpolitik and willingness to negotiate. Above all, the North Korean regime, having few allies and grappling with overwhelming poverty and occasional famine, was interested in survival and economic benefits, especially for the elite, as well as armaments. This was and remained the case until recently.

By the late 1990s, an impasse of sorts had developed. On August 31, 1998, North Korea tested its three-stage Taepodong-1 missile, which flew over Japan and landed in the Pacific Ocean. There was concern that North Korea might soon test a Taepodong-2, which could carry nuclear weapons to North America. In 1999, a small team of US experts, headed by former secretary of defense William Perry, visited Pyongyang as another long-range missile test appeared to be imminent. The reception in Pyongyang was hostile, but North Korea did not close the door to further dialogue. In October 1999, Perry released his report stating that it was in the interest of the United States to build on the Agreed Framework, to engage in discussions with North Korea to relieve tensions, and eventually to end sanctions and normalize relations. Meanwhile, South Korea had elected as president Kim Dae-jung, a former dissident during South Korea's military government, who established a policy of increased engagement with North Korea known as the Sunshine Policy.

In January 2000, a US State Department delegation met with North Korean diplomats in Berlin. Eight months earlier, the Perry delegation had invited North Korea to send a high-level envoy to Washington. The State Department delegation drafted a possible joint statement should such a visit take place and gave it to the North Koreans. It included the declaration that neither government would have "hostile intent" against the other and emphasized the desire of both countries to "build a new relationship free from past enmity." During the meeting, North Korean officials indicated that the DPRK was willing to observe a moratorium on further testing so long as the dialogue continued. The next month, a senior North Korean official stated publicly that the country now had sufficient military strength to concentrate on economic development. The State Department experts concluded that this meant that North Korea had a serious economic problem and that negotiations were now possible.[23]

The real turning point came in June, when Kim Dae-jung flew to Pyongyang for a summit meeting with Kim Jong-il. This meeting was arranged in secret; the United States was not informed in advance. The two leaders met at Pyongyang Airport and rode into town in an open car on a road flanked by cheering onlookers. The meetings were cordial, and the parties agreed to a five-point plan on eventual reunification with an emphasis on economic development. The following month, the new president of Russia, Vladimir Putin, visited North Korea. Later, he met with President Clinton at a G-8 meeting and discussed Kim Jong-il's offer to negotiate on North Korea's missile program, which he had mentioned during Putin's visit to Pyongyang. Earlier, Kim Jong-il had told President Kim of South Korea that in his view the only way for North Korea to survive was to improve relations with the United States. If the United States would only guarantee the survival of the regime and allow North Korea to be introduced to the international community, then, Kim Jong-il reportedly said, his government would abandon everything, "including nuclear weapons, missiles, and weapons of mass destruction, everything."[24]

In October 2000, Vice Marshal Jo Myong-Rok of the Korean People's Army, the number two official in North Korea, was seated next to President Clinton in the Oval Office in Washington, thereby responding to the invitation from the Perry delegation. Other high-ranking US officials were also present, including Secretary of State Madeleine Albright and National Security Advisor Sandy Berger. The vice marshal wore his dress uniform covered with medals, and the president cordially greeted him. Jo was holding a brown folder when Clinton asked if the marshal had a letter for him. He promptly stood and formally handed the letter to President Clinton. The president opened the folder and read the letter. He pronounced it to be a "good letter." In it, Kim Jong-il stated that he was prepared to stop the production, export, and use of long-range ballistic missiles. Then Jo unveiled a surprise. He invited President Clinton to Pyongyang to sign an agreement. He said that if President Clinton would come, "Kim Jong-il will guarantee that he will satisfy all of your security concerns," going on to say, "I really need to take back a positive answer." Clinton was noncommittal, but he generally spoke positively; he wanted the North Koreans to understand that they could work with him. The vice marshal visibly relaxed. It was clear that his real mission was to persuade the United States to take North Korea seriously. All in the room sensed the possibility of a deal that could lead all the way to normalizing relations. After the meeting, a joint US–North Korean communiqué was released, stating that neither government would have "hostile intent" against the other and that they were intent on building a "new relationship free from past enmity," based on the January draft. This document was of great importance to North Korea; they regarded it much the same way as the Chinese regarded the Shanghai Communiqué of 1978, as the cornerstone of a new relationship. Clinton put off a visit for the time being, but several weeks later he sent Secretary Albright with a small team to Pyongyang to convey his views and prepare for a possible visit by the president.[25]

Secretary Albright arrived in Pyongyang on October 23, 2000. She and her delegation were warmly received and held two days of talks with Kim Jong-il. She gave him a letter from Clinton urging a halt to all exports of ballistic missiles of all ranges and a termination of the development of long-range ballistic missiles (which could potentially threaten the United States with nuclear weapons). In return, the North Koreans said that they wanted a normalization of relations, no hostile intent (from the communiqué), and some benefit from normalizations. Kim Jong-il, who was the spokesman throughout on the North Korean side, said that North Korea could agree to an export ban and could join the international Missile Technology Control Regime, which governs the size and range of missiles sold for export. He said that missile sales to other countries helped to pay for the North Korean military, but a broad relaxation of future relations with the United States could possibly compensate. And because the United States would no longer be a threat, missiles would become insignificant.

Technical details of a missile agreement were left to a future meeting of technical experts, but the US participants leaving Pyongyang believed that a presidential visit could close a deal on missiles and take the two countries in the direction of ending fifty years of hostility. President Clinton was interested in going, but senior advisors thought there were too many details left unresolved. President Kim Dae-jung urged Clinton to go, and other US advisors were convinced a deal was within reach if he went. The State Department experts who had made the overtures in January believed that the missile deal was diverting attention from an even more important issue. Kim Jong-il was clearly signaling that he wanted agreement to a fundamental shift in relations: North Korea desired improved relations with the United States. Then came Election Day in the United States, November 7, 2000. On that day, a commentary in Pyongyang's official newspaper, *Rodong Sinmun*, asserted, "the improved relations between the two countries are in line with the desires and interests of the two peoples."[26]

The long stalemate after Election Day significantly affected the debate within the administration as to whether President Clinton should take the offer from North Korea, travel to Pyongyang, and hopefully sign an agreement with Kim Jong-il, ending the threat of North Korea's missile program and perhaps a broader agreement on US-DPRK relations as well. Many officials thought the president should accept the risk and go, as did some foreign leaders such as Kim Dae-jung.

Others thought there were too many unresolved issues. President Clinton wanted to go, but he had some hesitation and wanted to brief the new president before he went. But that was not possible until the new president was determined. (The close 2000 presidential election results necessitated a recount of votes in the state of Florida, which delayed George W. Bush's official victory by several weeks.) So, Clinton decided to send Secretary Albright's assistant, Wendy Sherman, with a delegation and Clinton's arrival date in her pocket once the verification issues for the proposed missile agreement were resolved. The events that followed made a possible Clinton visit less likely. Vice President Gore conceded the election after a ruling by the US Supreme Court and President-Elect Bush selected General Colin Powell to be secretary of state. Not long after, President Clinton mentioned a possible trip to North Korea, but Bush was lukewarm to the idea, and in the end there was no trip.

As the Bush administration took office, North Korea tried to signal that it looked forward to dialogue with the new president. On February 8, 2001, at the Atlantic Council in Washington, DC, the North Korean UN representative said, "We hope that the Bush Administration maintains the U.S. engagement policy towards North Korea."[27] At the time, the North Korean government remained reassured by the existence of the communiqué signed just a few months before by President Clinton and Vice Marshall Jo pledging "no hostile intent" between the two countries.

But the incoming staff for the National Security Council made no secret of their distrust of North Korea in general and of Kim Jong-il in particular. They wanted to terminate the Agreed Framework as soon as possible. Secretary Powell, however, while thinking a trip to North Korea by President Clinton would have been a mistake, nonetheless wanted to continue the engagement policy.

Early in his tenure, President Bush began making calls to foreign leaders. In early February 2001, he called President Kim Dae-jung of South Korea. The call did not go well. Kim used the opportunity to stress the importance of his Sunshine Policy. Bush did not relate at all to Kim's positive approach to North Korea. Late that night, Condoleezza Rice, Bush's national security advisor, called one of the North Korean experts at the State Department and asked him to prepare a memorandum on President Kim Dae-jung for President Bush detailing his background and explaining his motivation for what he said on the call.[28] President Kim was concerned about a possible change in Washington's engagement policy that could create serious difficulties for his Sunshine Policy. Against the advice of US experts in and out of government, Kim sought an early meeting with President Bush. With all that he had been through in his life, Kim was convinced that he could persuade Bush.

The meeting was set for March 7, and in preparation, the South Korean foreign minister met with Secretary Powell in Washington. Powell reassured him that the United States intended to stay with the Agreed Framework and support President Kim's Sunshine Policy. On the day of his arrival in Washington, Rice gave an interview to the *New York Times* as an unnamed senior government official in which she stated that North Korea and Kim Jong-il were "a problem," while Powell met with reporters and indicated that the Bush administration planned to pick up with North Korea where the Clinton administration left off.

The next morning, Powell hosted a breakfast with President Kim at Blair House. The meeting was highly positive; President Kim and Secretary Powell seemed comfortable with one another. Kim tried out on Powell the remarks he planned to use with President Bush, and those American officials attending thought them excellent. But the situation was to change quickly. Just before leaving Blair House for the White House, Powell received a call from Rice demanding that he immediately set things straight with the press—for, in response to Powell's remarks, the *Washington Post* was running a front-page story about the administration's plans to resume missile talks with North Korea. Thus Powell had to leave the Bush-Kim meeting and inform a group of reporters waiting outside that the administration would not be resuming negotiations anytime soon. At the meeting itself, after Kim delivered the remarks he previewed at Blair House, Bush responded by challenging Kim and his ideas and made it clear that he would not continue the Clinton policies toward North Korea and would not resume the missile talks in the foreseeable future. His position was basically that his administration detested Kim Jong-il and did not agree with Kim's Sunshine Policy.[29] At their joint press conference afterward, Bush, calling him "this man" (instead of referring to him as President Kim), indicated that the two had discussed the issue of North Korea and had disagreed. Kim said the same thing in more diplomatic language. All in all, it was a catastrophe.

This treatment deeply offended President Kim, who was upset about it for years. And it had two results: North Korea realized that agreement with the United States was now impossible and vigorously resumed their pursuit of nuclear weapons, which likely included opening the uranium route to the bomb with the equipment that A. Q. Khan had transferred to them some years before and which had been up to this time largely confined to storage. Relations between the United States and South Korea were seriously damaged, the South Korean public being particularly incensed by the public trashing of their president, a seventy-five-year-old grand figure of their political system and the winner of the Nobel Peace Prize the previous year. Among the reasons that some Bush administration officials, the so-called neoconservatives, held the views about North Korea that they did was that the North Korean case at the time represented one of the best justifications for ballistic missile defense, which—along with the invasion of Iraq—was one of the two top priorities of the new administration.[30] In June 2001, after completing a North Korean policy review, President Bush indicated that the United States would be prepared to resume negotiations with North Korea, but only if its leadership agreed to specific conditions: improved verification of the Agreed Framework, a ban on missile exports, controls on missile forces, and reductions in conventional military capability. Furthermore, Bush did not renew the "no hostile intent" communiqué. This could not appear to North Korea as anything but intensely hostile.

After the terrorist attacks of September 2001, North Korea tried hard to distinguish itself from international terrorists by joining United Nations conventions it had not joined before. Nevertheless, the negative pressure continued to mount. President Bush made major public denunciations of Kim Jong-il and North Korea. His State of the Union "Axis of Evil" speech vilified North Korea. Also, in December 2001, the Defense Department created a list of states against which the United States might one day be required to use nuclear weapons: Iran, Iraq, Libya, North Korea, and Syria. Lastly, early in 2002, following up on the State of the Union message, the White House announced—for the first time since it was signed in 1994 and admittedly on no new information—that North Korea was not in compliance with the Agreed Framework. This followed a certification of compliance issued by the Clinton administration in January 2001 (just a little over a year before) based on the same information.[31]

A few months later, after a visit by a senior South Korean official to North Korea, the DPRK indicated that it was willing to accept the Bush administration's call for negotiations. After another internal debate, the administration decided to send a delegation to North Korea headed by Assistant Secretary of State James Kelly to attempt comprehensive talks. Preparations for a resumption of negotiations came to a sudden stop, however: the Central Intelligence Agency informed the State Department and the White House that it suspected that North Korea was running a clandestine uranium enrichment program, which (to put it mildly) was highly contrary to at least the spirit and rationale of the Agreed Framework. The agreed July meeting date was postponed, and by the end of the summer, the CIA clarified its analysis, concluding that this program, when it had begun in the late 1990s, was a small research program and that it continued as such until 2002, when it became a much more serious program. North Korea was now conducting procurement of equipment for this program in other countries. The CIA briefed the National Security Council principals, and it was decided that the United States could no longer do business as usual with North Korea. The Kelly trip was revived, but with a new mission. There would be no negotiations. Kelly's mission was simple; he was to go to Pyongyang and accuse the North Koreans of conducting a secret uranium enrichment program. A date in early October was agreed upon with North Korea. On the way to Pyongyang, Kelly's statement was changed to also accuse the North Koreans of violating the Agreed Framework. The North Koreans were expecting negotiations, but negotiations were not what the Americans were offering. Normally at these meetings the North Korean government would host a lavish dinner the first night and the visitor would reciprocate the second night. When it became clear that the United States would not reciprocate, the American delegation was housed at a second-rate downtown hotel rather than at the government guesthouse. The meeting began on a sour note only to become bitter.

At the first meeting the next afternoon with Kim Gye-gwan, one of several vice ministers and a frequent interlocutor with Americans, Kim invited Kelly to begin. It was meant to be a short discussion. Kim said that he wanted to learn about current US policy toward North Korea and to understand the true intentions of the United States with respect to dialogue with his country. Kelly decided to read his prepared script rather than engage in an introductory discussion. The basic message was that President Bush had planned to have serious discussions with North Korea about transforming the US–North Korea relationship, but now that the United States had irrefutable evidence that North Korea had embarked on a secret program to acquire nuclear weapons through uranium enrichment, dialogue was no longer possible. Kelly's brief also covered other subjects such as terrorism, missiles, and human rights. After this presentation, Kim asked for a break and left the room.[32]

Upon his return, Kim rejected the HEU program charge and then delivered standard points on the US–North Korea relationship. The government dinner that night passed uneventfully. The next morning began with a somewhat longer meeting with Kim. Kelly repeated essentially the same presentation as the previous afternoon. Kim responded that it was clear that the United States was embarked on a program of "strangulation" of North Korea and intended to change his country's system by force. Therefore only a hardline response would be appropriate.

Not long after this discussion, the US delegation met with First Vice Minister Kang Sok-ju. This was a pivotal meeting in the long and tortured history of US–North Korean discussions. Kang said that he had been thoroughly briefed and worked through the night to prepare an official response. He said that the United States had destroyed the Agreed Framework by designating North Korea as part of the Axis of Evil, establishing a preemptive nuclear strike policy, and singling out North Korea for nuclear attack. He noted that Article III of the Agreed Framework provided that the United States would not use or threaten to use nuclear weapons against North Korea, and that the new US policy was in direct violation of this provision. North Korea had no choice but to modernize its armed forces. As for US claims that North Korea had a uranium enrichment program for the construction of nuclear weapons, North Korea was now convinced that it needed to prepare even more advanced weapons and to put itself on an equal footing with the United States before it could discuss denuclearization. It perhaps is noteworthy that this is consistent with the policy of Kim Jong-il's son and successor as currently pursued in 2017.

Kang said, "We are part of the Axis of Evil and you are gentlemen. This is our relationship. We cannot discuss matters like gentlemen. If we disarm ourselves because of U.S. pressure, then we will become like Yugoslavia or Afghanistan's Taliban to be beaten to death." At the end of the discussion, Kang insisted that North Korea had to counter the United States' "physical declaration of war" and that, in addition to enriched uranium; there were many other things ready to be produced.[33]

All eight members of the US delegation took Kang's remarks as an admission to having an HEU program. North Korea officially and consistently denied this afterwards. But there was the agreement with A. Q. Khan in 1993, the surge in international purchases of dual-use equipment after early 2002, and the unveiling of a uranium enrichment plant in 2009; these are facts, not interpretation. The issue is not whether North Korea had an enrichment program, but rather when did it become a serious program and how far has it gone.

After the delegation returned, the United States arranged to have the heavy fuel oil shipments suspended, which pursuant to the Agreed Framework were designed to offset North Korea's loss of energy output resulting from the shutdown of the Yongbyon reactor. This termination was announced as justified because North Korea was building nuclear weapons. The response by the DPRK was not long in coming. In December, the DPRK expelled the IAEA monitors at Yongbyon and removed the monitoring devices. On January 10, 2003, North Korea announced that the ninety-day withdrawal notice period—which had begun ten years earlier—had now been completed and that the DPRK was no longer a party to the NPT. The Yongbyon reactor was restarted, and reprocessing campaigns were pursued in 2003 and 2005, resulting in enough plutonium acquired for up to twelve nuclear weapons. In 1994, the Clinton administration had been prepared to go to war to prevent the reprocessing of the fuel rods that North Korea had pulled from the Yongbyon reactor. In 2003 and thereafter, the political environment was changed. Guided partly by its own rhetoric that the administration "does not negotiate with evil but rather destroys it," the Bush administration stood idly by, hoping for regime change and pursuing missile defense. Meanwhile, North Korea became, in effect, a potential nuclear weapon state.

In 2004, the five regional states and the United States began the Six-Party Talks, which lasted to the end of the Bush administration in December 2008, and had the objective of ending the nuclear weapon program in North Korea. Little was accomplished over the years, although there were some brief positive moments. In September 2005, with the United States downplaying the HEU issue, North Korea in principle agreed to end their program, but a long period of stalemate followed. In April 2005, President Bush in a press conference had again attacked Kim Jong-il personally, saying, "Kim Jong-il is a dangerous person. He's a man who starves his people. He's got huge concentration camps and there is concern about his ability to deliver a nuclear weapon." He spoke too soon. On October 9, 2006, the North Koreans carried out their first nuclear weapon test. Although a failure, as a planned 4-kiloton test came in at less than a kiloton, this test nonetheless signaled a new, more threatening era in which one of the world's most dangerous and unstable states was evolving into a power capable of delivering nuclear weapons by ballistic missile against all of its regional neighbors and later beyond.

A short time afterward, under pressure from China and with some skillful diplomacy by the US negotiator, Ambassador Chris Hill, North Korea signed an agreement to close the Yongbyon reactor and begin terminating its nuclear program (of course, the HEU program may have been marching along). The reactor was shut down in July 2007 in the presence of IAEA inspectors. At the time, Secretary of State Rice had sufficient clout with President Bush to keep the focus on negotiations and resist continued White House pressure for regime change.

In 2007, North Korea agreed to make a complete declaration of its nuclear program by the end of the year; it missed the deadline but delivered the declaration in June 2008. There was considerable information on the Yongbyon reactor program but nothing on the HEU program or the building of the reactor—more or less a carbon copy of the Yongbyon plutonium production reactor—in Syria by North Korea that was destroyed by Israeli warplanes in 2007, years before the declaration. As had been agreed, President Bush gave the forty-five-day notice to remove North Korea from the State Department's list of state sponsors of terrorism. But the United States was now insisting on a verification agreement for the declaration, and when at the end of the forty-five days North Korea had not agreed to this, Bush took no action on the State Department list. In September, the United States indicated it would not take North Korea off the State Department list without a verification agreement permitting full access to "any site, facility, or location," along with the right to acquire and keep samples. David Albright, the US nuclear expert, called this demand a "verification wish list" comparable to what Iraq had agreed to "only after it was bombed." North Korea offered a counterproposal but objected to two key provisions: visits to undeclared facilities and acquisition of samples.[34]

For its part, North Korea began plans to restart the Yongbyon reactor in view of the impasse. In October, after North Korea banned inspectors from Yongbyon and with the presidential election pending, the United States suddenly announced that a verification agreement had been reached—although the text of this agreement was never produced—and on October 11 removed North Korea from the State Department list. North Korea then readmitted the IAEA inspectors, and the disarmament process seemed to be resuming. North Korea continued to refuse allowing inspectors to remove samples from the Yongbyon nuclear complex, officially stating that it had never agreed to sampling. In December, the DPRK refused to agree to a written verification plan, thereby ending the nuclear disarmament process on the Korean Peninsula for the Bush administration. This left a completely unconstrained situation for President Bush's successor.

In the spring of 2009, North Korea conducted what it described as the launch of a communications satellite. Experts concluded that this was in fact a test of the Taepodong-2 missile, which in theory was capable of reaching North America. North Korea had called it a satellite launch to get around UN sanctions.

Later in 2009, North Korea conducted a second nuclear weapon test, this one more successful, coming in at about 6 kilotons, and announced that it was now a nuclear weapon state. In November 2010, Stanford University professor and former director of Los Alamos National Laboratory Siegfried Hecker and two colleagues from Stanford who were visiting North Korea were unexpectedly given a tour of a secret enrichment facility with perhaps up to two thousand centrifuges. Hecker said he was "stunned" that North Korea had built such an advanced plant so quickly. US officials regarded this plant as "significantly more advanced" than what Iran possessed, and senior US and South Korean officials believed this plant could not have been built so quickly without a network of secret sites elsewhere.[35]

The evidence was clear. An active nuclear weapon program now existed in North Korea with both the plutonium and uranium routes open, with an active ballistic missile development program, with potential long-range capabilities. With negotiations nowhere in sight, the program continued unabated.

North Korea carried out its third nuclear weapon test on February 13, 2013, after having successfully tested its long-range rocket in December 2012. This nuclear weapon test for several reasons represented somewhat of a sea change for the DPRK. It indicated unequivocally that Pyongyang was on its way to acquiring the capability to deliver nuclear weapons at short and medium range and in due course over longer ranges to China, Russia, and the United States. There were calls in the international community for North Korea to return to the Six-Party Talks, by then over four years in abeyance. North Korea expressed no interest in doing so. The DPRK called the test device a miniaturized atomic bomb, and the yield was judged to be 6–10 kilotons. There was no question that this was a successful test.

A report in the *London Times* alleged that, according to Western intelligence services, Iran's leading nuclear scientist, Mohsen Fakhrizadeh-Mahabadi was believed to have traveled to North Korea to observe the DPRK's third nuclear test.[36] Fakhrizadeh-Mahabadi headed a project within Iran's nuclear program to develop a warhead small enough to fit onto one of the ballistic missiles developed by Iran from North Korean prototypes. The article cited Japanese government sources and defense officials in South Korea to the effect that the main purpose of the third test by the DPRK was to develop a missile-ready warhead.

Iran has refused to make the scientist available for interviews by the IAEA during its investigations of Iran's nuclear program. The article reports that his name appears in UN Security Council documents, which have identified him as a "person involved in nuclear or ballistic missile activities." He was apparently able to travel to Pyongyang, probably through China. UN Security Council resolution 1747 urges member states "to exercise vigilance and restraint" in allowing

Fakhrizadeh-Mahabadi entry or transit and requires member states to notify a UN sanctions committee if he is on its territory. In granting him transit, China made no such report.[37] The article cites Andrei Lankov, identified as an expert on North Korea at Kookmin University in Seoul, as saying "denuclearization is clearly a pipe dream. North Korea will stay nuclear as long as it is run by the Kim family."[38]

I encountered the ambassador from South Korea on the margins of a conference in Washington shortly after the *Times* article appeared and asked whether he believed this report to be true. The ambassador replied, "of course, Iran and North Korea have cooperated on missiles for a long time, why not on nuclear weapons?" James Acton, of the Carnegie Endowment for International Peace, said on February 14, 2013, that Seoul and Tokyo would press Washington to more vigorously push North Korea toward denuclearization. But such a move would be a mistake, according to Acton, because now this goal was not attainable, "at least not until the North Korean regime collapses, as it eventually must. . . . The North Korean regime appears to have concluded that nuclear weapons are simply too vital to its own security to trade them away."[39] Acton urged that Washington needed to put the emphasis on non-proliferation for now. He noted that the DPRK has a terrible record on non-proliferation: many ballistic missile sales, uranium to Pakistan, and the sale of a plutonium producing reactor to Syria, which the Israeli Air Force destroyed in 2007.[40]

Acton's analysis turned out to be right. On March 31, 2013, at a plenary meeting of the Central Committee presided over by President Kim Jong-un, a "new strategic line" was set that called for both a stronger economy and a more powerful nuclear arsenal. The committee declared that North Korea's "nuclear armed forces represent the nation's life, which can never be abandoned as long as the imperialists and nuclear threats exist on Earth."[41] Kim Jong-un also asserted, "Nuclear weapons guarantee peace, economic prosperity, and the people's happy life." He called for increasing the "pivotal role of nuclear weapons in war deterrent strategy and war waging strategy."[42]

A year before, on April 13, 2012, the DPRK's constitution had been revised to refer to North Korea as a "nuclear state."[43] In accordance with the priorities enunciated by Kim Jong-un at the Central Committee meeting, the North Korean munitions industry shifted its focus from conventional weapons to the development and production of nuclear weapons along with long-range delivery vehicles and cyber weapons. There was also an emphasis on miniaturization—small nuclear weapons—because smaller weapons are more broadly usable and more economical, according to the North Koreans.[44]

The following broad national nuclear weapon target list priorities can be discerned from official North Korean statements: (1) US military bases in South Korea, (2) US military bases in the Asia Pacific operational area, (3) US military bases on Guam, (4) US military bases in Hawaii, and (5) US military bases on the US mainland. If one takes this list of North Korean nuclear weapon target priorities at face value, it is clear that the DPRK is planning for nuclear war against the United States and that, despite the objective economic difficulties, the North Korean regime may be planning a much larger force than Western analysts assume in pursuit of a first-strike capability as part of a counterforce strategy.[45]

After careful study of all this information, one is confronted with the centrally important conclusion that, in all likelihood, North Korea will not be willing to relinquish its nuclear weapons even for a meaningful package of credible incentives. Kim Jong-un has publicly stated, "Our nuclear arsenal is not a bargaining chip and cannot be negotiated away, regardless of the price."[46]

Another perspective on this matter is presented by Victor Cha, former director for Asian affairs at the National Security Council and senior professor at Georgetown University. In his 2013 book *The Impossible State*, he contemplates the eventual end of the Kim dynasty in North Korea. He writes, "Despite what appears to be a stable power transition to a new generation of Kim-family rule, I still believe that a dead end awaits the regime. With no real reform apparent in North Korea, we see a leadership exercising a more rigid ideology, seeking greater control over both an increasingly independent minded society and disgruntled elements of the military. This is not sustainable." But Cha also predicts that a collapse of North Korea could precipitate a major crisis that would involve, among other things, an uncontrolled nuclear arsenal, for which possible crisis there has been virtually no preparation. Thus he concludes "President Obama may find his 'pivot' to Asia absorbed by a new crisis on the Korean peninsula."[47]

On January 6, 2016, North Korea announced that it had conducted its fourth nuclear weapon test, claiming it to be a hydrogen bomb test. If true, this could be a real game-changer, but the claim was viewed with considerable skepticism around the world owing to the small size of the test. The Comprehensive Nuclear-Test-Ban Treaty Organization measured the nuclear explosion as slightly less powerful than North Korea's 2013 nuclear weapon test, which had a yield of 6 to 10 kilotons. But as Daryl Kimball, executive director of the Arms Control Association, asserts, "With every successive underground nuclear test, North

Korea's nuclear scientists undoubtedly learn more about how to design smaller warheads that can be delivered by missiles. . . . Today, it likely has 10 to 16 nuclear weapons. By the end of this decade, it could have more than 50." Kimball argues that although there will be UN Security Council action this time, there must be tougher measures and unlike what has been the case in the past, there must be fully enforced sanctions.[48]

Many called for much stronger sanctions. The president of South Korea said that the United States and its allies were working on sanctions to inflict "bone numbing pain" on North Korea after its latest test.[49] Japan's ambassador to the United Nations told reporters, after a Security Council meeting that condemned the test, that he expected the council to adopt a robust resolution on North Korea. The response from the Security Council was mixed. The Russian ambassador said only that a "proportionate response" was necessary. Beijing, in an uncharacteristically strong statement said, "China strongly opposes this act." Nevertheless, the *New York Times* called this array of responses a "now-familiar set of rituals."[50]

On Saturday, February 7, 2016, North Korea conducted another test of its intercontinental ballistic missile, again referring to it as the launch of a communication satellite, again a designation intended to avoid UN sanctions. However, the following day in New York members of the Security Council accused North Korea of defying repeated warnings with an action that constitutes "a clear threat to international peace and security."[51] Further, US Intelligence Chief General James Clapper on Monday, February 9, told the Senate Arms Services Committee that Pyongyang was committed to developing a long-range, nuclear-armed missile "capable of posing a direct threat to the United States."[52] Then, on February 24, the United States and China in principle agreed to a UN resolution that apparently had wide support and would impose significant new sanctions on North Korea in response to its recent nuclear and missile tests. US Ambassador Samantha Power submitted a draft resolution the following day, on February 25. On March 3, 2016, the council unanimously adopted a broad and much tougher sanctions resolution on North Korea than those in the past. Shortly thereafter, North Korea fired six short-range missiles into the sea as a show of defiance, and on March 4, North Korean state media announced that Kim Jong-un had ordered his country to prepare to use its nuclear weapons and for the military to be in "pre-emptive attack" mode in the face of growing threats from its enemies.[53]

Any future hope for nuclear disarmament—for an NWFZ in northeast Asia—will require that the world community, particularly the United States, bring the DPRK back to the NPT. In addition, North Korea will ultimately need to agree to being a law-abiding and constructive member of the world community. This goal should be realized through diplomacy, but if that is not possible, then by force. A senior US expert on North Korea, Joel Wit, asked:

> What does all this mean for America's future policy toward North Korea? Immediate strong responses to provocations are fine. So are public statements of indignation, bigger and better sanctions, more pressure on the North's Chinese allies to support these measures, military steps to show the North Koreans and our allies that we are resolute. These are all warranted. But the North Koreans are in this for the long haul. They feel their country and its government's survival is at stake. Unless Americans take them seriously and formulate a long term strategy for stopping this threat, rather than adopting ad hoc tactical responses, when North Korea conducts its fifth test a few years from now, the United States will find itself, like Captain Renault in [the movie] *Casablanca* rounding up the usual suspects.[54]

Part of this strategy must be to ultimately dismantle what is known as North Korea, Inc., a shadowy group of special state-owned trading companies and middle men, operating mostly in China, that maintain a steady flow of cash and acquisitions for the nuclear weapon program. The new sanctions resolution mentions this problem but does little about it. As two researchers put it, "The key to stopping North Korea's weapons program is stopping the private Chinese firms that help import illicit goods."[55]

Two days prior to the publication of Wit's opinion piece, Victor Cha and Robert Gallucci, the US government negotiator for the Agreed Framework and former dean of the School of Foreign Service at Georgetown, published their views on North Korea. They noted that during the Six-Party Talks in 2005, a North Korean diplomat let it slip that "The reason [the United States] attacked Iraq is because they didn't have nukes. And look what happened to Libya. That is why we will never give up ours." The two authors commented that North Korean government leaders believe that nuclear weapons will prevent others from attacking them, but this belief is deeply misguided. North Korea is reducing its conventional forces to focus on nuclear weapons. This focus could lead to a rapid escalation to the nuclear level in time of crisis, which "could mean either pre-emptive action by the United States, or, if North Korea ever used nuclear weapons, a massive retaliation." The authors concluded, "North Korea thinks that nuclear weapons make it more secure. That's wrong. North Korea's only path away from isolation and insecurity will require negotiation on all issues, including security, human rights, and economics. In order to help it understand this, the United States must use the nuclear test Wednesday to force the North back to the table."[56]

After the end of the Cold War, presenting serious proposals for negotiating an NWFZ for northeast Asia became possible. The first such proposal was put forth by John Endicott, a senior professor at Georgia Tech University leading a research group in 1995. His group's concept was a circular zone with a 2,000-kilometer radius centered on Pyongyang in which the negotiated obligations would apply. This concept was limited to tactical nuclear weapons but with some obligations placed on nuclear weapon states with land areas in the zone along with the obligations on non-nuclear states. The Endicott group returned two years later with a modified proposal involving a league of non–nuclear weapon states in the region establishing a limited NWFZ. Endicott led a Track II diplomatic effort to advance these proposals. Dr. Hiromichi Umebayashi of Nagasaki University proposed a trilateral NWFZ treaty involving Japan, the ROK, and the DPRK with negative security assurances from China, Russia, and the United States, and in 2004 he publicly presented a model treaty based on this concept.

The most recent proposal was introduced in a 2011 article by Mort Halperin, senior advisor to the Open Society Institute. Subsequently, discussions of this concept were held in Washington, DC, in October 2012 and in Nagasaki in December. Halperin's proposal involved a comprehensive agreement on peace and security for northeast Asia covering all outstanding issues. It generally appears to be a revival of many of the issues resolved with North Korea and then subsequently abandoned by the George W. Bush administration.[57] None of these proposals got past the Track II discussion stage.

So, what can be done, and what are the prospects of expanding the NWFZ movement into northeast Asia? Of the states relevant to the area, China, Russia, and the United States are part of the P-5 group. Presumably, if an NWFZ could be achieved, these three states would adhere to treaty protocols placing their territories and bases within the treaty zone under the obligations of the treaty, as they did pursuant to other NWFZ treaties. Japan and South Korea are NPT non–nuclear weapon states in good standing, if uneasily so because of the behavior of the DPRK. These two states could quickly become nuclear weapon states given the advanced state of their nuclear capability.

It comes down to North Korea and the prospects of persuading this regime to return to the NPT, a prerequisite for making an NWFZ in northeast Asia possible. As recounted above, President Clinton had this issue virtually resolved. Kim Jong-il, the present ruler's father, was apparently persuaded that the way to security for his nation was through a good relationship with the United States. But the succeeding Bush administration rejected the emerging results of Clinton's diplomacy. That, plus the change of regime upon Kim Jong-il's death some years later, strongly suggests that this view of the road to security for the DPRK is not shared by the regime of his son, Kim Jong-un. During the first two Kim family regimes, negotiations with North Korea seemed possible from time to time; their objectives were largely limited to regime survival and money. This is not the case with the current regime, which seems intent on making itself a nuclear weapon state able to confront even the United States. But this is an illusion, a fantasy.

As Victor Cha and Robert Gallucci suggest in their column, if pressed too far such a policy could lead to nuclear preemption or nuclear retaliation by the United States, which would end seventy years of Kim family rule. Add to this what Victor Cha asserts in his book: that the North Korean people, highly literate and connected by cell phones, one day will end the Kim family dynasty in the DPRK. If or when the Kim regime ends—either through war or hopefully through the action of the North Korean people—an NWFZ agreement for northeast Asia may become possible, but an end to the Kim regime is also likely to lead to chaos and a major international crisis. The world community should prepare itself to manage such a situation should it occur.

In the meantime, perhaps the best approach for the immediate future is to keep heavy pressure on North Korea, preferably through the UN Security Council to the extent that Russia and China will allow this to happen. And, at the same time, hope that Victor Cha is right about the North Korean people and that the demise of the Kim family regime will be sooner rather than later.

In early May 2016, however, the Workers' Party of Korea held the Seventh Party Congress, the first since 1980. At this congress, North Korea leader Kim Jong-un was further elevated. He said the following about nuclear weapons in a speech: "As a responsible nuclear weapons state, our republic will not use a nuclear weapon unless its sovereignty is encroached upon by any aggressive hostile forces with nukes, as it has already declared, and it will faithfully fulfill its obligations for non-proliferation and strive for the global denuclearization." In other words, he said that North Korea is a nuclear weapon state just like the United States and the other P-5 states.[58]

On Friday, September 9, 2016, North Korea conducted its fifth nuclear weapon test. Jeffrey Lewis, director of the East Asia Nonproliferation Program at the James Martin Center for Nonproliferation Studies in Monterey, California, estimates the size of the test at between 10 and 20 kilotons. If confirmed, this would make it the largest of North Korea's five tests. South Korea's president Park Geun-hye said, in part, "North Korea's provocations will do nothing but accelerate its self-destruction."[59] An article in the *New York Times* on Sunday, September 11, 2016, notes that "North Korea's provocations introduce tremendous danger, but stave off what Pyongyang sees as the even greater threats of invasion or collapse."[60] This is a danger that we must all live with.

On March 11, 2017, the *Washington Post* published an article about North Korea.[61] It was now being reported that the fifth nuclear weapon test by North Korea in September in fact came in at about 30 kilotons, more than twice the size of the weapon that devastated Hiroshima. And the country's nuclear weapon arsenal was judged to contain up to twenty weapons. It was asserted that North Korea was working on the development of a long-range ballistic missile that could deliver a nuclear weapon against the continental United States. The *Post* article was titled "Anxiety Grows over North Korea's Arsenal," and so it was.[62]

Chapter 11
South Asia

Of the three areas where advancement of the nuclear weapon–free zone process—or its equivalent—is essential to achieving a nuclear weapon–free world,
South Asia is the most complicated and most difficult. In the Middle East, the
outlines of a peace agreement for Palestine have been well understood for nearly
two decades. And it is further understood that continuing with the status quo
or opting for the one-state solution will only lead to recurring violence. It would
take just two political leaders in place at the same time who are strong enough
and wise enough to make a peace agreement happen: a new Mandela and a new
de Klerk for the Middle East.

In the Middle East, as far as the prospects for a Palestine peace settlement are
concerned, the principal antagonists are Israel and Iran, both possessing highly
literate populations and both heirs to a great culture. This is not true with respect
to the lone problem state in Northeast Asia, North Korea. North Korea has a
highly literate population, but it is not heir to a great culture deriving from the
DPRK and its national ethos. Its government behaves more like a Mafia organization than a modern government. It currently seems set on a course that—if
diligently pursued—can only lead to catastrophe for North Korea. But a solution
can be imagined. As Victor Cha says in his book, the current regime is simply
not sustainable, and one day the North Korean people will put an end to it, or
the reckless policies of the DPRK government itself will bring down the regime.

South Asia is another matter. Any solution is difficult to imagine. If Pakistan
were to give in and concede that the Muslim population of Indian Kashmir will
remain forever part of Hindu India—despite having voted to join Pakistan in
1947—Pakistan will be giving up something fundamental to their raison d'être as
a state. Likewise, should India concede that Indian Kashmir will become part of
Pakistan, why shouldn't other Indian states with large Muslim populations consider a separate arrangement with Pakistan? For that matter, perhaps the Tamil

states in the south would want independence from Hindu India. The integrity of the India Union could be called into question.

Add to this the fact that both India and Pakistan have substantial arsenals of nuclear weapons, with ballistic missiles to deliver them. The near probability of nuclear war between these two principal states of South Asia, if it ever were to happen, would be the greatest human calamity of all time. Dangerous as it is, the situation is worsened with the significant presence of violent nonstate actors in Pakistan, such as the Taliban, thereby including the risk of nuclear terrorism should one of these groups achieve access to the Pakistani arsenal. It will take great feats of statesmanship to sort all this and a long period of time to create conditions that would permit consideration of an NWFZ in South Asia. But such a zone would be immensely in the interest of both India and Pakistan. The two countries are far less secure than before they acquired nuclear weapons; they have created a situation where every border clash over Kashmir carries with it possible escalation to nuclear war and the death of millions.

If there were a bright side to this story, it would be that India and Pakistan are the only countries in the region that possess nuclear weapons. Bangladesh, Nepal, and Bhutan are all too poor or too small to contemplate this possibility. Therefore tackling the core issues of the India-Pakistan conflict could present opportunities for the establishment of an NWFZ in the area. Admittedly, however, this is an uphill battle. There has been great antipathy between India and Pakistan ever since independence and partition in 1947, when in the range of a million people were killed and many millions more were made refugees. Nearly seventy years later, we face a situation where there have been four wars, many cross-border terrorist attacks, innumerable bloody ethnic clashes, and a confrontation that holds millions of people hostage to two rival nuclear arsenals that are far from stable. Truly a witch's brew. What one can say with confidence is that the 1947 partition decision upon the gaining of independence by British India was one of the most unwise political acts of the twentieth century.

INDIA

Many experts believe that India acquired nuclear weapons to offset China. China tested its first nuclear device in 1964, and India's first nuclear explosion was in 1974. Yet, while China promptly built an arsenal of some several hundred weapons, India did not do the same until nearly twenty-five years after the first explosion in 1974—in the wake of the 1998 tests.

India's path to an eventual nuclear weapon began decades ago and proceeded in fits and starts. Dr. Homi Bhabha, generally regarded as the father of the Indian nuclear program, left India to study at Cambridge, beginning with engineering but instead achieving a doctorate in physics in 1935. He did important work in the area of cosmic rays and later significantly contributed to the study of a particle called the meson, which he first discovered during his work on cosmic rays. The outbreak of World War II in 1939 found him trapped in his home country, thereby preventing the continuation of his principal work in European laboratories. Prior to his return to India, Bhabha had visited the institutes and laboratories of some of Europe's greatest physicists. Some of these men—Niels Bohr, Enrico Fermi, and James Franck—later played important roles in the US Manhattan Project. From afar, Bhabha could deduce this a few years later. They represented an elite community of world-class scientists to which Bhabha was drawn because of his talent and education, but to which he could not belong because of his country of birth. If Indian scientists could not be part of this elite group, they could assemble in India and establish their own.[1]

With WWII already raging and Bhabha in India with nowhere else to go, he accepted the position of "reader" in theoretical physics at the Indian Institute of Science in Bangalore. Two years later, in 1941, at the age of thirty-one, he was appointed professor of cosmic ray research and also elected as a fellow of the Royal Society. In 1944, he wrote to the Sir Dorabji Tata Trust urging a philan-thropic grant to establish a nuclear research institute to develop Indian expertise. When nuclear power production became feasible in "a couple of decades," this institute would allow India to develop a national program without relying on foreign assistance. Though his initial interest was nuclear power, he later came to believe that the nuclear weapon option would be good for India. So, when the government became interested in supporting nuclear power and, if necessary, nuclear weapons, a leader to undertake such efforts was already in place.[2]

Bhabha's letter to the Tata Trust was carefully written. He said that he had been motivated to take a position at a "good university in Europe or America" but instead decided to stay in India, "provided proper appreciation and financial support are forthcoming." The Tata Trust responded positively, and in 1945 the Tata Institute of Fundamental Research opened with Bhabha as director. Later, Bhabha frequently referred to the institute as "the cradle of the Indian atomic energy programme."[3]

The following year, Bhabha assumed a second position, that of chairman of the newly formed Atomic Energy Research Committee, which had been created to promote physics education in Indian colleges and universities. Then, in 1948, Prime Minister Jawaharlal Nehru, who had written, "The future belongs to those who produce atomic energy," submitted legislation to create India's Atomic Energy Commission (AEC). The Atomic Energy Act established the legal framework within which the commission would operate and thereby created a regime of secrecy far surpassing the restrictions in British and US legislation. The veil of secrecy was imposed not only over processes, technologies, and designs, but also over atomic energy research and development. This legislation established government ownership of uranium, thorium, and all other relevant raw materials. Nehru argued that this secrecy was necessary to protect the nation's raw materials for the development of nuclear energy from colonial exploitation as well as to persuade foreign nations, with whom India might cooperate in nuclear commerce, that their secrets would be safe in Indian hands.

The Atomic Energy Act established the basis for the extreme secrecy that would envelop the Indian program in the years ahead. Its consideration by the national legislature, the Lok Sabha, led to a bitter debate before it was finally adopted. As George Perkovich reports in his important book *India's Nuclear Bomb*, one of its most forceful critics, S. V. Krishnamurthy Rao, objected to the "extraordinary powers" that the government was seeking over nuclear research in India. He asked why India was planning to impose even greater secrecy than the United States and the United Kingdom, which were (unlike India) also building nuclear weapons. He noted that the oversight and balancing mechanisms even in the US Atomic Energy Act were not present. Rao asked, why is it that "secrecy is insisted upon even for research for peaceful purposes?" To which Nehru responded, "Not theoretical research. Secrecy comes in when you think in terms of the production or use of atomic energy. That is the central effort, to produce atomic energy." The exchange continued, with Rao arguing, "In the Bill passed in the United Kingdom, secrecy is restricted only for defense purposes." "I do not know how you are to distinguish between the two," Nehru rebutted.[4]

The debate stopped here, with Nehru acknowledging that there is a dual purpose to the development and application of nuclear technology. With this observation, Perkovich continues his account by reporting the bill's passage and an ensuing important exchange. Professor Shibban Lal Saksena asked for the floor and proceeded to criticize the naïveté of the debate:

Science is power, both for good and for evil. . . . If we have not got the knowledge and the ability to use this power, there is no virtue in our saying that we shall not use it for destructive purposes and that other people should not so use it. . . .We all know that atomic energy is today the most important scientific discovery. Unless we spend upon it lavishly and unless we use all our resources, both in men and materials, for its development, we shall not be making the best use of our talents and materials. . . . Until we have the capacity to use atomic energy for destructive warfare, it will have no meaning for us to say that we shall not use atomic energy for destructive purposes.

Nehru stepped forward for his reply. He did not insist on the peaceful nature of the Indian nuclear project. He acknowledged that the nuclear project in India, as in the United States and Great Britain, was a potential source of military as well as economic power:

> The point I would like the House to consider is this, that if we are to remain abreast in the world as a nation which keeps ahead of things, we must develop this atomic energy apart from war—indeed we must develop it for the purpose of using it for peaceful purposes. It is in that hope that we should develop this. Of course, if we are compelled as a nation to use it for other purposes, possibly no pious sentiments of any of us will stop the nation from using it that way.[5]

Perkovich rebuts the assertion that India built nuclear weapons to offset China's arsenal or to establish a hedge against a military threat from Pakistan. Here was Nehru in the 1948 debate over the Atomic Energy Act in the Lok Sabha, acknowledging the potential military use of nuclear power. He recognized that the reactors, facilities, and experts that make up nuclear establishments inherently have a dual purpose. It is not technically possible to argue that a nuclear program is inherently peaceful. Intentions are what determine usage. Some programs are far more advanced and sophisticated than others, but a high level of nuclear technical expertise is not required to construct a crude gun-type weapon such as the one used against Hiroshima. Of course the capability—developed over many years—of being able to deliver such weapons at long range by ballistic missiles, which are virtually impossible to defend against, greatly multiplies the threat of any such program. Military potential exists in any nuclear program, regardless of stage of development—something that Nehru recognized in 1948 and did not rule out. Therefore, contrary to most historical analysis and conventional wisdom, the founders of India's nuclear establishment acknowledged and welcomed a military dimension from the beginning, despite Nehru's genuine hope that India's program could retain a purely peaceful character. India's foundational debate over a nuclear program occurred in 1948, before the communist takeover in China, before any military threat from China or elsewhere was apparent.[6]

Debate over the Atomic Energy Act unraveled the essential duality toward the consideration of nuclear energy that has afflicted the Indian program ever since: India must have nuclear technology and be able to produce peaceful nuclear energy if it is to remain a first-class nation. The intention is that nuclear energy will always be used that way in India and eventually everywhere. It brings enormous benefits to humanity not realizable any other way. But it *is* dual purpose, and someday another state could threaten India, necessitating its use for military purposes. Should that bleak day ever come, India will be glad to have it. But should India test an explosive device? And should it take more sophisticated technical steps and build a stockpile? Or should India agree not to use nuclear weapons first? To never test again? Different Indian administrations looked at these questions differently. Should the day ever come when an NWFZ could be considered for South Asia, the Indian viewpoint toward nuclear energy could pose problems.

Nuclear science and technology assumed a special place in the plans for the technological development and modernization of India. The need to vastly increase the amount of available electrical power was clear to both Nehru and Bhabha, who saw nuclear energy as the most effective means of achieving this goal. No field of science and technology appeared more promising and prestigious than nuclear energy. Bhabha, like Nehru, whom he first met in 1937, regarded mastery over the energy potential in the atomic nucleus as the apogee of science. In their view, the colonial British regime had purposely retarded Indian industrial development, but they envisioned science as the way to overcome this legacy and achieve for India the highest symbol of modernity.[7]

It was Bhabha who—brilliantly and with great energy—drove the Indian program. He developed plans in the early 1950s for acquiring plutonium before there was any commercial or economic justification for doing so. His analysis of how a nation could produce nuclear weapons despite international safeguards represented a deliberate strategy for developing India's nuclear weapon option. In the late 1950s, he was already stating privately his desire that India should build nuclear weapons. Many have argued that Nehru, as a world leader of singular moral stature and the heir to Mahatma Gandhi, was above developing nuclear weapons, yet in a 1946 speech in Bombay he declared:

> As long as the world is constituted as it is, every country will have to devise and use the latest scientific devices for its protection. I have no doubt India will develop her scientific researches and I hope Indian scientists will use the atomic force for constructive

purposes. But if India is threatened she will inevitably try to defend herself by all means at her disposal. I hope India in common with other countries will prevent the use of atomic bombs.[8]

And so the Indian program in the 1950s and 1960s proceeded with vigor, led by the redoubtable Homi Bhabha.

Nehru and Bhabha had a conversation in 1960 with a retired US general named Kenneth D. Nichols, who had overseen the design and construction of plants used in the Manhattan Project to enrich uranium and extract plutonium. In 1960, Nichols was chairman of Westinghouse International Atomic Power Company in Geneva, Switzerland. At Bhabha's request, Nichols was invited to India to discuss plans for building India's first nuclear power plant. While discussing the plant with Bhabha and a few of his associates, Nichols touted the advantages of American light-water reactor technology. After these discussions, Bhabha and Nichols met with Nehru.

According to Nichols, during the meeting, Nehru asked Bhabha, "Can you develop an atomic bomb?" Bhabha assured Nehru that he could and under further questioning said it would take about a year. Nehru then asked Nichols whether he agreed with Bhabha. Nichols replied affirmatively—that he knew of no reason why Bhabha could not do it. Nehru then said to Bhabha, "Well, don't do it until I tell you to."[9]

Construction of the first reactors began with duality of purpose at the core of the program. Nuclear power was considered central to the modern development of India. It also was seen as placing India in the first rank of national intellectual achievement. In Nehru and Bhabha's view, the program would bring great economic benefits to the country. It should remain a peaceful program, but if India were at any point threatened, it must have the ability to defend itself with, among other things, all the scientific expertise at its disposal. In international fora, India would always argue against nuclear weapons and in favor of their elimination while emphasizing the peaceful benefits of nuclear power. But again, as stated by Professor Saksena in the Lok Sabha after the debate over the Atomic Energy Act, "Until we have the capacity to use atomic energy for destructive warfare, it will have no meaning for us to say that we shall not use atomic energy for destructive purposes." To some in India, this is an important part of the rationale for the nuclear program. In other words, the economic well-being of India depends on its mastery of nuclear technology, which would place it in the first rank of modern states. But it is also having the nuclear option—not necessarily exercising it—that truly makes a first-class state. Thus the acquisition of nuclear energy and the nuclear option have been woven into India's culture and social consciousness in a unique way: as a reaction to colonialism and perceived racism. India cannot think well of itself unless it has these things. An argument for taking the nuclear option away from India under any circumstances would be difficult to win.

In 1958, Nehru's government adopted Bhabha's plan to employ nuclear energy to stimulate economic development. The first stage would be to acquire Canadian CANDU natural uranium-fueled reactors to produce power and plutonium. The second stage would involve a second set of reactors, fueled by recycled plutonium and thorium—of which there was much in India—to produce U-233 (a fissionable by-product of the uranium nuclear fuel cycle). The U-233 would be used in a third set of reactors with more thorium and produce more U-233 than was consumed by the fission process. An unlimited amount of U-233 would be created. This at least was Bhabha's vision.

Canada offered to build a 40-megawatt CANDU research reactor on India's peaceful uses assurance, but without significant restrictions on the plutonium produced by the reactor. The reactor was called CIRUS (Canadian-Indian-US). While CIRUS was under construction in 1958, Bhabha ordered the construction of a plutonium separation plant at Trombay. In June 1964, shortly after the death of Nehru and shortly before the first Chinese nuclear weapon test, the first spent fuel from CIRUS entered the Trombay plant for plutonium separation. In 1963, Canada reached an agreement to build a natural uranium-fueled CANDU power reactor in Rajasthan, and the United States agreed to build two light-water power reactors at Tarapur, north of Trombay.[10]

After the first Chinese nuclear weapon test on October 16, 1964, there were demands in the Lok Sabha for India to press ahead for a nuclear weapon. Bhabha asserted on All-India Radio, "atomic weapons give a state possessing them in adequate numbers a deterrent power against a much stronger state."[11] But Nehru's successor, Prime Minister Lal Bahadur Shastri, was opposed to India constructing nuclear weapons. A resolution was introduced in the Lok Sabha on November 27 by the opposition Hindu (Jana Sangh) party calling for atomic weapons, but it was defeated by a voice vote, which is what Shastri wanted. He believed India should press for nuclear disarmament rather than become part of an arms race. But he noted in parliament that, if India so chose, it could build a weapon in two to three years. Bhabha continued his efforts and India's peaceful program moved forward, but not for much longer. The next year, 1965, Bhabha was killed in a plane crash near Switzerland. Shastri had died from a heart attack two weeks earlier, and Indira Gandhi had become India's prime minister. She had to reconstitute the nuclear establishment after Bhabha's death and fill the many jobs he had held, a necessity that led to a significant slowdown of the program for a time.

In 1968, progress resumed. As Prime Minister Gandhi and the government were focused on the NPT, a small group of scientists at the newly named Bhabha Atomic Research Centre (BARC), in homage to their late leader, began a program of technical work as part of a concerted effort to bring India into the nuclear club. This meant developing the expertise to shape plutonium from Trombay into bomb cores, developing the chemical high-explosive device needed to implode the plutonium core, and developing the equations of state for plutonium, among other things.[12] Initially, the spent fuel came from CIRUS, poisoning Indo-Canadian relations for some thirty years. Though not all the scientists at the center participated in this work (some were opposed to building bombs), the technical work continued and intensified. Dr. Homi Sethna, who had recently succeeded to the position of AEC chairman after the death of Bhabha's successor, gave the green light to Dr. Raja Ramanna, the technical leader of the scientific team, to construct a nuclear device. In September 1972, Sethna invited the prime minister to Bombay for a tour and showed her a model of Smiling Buddha, India's first nuclear device. "Should we do it or not?" he asked Prime Minister Gandhi. "Get it ready. I will tell you whether to do it or not," she replied. Soon after, a search for a test site would begin.[13]

The decision to test a nuclear weapon was the prime minister's alone to make. In the early 1970s, the device was referred to as a PNE, or peaceful nuclear explosive, though, in fact, the difference between a nuclear device to be used for peaceful purposes (e.g., digging a canal) and a nuclear weapon, as was discussed earlier, is nil. A test site was chosen in 1973—located at Pokhran in Rajakstan— and its physical preparation began in September of that year. Few in the Indian government were part of or even knew about this process, and definitely not the military. The cabinet was neither consulted nor informed. The defense and foreign ministers learned of it only shortly before the test. The final decisions were made in early 1974 with few people participating: several close aides, Sethna, and Prime Minister Gandhi.

In the first of these final meetings, the possible international repercussions were considered. The United States and Canada had made it clear to India that a nuclear test would violate their understanding of the bilateral nuclear cooperation agreements and thus have potential consequences. Nonetheless, India was still surprised at the ensuing international reaction: the United States abrogated its treaty with India to supply fuel to the completed Tarapur reactors; Canada effectively cut off all further nuclear cooperation with India. It took the Canadians nearly thirty years to cool down. And there was strong worldwide condemnation, which in the end likely strengthened the NPT by bringing so much governmental attention to the treaty around the world.

The test was not Indira Gandhi's idea. It was pressed by the scientific community, and she did it for them. It was not done for security reasons concerning China or Pakistan or any other state. Nor was the Indian military involved. In an interview with the American writer Rodney Jones a few years later, Gandhi said, "The PNE was simply done when we were ready. We did it to show ourselves that we could do it. We couldn't be sure until we had tried it. We couldn't know how to use it for peaceful purposes until doing it. . . . We did it when the scientists were ready."[14] This corresponds with the recollection of Raja Ramana, who said in describing a final meeting during which opposition was expressed by two senior aides, "Fortunately for my team Mrs. Gandhi desired that the experiment should be carried out on schedule for the simple reason that India required such a demonstration."[15]

The Indian military at the time of the test declared that they had no plans for weapon application of the demonstrated nuclear explosive capability. Gandhi had been clear in her 1978 interview with Rodney Jones that military considerations had played no role in her decision: "No," she said, "we don't want nuclear weapons. They only bring danger where there was none before."[16]

Thus, in mid-May 1974, some two dozen Indian scientists and engineers, led by Dr. Rajagopala Chidambaram, were encamped near the Indian village of Pokhran. On May 13, the scientists began assembling the device and on May 15 lowered it into the shaft, where it would be detonated underground, and then sealed it with sand and concrete. For the next three nights, Chidambaram and his colleagues worried that these plans would be or had already been uncovered by an American satellite and would be obstructed by American pressure. But this was not the case. US intelligence agencies had monitored the Indian nuclear program for years but had accorded it a low priority, both technologically (how frequently satellites were focused on India) and analytically (how many studies were conducted). A 1972 interagency study said, "Our intelligence assessment is that, over the next several years, the chances are about even that India will detonate a nuclear device."[17] Yet when the test did take place, the United States was caught entirely by surprise.

At 8:05 a.m. on May 17, India carried out its first nuclear test, and at 9:00 a.m. All-India Radio reported that India had successfully conducted a peaceful nuclear explosion in western India. New Delhi claimed a yield of 10 to 15 kilotons, though further information obtained by the United States not long after indicated a yield of 10 kilotons. The Indian press was ecstatic, which was echoed in public opinion polls. The overall result was that the Indian nation—at least in urban centers—believed that its aspirations for global greatness had been achieved.[18] Meanwhile, the US intelligence community, resulting from the failure to detect the test in advance and warn senior US policy makers, elevated India and proliferation more generally on its list of priorities.

In 1981, Gandhi returned as prime minister with a continued interest in nuclear weapons after four years out of office. Gandhi's immediate predecessor, Morarji Desai, had supported improving the design of the nuclear explosive device, but promised the US ambassador when pressed that he would "never develop a bomb." Gandhi pressed ahead, however. Ramana proposed the testing of two devices representing streamlined versions of the 1974 device. Two new shafts at Pokhran were approved, and US satellites watched closely as they were dug. In May 1982, Gandhi approved the tests, only to call them off hours later. A few days earlier, India's foreign secretary, Maharaja Krishna Rasgotra, had been in the United States meeting with Undersecretary of State Lawrence Eagleburger. Eagleburger took out satellite pictures of Pokhran and noted the activity going on there. He asked whether India was going to test again and implied negative consequences for India if it did. Upon his return, Rasgotra briefed Gandhi on his conversation just after she had approved the planned tests. A few hours later, she canceled all of them.[19]

In 1982, US intelligence sources leaked reports that India had prepared a plan for an attack on Pakistan's uranium enrichment plant at Kahuta, a report that became the subject of a front-page story in the *Washington Post.* The Indian government publicly denounced the story as "absolutely rubbish." But Pakistani leaders remained concerned. In early 1983, Gandhi was again under pressure from the Indian scientific community to test a new, much lighter design for a nuclear weapon. She held a meeting with Ramana, now the head of the Bhabha Centre, and the chief of the Defense Research and Development Organization (DRDO) V. S. Arunachalam, who urged a test of the new design. The military was involved this time. Gandhi tentatively approved a new test, but for unclear reasons she changed her mind twenty-four hours later.[20]

Beginning in 1983, however, India began attempts to produce ballistic missiles. The military was involved in this effort. A series of missile projects were planned, including two particularly ambitious projects: the Prithvi tactical surface-to-surface missile and the longer-range Agni missile designed to carry nuclear weapons to the 1,500- to 2,500-kilometer range. The Prithvi was not originally conceived as a nuclear weapon carrier, and the Agni was a technology project. Later on, they both became nuclear weapon delivery vehicles. At the time, India's means of nuclear weapons delivery was limited to aircraft, for which there still was no demonstrated nuclear technology. In March 1983, Prime Minister Gandhi continued to insist publicly, in an interview with French journalists, that India would not build nuclear weapons.[21] But the next year, the Pakistan threat appeared to loom larger. A. Q. Khan gave an interview to an Urdu-language newspaper in Pakistan, *Nawa-e-Waqt*, in which he claimed Pakistan could build a nuclear weapon if it so chose, saying that, if necessary, Pakistan has "the capability of doing it."[22]

In 1984, a Sikh separatist movement in the state of Punjab was suppressed by the Indian Army with considerable loss of life and damage to the holiest Sikh shrine, the Golden Temple. Gandhi was assassinated four months later by her Sikh bodyguards. In October 1984, her son Rajiv Gandhi succeeded her. During the early stage of his tenure, Rajiv Gandhi was "totally against" nuclear weapons. Even if Pakistan built a bomb, Indian policy might not change. Rajiv preferred to advocate nuclear disarmament. Indian scientists, however, continued to develop India's capability. Meanwhile, under General Zia and A. Q. Khan, the Pakistani program continued. On a visit to the United States, Rajiv achieved agreement with President Reagan to purchase advanced computer capability, which could (among other things) be used in a nuclear weapon program. India's scientists were also investigating the possibility of boosted fission weapons. Despite his anti–nuclear weapon views, in 1985 Rajiv requested that a small task force be formed to assess the costs of a nuclear deterrent. In September, a secret committee began considering China's capability and the threat from Pakistan. In the end, even after the committee submitted a report on a possible deterrent force and what it would cost, the top leaders of the nuclear scientific community concluded that India had a known nuclear explosive capability and could readily assemble air-delivered weapons if the need arose. This was sufficient. It corresponded with Rajiv's calculations. In November 1985 on a visit to Japan, Rajiv noted, "We lived with Chinese weapons for long. But our relation with Pakistan is more turbulent. [Nevertheless] we would like not to develop a weapon and we are not developing a weapon." In December, Rajiv met with General Zia in New Delhi, and the two signed an agreement to improve relations, which significantly included a commitment not to attack each other's nuclear facilities.[23]

In 1986, the prime minister and General K. Sundarji, the military's most vocal advocate of nuclear weapons, put aside their disagreements over the program and agreed to conduct India's largest-ever conventional arms exercise to show off India's growing conventional capability. It was called Operation Brasstacks and was a massive demonstration involving two armored divisions, a mechanized division, and six infantry divisions in a large area in the Rajasthan Desert near the border of the Pakistani state of Sundh. India did not inform Pakistan of the huge scope of the exercise. Pakistan misinterpreted it and moved its two major army groups to the Indian border opposite the Indian exercise. India began to plan reinforcements. War seemed likely until both sides signaled they did not want war. At the end of January 1987, the two sides agreed on talks, and on February 4 they agreed on a sector-by-sector withdrawal of troops from the border.

Indian leaders discovered only after the crisis that A. Q. Khan had attempted to inject a nuclear weapon element into it. He had already increased the tension of the situation prior to the crisis. The September 1986 *Times of India* reported that, in an August 31 interview with a Pakistani Urdu-language newspaper, he had said that Pakistan "now is a nuclear power." On January 28, he had given an interview to an Indian journalist in which he said that Pakistan had enriched uranium to weapons grade and could do a laboratory test of an atomic bomb at any time and that "we shall use the bomb if our existence is threatened."[24] Fortunately, this interview was not published until March 1, when the crisis had already dissipated. In its aftermath, amid the tumult in the legislature, the prime minister made clear that he did not want India to give up the nuclear option, but he did not want to use it except as a last resort. Rajiv resisted moving toward nuclear weapons, as he had his own idea about how to deal with Pakistan. Pakistan might launch an attack and take some territory, but they couldn't keep it because of the conventional strength of the Indian army. Rajiv believed that India just needed to make sure that Pakistan understood, publicly and privately, that if Pakistan in some crisis ever turned to nuclear weapons, India would "blow your country off the map." That was all India needed.[25]

A 1986 article by US researcher Gary Milhollin alleged in detail that India had clandestinely purchased large amounts of heavy water to use as a moderator in various reactors. The initial rebuttal by K. Subrahmanyam essentially said, "What if we did?" because India is not a signatory to the NPT. This touched off a larger debate about the NPT. Raja Ramana raised the vital issues of race and colonialism: "We are all used to white people having a low opinion of us and I can see how jealous some of them become when we achieve total independence in our nuclear requirements." Because India violated no legal commitments in importing heavy water, Milhollin's allegations seemed like missionary non-proliferation bigotry. Many Indians believed that the NPT was predicated on the assumption that dark-skinned people are somehow less capable of managing nuclear technology than Americans, Britons, the French, Israelis, and Russians. The absence of any significant non-proliferation pressure on Israel as opposed to India and Pakistan was proof of the racial bias in US policy.[26]

Moving to the end of the decade, Perkovich makes clear that neither India nor Pakistan changed its declared nuclear policies or the associated rhetoric. India began flight-testing the Prithvi and Agni missiles, which were both now being developed with a nuclear weapon delivery capability in mind. And the scientific community continued to enhance its nuclear weapon capabilities in laboratories and on test ranges. Between 1988 and 1990, India apparently readied some two dozen nuclear weapons for quick assembly and potential dispersal to air bases for delivery by aircraft against Pakistan. American intelligence noted that Indian strike aircraft had practiced the "flip toss" or "bomb toss" maneuvers, which would be required to deliver nuclear weapons. This appalled some high-ranking US Air Force officers, one of them saying, "we had a lot of worries whether they could bolt it on right. It scared the bejesus out of me that they would have it fall on their own soil. Believe me, it's easier to have that happen than you think. We've done it, I know." It has been reported that between 1950 and 1968, eleven nuclear weapons fell out of or crashed with US aircraft and were never recovered."[27] Pakistan, in its turn, proceeded with its nuclear-capable tactical ballistic missile called HAFT. HAFT-1 and HAFT-2 had ranges of 80 and 300 kilometers, respectively. Pakistan was also developing its nuclear weapons, if somewhat more slowly than A. Q. Khan had been saying in public.

In November 1989, the struggle revolved around an inconclusive election, but also one that saw a dramatic increase in the strength of the Hindu nationalist or BJP Party, which was the only party that advocated the building of an Indian nuclear weapon arsenal. With no party close to a majority, V. P. Singh and the National Front formed the government. The next year, conflict flared in Kashmir. India deployed 200,000 troops, which faced the primary armored tank units of Pakistan on the other side of the line. The Pakistani nuclear weapons arsenal was apparently placed on alert; the United States intercepted a message to the Pakistan Atomic Energy Commission (PAEC) to assemble at least one bomb. It is difficult to know how close the two sides were to nuclear war, but President George H. W. Bush was sufficiently concerned to send Deputy National Security

Advisor Robert Gates to the subcontinent to help the two sides back away from the crisis and adopt confidence-building measures.[28]

In 1991, there was a new election in India. The campaign began in January and ended in mid-June. But on May 21, a Tamil activist assassinated Rajiv Gandhi, and the resultant sympathy gave a victory to the Congress Party. This was despite a further rise for the BJP to 119 seats in the Lok Sabha versus roughly twice that many for the Congress Party. The successor to Rajiv Gandhi was Narasimha Rao.

During Rao's tenure, the two sides frequently exchanged fire between troops deployed on the Siachen Glacier, perhaps the highest-altitude serious battlefront in world history. The two countries continued their work on nuclear weapons and nuclear weapon delivery vehicles. Pakistan acquired the M-11 ballistic missile from China with a range of 300 kilometers, while India successfully tested the Agni in 1994 with an expected range of 2,000 kilometers. By the end of 1991, India's inventory of weapons-grade plutonium was 700 kilograms, enough for many weapons. In April 1995, Rao approved the development of the Agni II and instructed the army to prepare shafts at Pokhran to conduct two nuclear tests. As the shafts were being prepared, US KH-11 satellites were watching overhead. It was not completely clear to the satellite interpreters in the first months what the purpose of this activity was. By November, however, there was increased technical activity, and while US Ambassador to India Frank Wisner was in Washington paying a courtesy call on Secretary of State Warren Christopher, truly suspicious information appeared, consisting of cables running through tunnels, which suggested an underground test was being planned.

Politics could have been a motivator; Rao's party was facing a serious challenge from the BJP in the upcoming election. A secret cable from the State Department intelligence and research bureau observed, "Rao's effort to recover his political reputation and to refute BJP charges that he had compromised the defense of India could soon result in the testing of a nuclear device in the Rajasthan desert." Upon his return to India, Wisner met with Rao's private secretary on December 15 and told him that a test would backfire and bring sanctions. This was followed by a telephone call from President Clinton, and Rao backed off the tests.[29]

In the elections of mid-May 1996, however, the BJP finished with a plurality of seats and had their first opportunity to form a government. This outcome made the no-test assurances by the Rao government a dead letter. During the campaign, the BJP had promised to reevaluate India's nuclear policy. Atal Behari Vajpayee was sworn in and given fifteen days to achieve a confidence vote to establish his government. Much earlier, in 1964, when asked about the answer to China's first test, Vajpayee had said, "the answer to an atom bomb is another atom bomb, nothing else."[30] Almost immediately, Vajpayee told the scientists to proceed with the tests. But Vajpayee delayed the go-ahead until after the confidence vote. The BJP lost the vote, and a United Front government promptly replaced the BJP led government. But in March 1998, the BJP returned, winning 250 seats—just short of a majority but enough to win the ensuing confidence vote.

On March 20, 1998, Vajpayee and the BJP again assumed the control of the government. That same day, Rajagopala Chidambaram, chairman of the AEC, visited Vajpayee and made the case to conduct nuclear tests. On April 6, Pakistan tested its Ghauri missile, which was the No-Dong missile received from North Korea by A. Q. Khan in exchange for uranium enrichment technology. It was nuclear capable and could strike targets 1,500 kilometers away with a significant payload. Two days later, Chidambaram and the head of the DRDO, A. P. J. Kalam, were summoned to the prime minister's office and told to proceed with the tests. A contingent of one hundred scientists and engineers promptly headed to the site.

On May 1, an Indian Air Force plane carried the plutonium cores, produced by BARC and stored in underground faults in Mumbai, to the Jodhpur Airport. From there, trucks took them to the site where they were mated with all the necessary equipment. They were lowered into their shafts on May 10, the process being completed by 7:30 a.m. Everything was done under cover of darkness to minimize the risk of detection by US satellites. Back in New Delhi, senior officials were just learning about the tests: the defense minister was told on May 9 and the service chiefs and the foreign minister on the following day. The tests were scheduled for 9:00 a.m. on May 11. Because of a strong west wind, the tests were delayed until 3:45 p.m. At 5:00 p.m., Vajpayee announced that his government had just carried out three nuclear weapon tests. Later in an official statement by the government there were more specifics: the weapons included a fission device, a low-yield device, and a thermonuclear device with yields "in line with expected values."[31] On May 13, the government announced that two additional subkiloton tests had been carried out at Pokhran earlier that day. On May 17 at a press briefing, Chidambaram and other scientists claimed that the hydrogen bomb had a yield of 43 kilotons, that the fission device—significantly lighter and more compact—had a yield of 12 kilotons, and that the yield of the subkiloton device was 0.02 kilotons. A later BARC newsletter stated that the hydrogen bomb yield was 45 kilotons, the fission device 15 kilotons, and the three subkiloton devices, described as "experimental," were 0.02, 0.05, and 0.03 kilotons.

The Indian tests were a surprise once again. The CIA and other intelligence agencies had provided the policy community with no warning of the second round of tests. With these developments, a future Pakistani test was almost certain, and Pakistan would ultimately surpass India's number of tests. Despite heavy American pressure not to do so, on May 28 the Pakistanis carried out what were claimed to be tests of five devices simultaneously, just as India had done. Two days later, they conducted one more for a total of six, one more than the alleged number tested by India. The arms race between the two, if it perhaps had started before, had become institutionalized by now.

There was substantial skepticism in the US intelligence community that the Indian tests were what officials had claimed and whether the yields claimed had actually been achieved. Many experts believed that the alleged hydrogen bomb yield was closer to 30 kilotons than to 43, and some months later it was reported that experts had concluded that the hydrogen bomb test was a failure, that only the primary had detonated and not the full device, thus producing a low yield. The two alleged subkiloton tests on May 13 also came into question, as they were never detected at all. By then, analysts had believed for some time that the 1974 test had similarly been hyped with a measured yield of 6 to 8 kilotons, rather than the claimed 15 kilotons. Nevertheless, the US intelligence community began its crackdown to prevent future surprises. The CIA director, George Tenet, appointed a panel headed by Admiral David Jeremiah to analyze CIA's failure to provide advanced warning of the Indian tests and make recommendations for operational changes that would reduce the likelihood of this happening again. The report was completed in early June 1998, and Director Tenet accepted all the recommendations.[32] At the press conference announcing the completion of the report, the admiral was asked to what extent had this been an intelligence failure and to what degree it was attributed to India's success at keeping its plans secret. The admiral replied he would give each equal weight, and when asked whether advance warning could have been used to avert the tests, he said, "No, I don't think that you were going to turn them around."[33]

The initial public reaction in India to the tests was highly positive; a quick public opinion poll in six major cities registered 91 percent support. Vajpayee asserted that the threat from China motivated the tests, but anticolonial justifications immediately appeared. It was clear that the scientists and the nationalistic BJP government intended the tests to demonstrate to Washington and to the Indian people that India could not be pushed around. The exercise of the nuclear option, as Prime Minister Vajpayee proudly proclaimed on Independence Day 2000, "meant that 'the very countries that imposed sanctions against us . . . [now] view India with greater respect than in the past.'"[34] Thus the nuclear decision served several domestic objectives, including appearing strong and tough toward India's Muslim neighbors and unyielding toward Western powers that had pressed India for years to join the NPT. Though the tests had little to do with the threat from China or the danger posed by Pakistan, the 1998 explosions assuaged, at least according to India's leaders, India's enduring sense of inferiority and allowed it to gain a new sense of "respect."[35] In hindsight, this was no different from the way Britain and France had viewed the question forty years before; nuclear weapons confirmed their status as great powers and their right to be permanent members of the UN Security Council.

Not all observers within India were enthusiastic, however. Some saw it as a diversion of resources needed to supply health and education to India's masses of desperately poor citizens. Still others saw it as a moral retreat from the vision of the new India's founders and its commitment of many decades to nuclear disarmament and a peaceable world. Abroad there were many critics who were apprehensive about India's decision. One of those, President Bill Clinton, feared that with both India and Pakistan in possession of nuclear weapons, South Asia had become one of the most dangerous places in the world.[36] It was said that the decision to develop a nuclear weapons capacity was the most problematic of the BJP's accomplishment in the 1990s.

"Don't deploy nukes," said an editorial in the *Economic Times* before the tests on March 20, 1998. "The risk of accidental war will increase. . . . If India deploys weapons, so will Pakistan. And China will re-target many of its nuclear missiles at India. This cannot improve India's security." A *Business Standard* article in May said, "The BJP government has started India down a slippery slope. . . . India now comes under a darkening and lengthening nuclear shadow from both sides of its borders." And in response to the Pakistani tests, the *Economic Times* asserted, "Pakistan has just provided kilotons of evidence in support of this newspaper's position on the nuclear tests: It does not add to our country's security." The *Business Standard* further commented on May 29, "The balance of forces has been restored, so to speak, but at a higher level of terror. Indians and Pakistanis, who have lived under the shadow of conventional wars for the better part of their lives, will now have their respective nuclear umbrellas over their heads and the opponent's nuclear devices pointing at them." A senior columnist said, "India may have eighty bombs to Pakistan's eight, but in nuclear war, there are no winners."[37]

Arundhati Roy, the famous Indian writer, said in part:

It is such supreme folly to believe that nuclear weapons are deadly only if they're used. The fact that they exist at all, their very presence in our lives, will wreak more havoc than we can begin to fathom. Nuclear weapons pervade our thinking. Control our behavior. Administer our societies. Infuse our dreams. They bury themselves like meat hooks deep in the base of our brains. They are purveyors of madness. They are the ultimate colonizer. Whiter than any white man who ever lived. The very heart of whiteness. . . . India's nuclear bomb is the final act of betrayal by a ruling class that has failed its people. However many garlands we heap on our scientists, however many medals we pin to their chests, the truth is it's far easier to make a bomb than educate four hundred million people.[38]

Despite India's seeming international transgression in building nuclear weapons, India-US cooperation was not negatively affected. Washington in 2005 was looking for allies versus China. Also, there were substantial business interests that wanted access to the Indian markets, particularly those considered part of the military industrial complex: aerospace, weapon makers, and other Pentagon clients. India, on the other hand, had always been handicapped by the paucity of uranium reserves in the country, which limited significantly the speed of Indian nuclear weapon construction. The interests of the two governments came together in the US-India deal of 2005, which addressed objectives of both parties at the time. But the deal did nothing for the US nuclear industry as both sides claimed it would. In addition, it blasted a large hole in the NPT.

The framework for the US-India Civil Nuclear Agreement and the resultant 123 Agreement for nuclear cooperation was a July 18, 2005, joint statement signed by President George W. Bush and Indian Prime Minister Manmohan Singh, under which India agreed to separate its civil and military nuclear facilities and to place all its civil nuclear facilities under IAEA safeguards. In exchange, the United States agreed to work toward full civil nuclear cooperation with India. This took three years to accomplish. The outcome was that a state that possessed a substantial stockpile of nuclear weapons and had never joined the NPT could fully engage in nuclear commerce, including sensitive technology, while Iran, which was an NPT party and had no nuclear weapons, could not engage in such commerce at all.

The Henry Hyde Act and resulting agreement were truly contentious. First, the US Atomic Energy Act prohibits US nuclear commerce with states outside the NPT that have nuclear stockpiles and do not have full-scope IAEA safeguards on all of their activities. So, for India to be allowed to enter a partnership with the United States, this provision had to bypassed. The Henry Hyde Act took care of that by providing an exemption to this prohibition for India alone. Many members of the US Congress understood what this act would do to the health of the NPT regime, but the Indian and US business lobbies—hoping for substantial business deals in India—were strongly supportive and carried the process forward. The Hyde Act passed the House of Representatives on July 26, 2006, and the Senate approved it on November 16. President Bush signed the legislation on December 18. This legislation allowed for implementation of the civil nuclear cooperation agreement with India, signed by President Bush and Prime Minister Singh earlier in March of that year. The full text of the agreement was made public in August 2007. Nicholas Burns, the chief US negotiator, said that the United States has the right to terminate the agreement if India does another nuclear weapon test and that the United States in no way recognizes India as a nuclear weapon state. India rejected these comments, but Indian Foreign Minister Mukherjee did say that India would continue its moratorium on nuclear weapon tests.

The agreement was highly contentions within the Lok Sabha as well, perhaps even more so. India had been led to believe that it would be allowed, through trade with other countries, to maintain a strategic reserve of fuel. The United States was opposed to this because it could undermine future sanctions, and Congress was so informed. This resulted in a stipulation in the Hyde Act known as the "Barack Obama amendment" that the supply of fuel should be consistent with reasonable operating requirements. Thus the strategic reserve, important to India's civil nuclear program, was not in the deal. In the end, the agreement passed the Indian Parliament, but just barely: 275 to 256. And the Lok Sabha did not work out an acceptable nuclear liability regime until an agreement between President Obama and Prime Minister Modi in 2015.

The IAEA board of governors approved the Indian safeguards agreement on August 1, 2008. Next it was up to the forty-five-nation Nuclear Suppliers Group (NSG) to grant India a waiver from its full-scope safeguards requirement. There were initial objections from Austria, Iran, Ireland, Norway, Pakistan, and Switzerland, which presented clear problems because the NSG operates by consensus. A consensus was nonetheless achieved, though only after overcoming concerns expressed at the meeting by Austria, Ireland, and New Zealand, along with many others who had misgivings but remained silent. Granting a waiver to India for full-scope safeguards on all its nuclear facilities for both trigger list items (reactors, fuel, enrichment equipment, reprocessing equipment) as well as dual-use items (computers, etc.) was unprecedented for a country that had never signed the NPT. The United States seemed to be damaging the important non-proliferation rule it had initially championed: it took eighteen years before the US proposal to introduce the full-scope rule into the NSG was finally accepted, only to be waived now for India, based on the United States' own doing. In the end, despite all the effort invested in advancing this project, the US nuclear industry did not benefit at all until the nuclear liability issue was resolved in 2015. Likewise, the United States benefitted little from Indian strategic support vis-à-vis China.

India, on the other hand, has benefitted considerably. Starting with safeguards, New Delhi would only be required to place its fourteen civilian reactors under safeguards, keeping the remaining eight military-oriented reactors under no scrutiny. Although India has promised that all future civil reactors will be under safeguards, the Indian government alone determines which reactor is civil and which military.[39] Next, in terms of capacity and new capabilities, India possesses only 1 percent of the world's known uranium reserves, making it difficult for India to have both a nuclear weapons program and an aggressive nuclear power program. But if India can fuel its civil power program with imported uranium, it can use all its domestic stocks for its weapons program. This new capability was of great importance.

According to the calculations of one of the key advisors to the US negotiating team, Ashley Tillis,

> Operating India's eight unsafeguarded PHWRs [pressurized heavy-water reactors] in such a [conservative] regime would bequeath New Delhi with some 12,135-13,300 kilograms of weapons grade plutonium, which is sufficient to produce between 2,023-2,228 nuclear weapons over and above those already existing in the Indian arsenal. Although no Indian analyst, let alone a policy maker, has ever advocated any nuclear inventory that even remotely approximates such numbers, this heuristic exercise confirms that New Delhi has the capacity to produce a gigantic nuclear arsenal while subsisting well within the lowest estimates of its known uranium reserves.[40]

In responding to these developments, former president Jimmy Carter pronounced the US-India agreement to be a "dangerous deal. The proposed nuclear deal with India is just one more step in opening a Pandora's box of nuclear proliferation."[41] But some argue that there is still a positive side for non-proliferation. As noted by Professor Brahma Chellaney, an expert in strategic affairs, a professor at the Centre for Policy Research, and one of the authors of the Indian Nuclear Doctrine,

> While the Hyde Act's bar on Indian testing is explicit, the one in the NSG waiver is implicit, yet unmistakable. The NSG waiver is overtly anchored in NSG Guidelines

Paragraph 16, which deals with the consequence of "an explosion of a nuclear device." The waiver's Section 3(e) refers to this key paragraph, which allows a supplier to call for a special NSG meeting, and seek termination of cooperation, in the event of a test or any other "violation of a supplier-recipient understanding." The recently leaked Bush Administration letter to Congress has cited how this Paragraph 16 rule will effectively bind India to the Hyde Act's condition on the pain of a U.S.-sponsored cut-off of all multilateral cooperation. India will not be able to escape from the U.S.-set conditions by turning to other suppliers.[42]

The security situation in India makes decisions about its nuclear program, whether civil or military, all the more delicate. India has been subjected to several significant terrorist attacks that were believed to have originated in Pakistan—attacks that add pressure to the nuclear issue. Perhaps it will be enough to mention just one. On December 13, 2001, five assailants from the Lashkar-e-Taiba and Jaish-e-Mohammed terrorist organizations based in Pakistan assaulted the Lok Sabha. The six terrorists were killed along with six Delhi police personnel, two parliament security service personnel, and a gardener. The parliament had adjourned forty minutes earlier. Nevertheless, there were a hundred people still in the building, including several senior politicians. India considered a military response, but under the then current Indian military doctrine, which called for "holding corps" to stop any Pakistani advance, it took three weeks to get troops to the border. And a major crisis did ensue, with both sides undertaking large mobilizations. But essentially there was a stalemate at the border with large numbers of troops on both sides. By May 2002, the situation began to calm down.

But under the Indian military doctrine, Pakistan was prepared and the international community had time to intervene. Accordingly, in 2004, the Indian military began work on what they called the "Cold Start" doctrine. The idea was that, in the case of a major terrorist attack, there would be a quick but limited invasion of Pakistan. The intent was to launch the attack within forty-eight hours and to involve substantial armor and air forces possessing overwhelming firepower that would cross the border but proceed only a limited distance into Pakistan. The idea was to develop the capacity to launch a retaliatory conventional strike into Pakistan that would be punishing before the international community could intercede and, at the same time, pursue narrow enough aims to deny Islamabad the justification to escalate to the nuclear level. Perhaps India might penetrate in the range of 50 to 80 kilometers and use such an inclusion to extract concessions in postconflict negotiations in exchange for withdrawal. The problem with this concept is that—assuming sizable forces could actually act that quickly—it would be Pakistan, not India, that decides whether it would be appropriate to escalate to nuclear weapons. Pakistan has developed a tactical nuclear missile—the NASR (HATF-9)—a short-range, solid-fueled missile with a range of only 60 kilometers, which appears designed for battlefield use against invading troops. The existence of such a doctrine is denied by Indian officials, but there is evidence that it does exist, at least in theory. If such a plan were ever operationalized in the wake of a major terrorist attack, to call it a highly dangerous step would be a huge understatement.

So these two major countries sit side by side, exchanging live fire almost daily with high-level military and civilian leaders periodically issuing nuclear weapon threats in an area continually plagued with major terrorist violence, with intelligence that is not entirely reliable and with a somewhat unclear perception of each other's red lines. How much safer the two countries would be if somehow they could be persuaded to move away from nuclear weapons and toward a nuclear weapon–free South Asia?

PAKISTAN

Pakistan's continued insecurity, to a large degree, is a legacy of the two centuries of British rule in India. The region known today as Pakistan was conquered in the mid-nineteenth century after the disastrous First Anglo-Afghan War in 1838-41, one hundred years after the first British conquest of Bengal and the other parts of India by the army of the British East India Company. The British East India Company ruled India until the Indian Mutiny of 1857, in which Muslim soldiers in the company's army rebelled and whose defeat by the British Army of India brought direct imperial rule to the land, including by this time what is modern-day Pakistan. Shortly after the failure of the Afghan invasion in 1843, the British took Sindh, one of the four Pakistani provinces, and six years later seized the western Punjab, the largest province in Pakistan.

The conquest of northwest India was initially accomplished solely to provide security from marauding Afghan, Baloch, and Pashtun tribes. Britain was also influenced by the fear of tsarist Russia expanding into central Asia and intervening in India through Afghanistan. After two Afghan wars, the second in 1878-81, Britain needed to secure lines of communication. So, it turned northwest India into a garrison state ruled, in effect, by the army from Lahore, the capital of Punjabi province. Nearly half of the British Army in India was therefore based along the Balochistan/North-West Frontier Province (NWFP) border with Afghanistan.

In Punjab, the British used both patronage and repression. They allied themselves with a land-owning feudal class, for whom they built lavish canal and irrigation systems and recruited large numbers of the Punjabi peasantry for the army. Pakistan inherited this security state, which has been described by various scholars as being ruled in "the viceregal tradition" or perhaps (more accurately) as "a permanent state of martial law."[43]

Thus Pakistan's security crisis, which still plagues it today, is based on this garrison state mentality as well as on the fears, insecurities, and contradictions that were deeply rooted in Muslims living during the British Raj in India. Although Muslims as a group had once ruled India, they came to live in a Western colonial state after having been significantly defeated by the British, most notably in the 1857 uprising known as the Munity. Modern Muslim and elitist landlords, seeing a Hindu population favored by the British, began to think of themselves as a separate nation. This "two-nation" theory, which was to form the basis of the Pakistan movement, disregarded ethnic and religious differences and considered a separate religious identity sufficient to form the basis for a state—sufficient to create a new nation separate from the rest of British/Hindu India. But adherents to this view drew no support from the ulema, or religious leaders in the region, who saw Indian Muslims as inextricably linked to the ummah or the global community of religious leaders whose leadership lay with the Caliph in the declining Ottoman Empire far to the West. Thus these local religious leaders did not consider a separate state in the Indian subcontinent to be valid, although they changed their minds after Partition. This identity crisis became more severe as the Muslim League, established in 1906 by Pakistan's founder Mohammed Ali Jinnah, drew its principal support from Muslims in central and eastern India rather than the western regions that were to become the dominant provinces of the future Pakistan.

The Muslim League presented its demand for an independent Muslim state at its annual general meeting on March 23, 1940, when it passed the Pakistan Resolution. Seven years later, after the ill-advised Partition decision by the British Raj—a last calamitous act—Britain handed over a truncated Pakistan. This new Muslim-based state comprised Balochistan, the NWFP, Punjab, and Sindh, making up west Pakistan with the eastern province of Bengal being divided between India and Pakistan to create the geographically distinct east Pakistan 1,000 miles away. This was an unworkable situation, if ever there was one. Kashmir's status was left undecided by the British, with its regional ruler opting for India and its overwhelmingly Muslim populace favoring Pakistan. This led to immediate conflict between India and Pakistan. The nature of Partition and the speed with which it was enacted satisfied nobody. Millions of Hindus and Sikhs, living in areas that were to become Pakistan, migrated to India, while millions of Indian Muslims packed up and left to east and west Pakistan. Twelve million people in all left their homes and became refugees in either Pakistan or India. At least a million people were killed in the ensuing sectarian violence of Partition. It was one of the greatest tragedies of human history. "Pakistan emerged from a bloodbath of religious and ethnic hatred even as millions of Muslims chose to remain in secular India."[44]

Immediately, the question of Pakistan's identity arose. Was it to be a pluralistic, democratic country for Muslims and other religious minorities, or a theocratic Islamic state? Its founder Mohammed Jinnah made clear in his most famous speech in 1947 that he favored the former, stating, "You may belong to any religion or caste or creed—that has nothing to do with the business of the state."[45]

Jinnah died early in 1948, and since then many Pakistanis, particularly in the military, have ignored his wishes and the democratic founding of the country. No state-funded school's textbooks teach the words of the country's founder because this would infuriate the Muslim religious establishment, the mullahs. The military and the mullahs together in stressing the Islamic nature of Pakistan pervert the words of the country's founder and of history by claiming that Pakistan was created because of a religious movement. They proliferate this idea even though a large segment of British India's Muslim population chose to remain in India rather than move to Pakistan and that there are more Muslims in India than in Pakistan today. Qazi Hussain Ahmed, the leader of Jamaat-e-Islami, the most influential Islamic party in the country, said, "It is an established fact that Mr. Jinnah did not struggle for a secular Pakistan as it is against the basic creed and faith of a Muslim to sacrifice his life for such a secular cause. The driving force behind their tireless efforts was . . . setting up a country where people could practice Islam as their state ideology." The army trains its men to defend Islam rather than the nation.[46]

For half of the sixty years of the country's existence, Pakistanis have lived under four military regimes. The first free and fair elections took place in 1970, twenty-three years after Partition, only to be overthrown by generals. This trend happened again and again, with democratically elected leaders being repeatedly overthrown. Only in 2015 did this trend appear to end, with a successful transition, for the first time in the country's history, from one democratically elected leader to another.

Pakistan's failure to forge a national identity has led to an intensification of ethnic, linguistic, and religious nationalism. The province of Punjab, with 65 percent of the population, dominated the state, contributing the bulk of the army and bureaucracy. Smaller provinces have been in almost continual rebellion. There have been five insurgencies in Balochistan with Baloch nationalists seeking greater autonomy—all put down with brute force by the Pakistani Army. The NWFP gave rise to a Pashtun secular nationalist movement in the 1970s and many others since then, including the Taliban today. Since its birth in 1947, Pakistan has grappled with an acute sense of insecurity amid a continuing identity crisis. As a result, it has developed into a national security state in which the army has monopolized power and defined the national interest as keeping India at bay, developing nuclear weapons, and trying to create a friendly government in Afghanistan.

For the first twenty-four years of Pakistan's existence, its military, bureaucratic, and political elite carried out ruinous policies at home, alienating the ethnic minority through the heavy-handed, domineering policies of the ethnic majority, the Punjabis. These sets of policies sparked the 1971 uprising in east Pakistan, a crushing defeat at the hands of India and the most traumatic event in the country's history: the secession and subsequent establishment of Bangladesh. For the next thirty-five years, that same ethnic elite encouraged Muslim extremist movements with the idea of using them against India and to control Afghanistan, most prominently Osama bin Laden and al-Qaeda. These policies helped to prepare the ground for the 9/11 attacks. The United States, in part, contributed to this process. During the height of the Cold War, the United States poured enormous amounts of money into arming anyone who would oppose the Soviet seizure of Afghanistan in 1979, particularly Islamic extremists in Afghanistan, central Asia, and Pakistan.[47]

The 1971 debacle led to the temporary overthrow of the generals and the democratic election of Zulfikar Ali Bhutto, initially as prime minister and then as president. He initiated the first period of sustained democratic rule that Pakistan had ever known. He also began the Pakistani nuclear weapon program in 1972 and is famous for saying that the Pakistani people will have nuclear weapons even if they have to "eat grass." As far back as 1965, when he was foreign minister, Bhutto told the *Manchester Guardian*, "If India makes an atom bomb, then even if we have to feed on grass and leaves—or even if we have to starve—we shall also produce an atom bomb as we would be left with no other alternative. The answer to an atom bomb can only be an atom bomb."[48] And in his book *Eating Grass: The Making of the Pakistani Bomb*, General Feroz Hassan Khan recounted that the

Pakistani nuclear weapon program intensified considerably after India first tested a nuclear device in 1974.

At the core of the nuclear weapons acquisition narrative, according to Khan, is national humiliation, with the phrase "never again" being repeated over and over. For many nations, fears produced by past humiliations are frequently reinforced by concerns about nuclear blackmail. The Soviet Union, after experiencing the ravages of invading Nazi armies, refused to accept the danger it perceived as coming from an American nuclear monopoly. China's nuclear ambitions were fueled by a century of foreign interference: a brutal Japanese occupation and US nuclear threats in the 1950s. India's national humiliation stemmed from colonial subjugation, an embarrassing defeat in its border war with China in 1962, and strategic disparity following the Chinese nuclear test at Lop Nor in 1964. Israel is a state created to ensure that "never again" would the Jewish people face national extermination, and nuclear weapons were increasingly perceived as requisite in the context of enduring Arab-Israeli enmity.[49]

For Pakistan, the fall of Dhaka (the capital of east Pakistan), the loss of east Pakistan, and the capture of 90,000 prisoners of war by India are seared into the collective memory. The tragedies of 1971 left Pakistan reeling and were followed by the subsequent blow of the 1974 Indian test. Together, these events allowed nuclear enthusiasts to take charge and led to the ascendance of Zulfikar Ali Bhutto and his belief in the necessity of nuclear arms. Nuclear weapon efforts were redoubled after India's underground explosion at Pokhran in 1974. The asymmetry in strategic capability between India and Pakistan reinforced the feeling of insecurity that had lingered after Dhaka's fall. The Pakistani nuclear weapon program was the only way, according to General Khan, to prevent such humiliation in the future and to preserve Pakistan. "Never again" would Pakistan be subject to disgrace at the hands of others.[50] Khan asserted, "Today the national narrative around the need for nuclear weapons is intertwined with Pakistani nationalism to a level that it is almost treasonous to think otherwise."[51]

But there is another narrative, another way to look at nuclear weapon acquisition, as outlined by Perves Hoodbhoy in *Confronting the Bomb: Pakistani and Indian Scientists Speak Out*. In his chapter "Nationalism and the Bomb," Hoodbhoy writes,

> Nation building is the process of creating or reinforcing a national identity using the power of the state. . . . In much the same way, a few states see nuclear weapons as an instrument for building or consolidating a national spirit. . . .

Post-Hiroshima, the bomb became the symbol of ultimate power. Even countries allied to the U.S. felt at a disadvantage and rushed to make their own. . . . Britain, though devastated by six years of total war, became the world's third nuclear power. The notion that it would otherwise be considered a second-rank nation was simply intolerable. France, under Charles de Gaulle, thought similarly. . . .

This was evident in India when Indira Gandhi, extremely unpopular in 1974, tested India's bomb for the first time, releasing a burst of nationalist excitement that led to her popularity briefly shooting upward. India glowed again after its 1998 tests, with the BJP and Congress parties setting aside their difference to exult in "Indian greatness."

In Pakistan, the 1998 nuclear tests were celebrated with even greater fervour than in India. Missiles were paraded in Islamabad. . . . It was generally expected by Pakistanis that nuclear weapons would make their country an object of awe and respect internationally, and that it would acquire the mantle of leadership of the Islamic world.[52]

Bhutto remained in power until 1977, when he was overthrown in a coup by the army chief of staff—whom he had appointed—General Zia-ul-Haq. Two years later, Zia hanged Bhutto. General Zia's eleven-year reign has been Pakistan's longest, and it was by far the most destructive. He had a long-lasting and damaging effect on Pakistani society, an effect still evident today. Zia addressed the identity problem of Pakistan by imposing an ideological Islamic state on the population. Many of today's problems—the militancy of religious groups, the rise of powerful terrorist organizations (such as al-Qaeda, Lashkar-e-Taiba, and the Taliban), the mushrooming of radical *madrasas* (Arabic for "school") where many extremists and terrorists are educated, the spread of the drug and Kalashnikov cultures, and the huge increase in sectarian violence—can be attributed to policies adopted during Zia's tenure. The epithet that "all countries have armies, but in Pakistan the army has a country" aptly characterizes Zia's rule.[53]

Zia's longevity as a ruler was made possible by the unwavering support of the United States. First under the Carter administration and then under the Reagan administration, Zia made his Inter-Service Intelligence Directorate (ISI) available to act as a conduit for the arms and funds coming from the United States. Largely using the CIA, the United States armed the Mujahideen to fight the Soviet Union in Afghanistan, ultimately successfully. Vast sums of money to prosecute the war poured into Pakistan through the ISI, where widespread corruption enriched Pakistan through both the heroin trade and the CIA arms pipeline. Funds were also diverted to the nuclear weapon program. The United States made a devil's bargain with Zia by looking the other way as Zia, using most prominently A. Q. Khan, greatly ramped up the Pakistani nuclear weapon programs. This arrangement lasted so long as Zia kept the pipeline flowing and did not embarrass the US government by conducting a nuclear weapon test. The US Congress passed sanctions on Pakistan, but they were not implemented by the administration until a few months after the Soviets had withdrawn from Afghanistan.[54]

By 2002, because of Zia's policies, the Federally Administered Tribal Areas (FATA), a border region that is part of the NWFP of Pakistan along the Afghan border, became, in the words of renowned Pakistani journalist Ahmad Rashid, "a multilayered terrorist cake."[55] At its base were Pakistani Pashtun tribesmen, soon to become Taliban, who provided the hideouts and logistical support. Above them was the Afghan Taliban, who settled in FATA after 9/11, followed by militants from Africa, central Asia, Chechnya, China, and Kashmir, and topped by Arabs who forged a protective ring around bin Laden. FATA became the world's "terrorism central." Meanwhile, the nuclear program continued to expand. Nuclear weapon storage facilities were located not far from FATA, with the then head of terrorism central, Osama bin Laden, asserting that acquiring nuclear weapons was a "religious duty." Today bin Laden is dead, al-Qaeda is severely weakened, and the Pakistani Army has seriously taken up arms against the Pakistani Taliban. But Pakistan remains a dangerous place and is a stronghold of significantly capable terrorist organizations both in FATA and elsewhere.

A. Q. Khan, who was once described by CIA director George Tenet as "at least as dangerous as Osama bin Laden,"[56] appeared on the scene in Pakistan in 1975. He completed his university education in Pakistan and went to Europe for a graduate education. He received a PhD in metallurgy in 1971 and shortly thereafter went to work as a subcontractor of URENCO, the European enrichment corporation. Traumatized by Pakistan's defeat at the hands of India in 1971, he volunteered essentially to be a spy in 1974. Khan secretly transferred centrifuge plans and other sensitive information he had access to at URENCO to Pakistani agents. He returned to Pakistan in 1975. In less than a year, Khan established Engineering Research Laboratories (ERL) and began playing a significant role in the Pakistani nuclear weapon program, reporting directly to Prime Minister Bhutto but not to the Pakistan Atomic Energy Commission (PAEC), which Khan increasingly sidelined. Later that year, ERL established a secret plant at Kahuta, not far from Islamabad, and began helping Pakistan acquire nuclear weapons.

In 1976, Khan reached out to his "old boy" network of European friends and embarked on a vast nuclear weapon technology shopping spree for Pakistan.

Among other significant purchases, a Dutch firm sold Khan 6,500 tubes made of hardened steel for centrifuge rotors and a large, complicated system of pipes and vacuum valves to feed uranium hexafluoride gas into centrifuges from a Swiss firm that somehow obtained an export license. To take delivery of the latter item, Pakistan sent three C-130 cargo planes to Switzerland. After his buying campaign, Khan invited his "old boy" European friends to come to Pakistan to train the "local boys" on how to use the equipment. In 1977, construction began on a huge facility at Kahuta to house centrifuges and other equipment for uranium enrichment. The Pakistani nuclear weapon program was now truly underway.

By 1982, the US State Department had concluded that Pakistan was intent on acquiring nuclear weapons. Kahuta was too large for research and development. The CIA was aware by 1979 that Khan had assembled everything he needed to construct his own centrifuge plant. ERL in 1981 was renamed Khan Research Laboratories (KRL). Khan, whose major contribution to Pakistan's development of nuclear weapons enabled Pakistan to have a nuclear weapon capability by the end of the decade, became known in Pakistan as the "father of the Pakistani bomb." Despite close attention by US intelligence, it took over a decade to discover that Khan also served as a worldwide illegal middleman of nuclear proliferation.

By the late 1980s, Khan's proliferating sales outside of Pakistan had begun. Though Khan now had less need in Pakistan for his outside suppliers, they still needed his business, and with a surplus of P-1 centrifuges, arising from the upgrade to more modern P-2 machines, the opportunities were there. Khan had a large stockpile of P-1 machines to sell, and so he began to pitch sales to Iran, Iraq, Libya, and North Korea. On the margins of a state visit by Prime Minister Benazir Bhutto to North Korea, Khan made an agreement to exchange centrifuge technology for the technology and parts of the No-Dong missile, a North Korean medium-range ballistic missile, which could deliver a nuclear weapon to more than 1,500 kilometers. In Pakistan, Khan renamed it the Ghauri, where it had a significant impact on the balance of power with India.[57] Its range was such that it could cover much of India. It had a somewhat longer range than India's Prithvi missile, which could cover all of Pakistan given the smaller area.

Although the Reagan administration had looked the other way as Pakistan was developing its program, it nevertheless followed it closely. In the early 1980s, the CIA and British intelligence learned that Khan had obtained from China the design of a 20-kiloton nuclear weapon that the Chinese had tested in 1966. Many years later, Khan supplied this design to Libya and probably also to Iran. The CIA's penetration of the Pakistani program was so complete that as early as

1984 the agency could show a scale model of the Pakistani bomb to the country's foreign minister, and by 1989 a CIA official could say that "the president of the United States knew more about Pakistan's nuclear program than the prime minister of Pakistan."[58] This was without doubt the case: Benazir Bhutto, Ali Bhutto's daughter, became prime minister in an election following General Zia's assassination in 1988, but she lacked a clear majority. The army refused to let her govern— even though she was the head of the party with a parliamentary plurality and the obvious choice for prime minister—until she agreed not to reduce the military's budget and to allow the army to run foreign policy and the nuclear program.[59]

By early 1984, Kahuta had produced enriched uranium, according to General Khan. In March 1986, Kahuta was reportedly producing uranium enriched to 30 percent, still far from the 90 percent required for weapons-grade enrichment, but a significant step in that direction. Cold tests of an implosion device were conducted, and in 1987 Pakistan purchased a West German purification and production facility capable of producing 5 to 10 grams of tritium per day. In a 1987 interview, Zia asserted that Pakistan had not enriched uranium to weapons grade and did not intend to build nuclear weapons, but that it was "capable of building the bomb whenever it wishes." At the time of this interview, Pakistani scientists responsible for designing the bomb had been at work for seven years.[60] In the 1990s, Pakistan, in addition to acquiring the Ghauri ballistic missile, also obtained from China the efficient M-11 ballistic missile, with a range greater than 300 kilometers.

In June 1989, Prime Minister Bhutto came to Washington. During this visit she asserted the peaceful nature of Pakistan's nuclear program to a joint session of the US Congress. While there, she received a complete briefing on the Pakistani program from the CIA Director William Webster. General Beg, the army chief of staff, asserted that despite the agreement to have the army manage the nuclear weapon program, Bhutto was fully informed as joint chair of the "national command authority" along with President Ghulam Ishaq Khan. In contrast to this claim, Prime Minister Bhutto insisted to the West that the army did not keep her in the loop. President Khan and General Beg were unimpressed and even suspicious of the prime minister's fraternizing with US intelligence. Just a month after taking office, a CIA team gave her a briefing on the Pakistani program, but it was the briefing in Washington by the highest officials of the US government that laid the foundation of mistrust. This distrust contributed significantly to the deterioration of her relationship with the president and the army chief of staff and led to the dismissal of her government a year later.

Even so, General Beg insisted that Prime Minister Bhutto and President Khan were the architects of the Pakistani policy of nuclear restraint, developed prior to the prime minister's visit to Washington. It included five elements:

1. maintaining the minimum force posture necessary for a credible deterrent,

2. refraining from conducting hot tests,

3. freezing fissile stocks at the current level,

4. reducing uranium enrichment to below 5 percent, and

5. affirming that nuclear weapons do not replace conventional capabilities.[61]

Years later, in 2005, General Beg was asked whether there was a cap on warhead numbers in this policy. He replied ambiguously, "There was no cap on freezing . . . at the time we talked, the Indians had 50-70 warheads and what we had was good enough to deter."[62]

By 1987, the US government believed that Pakistan possessed either a nuclear device or all the components to make one. By May 1990, the US government had concluded that Pakistan possessed one or more nuclear weapons; by 1994, the government believed that Pakistan possessed enough material for six to eight nuclear weapons and could probably make one or two weapons per year.[63] Thus there have been no fundamental surprises for the United States with respect to the Pakistani program, either in 1998 or at any other time. During this time, the Pakistani government to some degree adhered to the Khan/Bhutto policy of nuclear restraint (obviously playing down the points on not increasing fissile stocks or conducting uranium enrichment above 5 percent) and continued to slowly increase the size of the stockpile. Amid all of this, China's role in helping Pakistan was pivotal. China's help came generally through technology transfers and specifically by giving Pakistan the 1966 nuclear weapon design, enough HEU for two weapons, and the M-11 missile. By 1987, A. Q. Khan declared that Pakistan already possessed a nuclear weapon capability. He boasted in a press interview, "What the CIA had been saying about our possessing the bomb is correct."[64] He was nevertheless just a little ahead of himself.

In May 1998, India conducted five nuclear weapon tests at Pokhran. It seemed clear to US intelligence analysts that India's nuclear tests made Pakistani tests a certainty, and sooner rather than later. The State Department intelligence bureau commented on May 13 that "though some Pakistani officials will counsel patience to allow the weight of the international opprobrium to fall exclusively on India, mounting domestic political pressure makes a Pakistani test virtually inevitable." The following day, various sources indicated that the current prime minister, Nawaz Sharif, had given the "green light" for tests.[65]

Two days after the first three announced Indian tests on May 13, 1998, the Defense Committee of the Cabinet (DCC) held a long meeting, and just as it was ending, India announced two more subkiloton tests. Pakistani seismic stations recorded no activity, and so PAEC assumed the alleged tests were experiments or safety tests for low-yield weapons. This assessment was later confirmed by Western sources.

In addition to these assessments, the DCC analyzed possible Indian motives for conducting the tests and settled on five points:

1. India has forced itself into the nuclear club simply to be on par with the nuclear weapon states of the NPT.

2. Without signing the NPT, India had none of the legal obligations to the treaty.

3. The tests were status oriented to claim permanent membership on the UN Security Council.

4. India's policy toward Pakistan would now be aggressive, especially on the issue of Kashmir.

5. India wanted to push Pakistan to follow suit and be faced with the political and economic consequences of sanctions.[66]

As the members of the DCC saw it, Pakistan was in somewhat of a trap. If Islamabad followed suit and conducted tests, Pakistan's already weak economy would be subject to economic sanctions, which in turn would weaken Pakistani conventional forces. On the other hand, if Pakistan did not test at the time, the nuclear deterrent would be undermined, and India would take aggressive action in Kashmir and against Pakistan in general. The regime's political survival would have also been in question.

Samar Mubarakmand, the number two scientist at the PAEC, assured the DCC that if the decision were made to test, the PAEC would need only ten days of preparation. A. Q. Khan argued that KRL deserved the honor of carrying out the test if conducted. The prime minister at the time was too focused on the decision itself, and no decision was made as to who would conduct the test. President Clinton had already made two phone calls to Prime Minister Muhammad Nawaz Sharif urging him not to test and sent Deputy Secretary of State Strobe Talbott to Islamabad to reinforce his message. Talbott stayed only a short time on this first visit, but he returned soon after, accompanied by a small team that included General Anthony Zinni, the commander of the US Central Command. General Zinni was prepared to make a serious substantive effort to persuade Pakistan not to test.

According to Khan's account, Pakistani officials found it difficult to believe that the United States, with all its resources, would not have known beforehand that India was planning to test. It seemed to them that India was granted "silent consent," while strong economic sanctions were to be applied to Pakistan—a devastating prospect considering the weak state of the Pakistani economy. By the time the Talbott team arrived, it was already clear the direction the decision was going to take. The United States urged Pakistan to take the political high ground, spurning a "tit for tat" with India, and thereby escape from economic sanctions. From Pakistan's perspective, not responding to India's tests was domestically unpopular and, from the strategic standpoint, would weaken Pakistan's deterrent. Many also remembered previous abandonment by the United States at times of crisis, thus making Washington's offers lack credibility. Khan notes that these skeptics were proved correct when in March 2005 the United States offered India an unprecedented nuclear deal resulting in the US-India Peaceful Atomic Energy Cooperation legislation. Accordingly, the US team left Pakistan empty handed.[67]

On May 16, 1998, after the Talbott delegation departed, Prime Minister Sharif held another secret DCC meeting. He gave instructions to the director of the Special Development Works (SDW) to make the necessary arrangements at the site. On May 18, he summoned PAEC chairman Dr. Ishfaq Ahmed to his office and ordered him to "carry out the explosion."[68]

Dr. Samar Mubarakmand led the tests. A. Q. Khan complained with vigor to the prime minister and the army chief of staff that PAEC was conducting the test and not KRL. As a result, a KRL group was added to the PAEC team, but PAEC remained in the overall lead. The date and time were set for May 28. Prime Minister Sharif called President Clinton and apologized for what was about to happen. He had no choice but to go ahead with the test, he asserted.

At dawn on Thursday, May 28, an air alert was declared over Pakistan. Based on a message from Saudi Arabia, air defense fighter planes were ordered to remain on alert in case of a nuclear attack by Israel on the test site. Pakistan approached the United States over this, and Washington contacted the chief of the Israeli Defense Force, putting him in touch with the Pakistan ambassador in Washington to lay this fear to rest.

It had been decided that there would be six nuclear tests, each with different designs. As Khan has it in his account, the PAEC could not afford to explode six bombs from its inventory, so only two bombs were selected, and the four remaining designs were to be tested with triggers and natural uranium wrapped around the weapon. Five weapons were to be tested on May 28 and the sixth two days later, on May 30, for a total of one more test than India had claimed. At 3:16 p.m. on May 28, after the "all clear" signal had been given, the button was pushed and the computer took over the system. Thirty seconds later, the mountain where the five devices were buried shook and changed color—dark granite turning white from oxidation—followed by a huge thick cloud of dust enveloping the mountain.[69]

That evening, Pakistan announced five tests of boosted fission HEU devices with a total yield of 40 kilotons, 35 from the main device, the other 4 of low yield. The prime minister announced in a television address, "Today we have evened the score with India." On May 30, the sixth device was tested by Pakistan with the yield being 18-20 kilotons, thereby topping its adversary.[70]

As with India, Western analysis did not agree with the yields attributed to the devices by Pakistan. Pakistan's claims were also subject to scrutiny and skepticism. Like India's May 11 test, the Pakistani May 28 tests emitted a single signal, which could have been caused by a single detonation or the five simultaneous explosions claimed by Pakistan. The US data indicated that the magnitude of the explosive yield of the explosion or explosions was 9 to 12 kilotons. One US official commented, "We don't believe either nation is really telling the truth about what they did."[71] These controversies about the yield of the Indian and Pakistani explosions continued for years.

Shortly after the Indian tests in May 1998, Prime Minister Atal Bihari Vajpayee announced that henceforth India would observe a nuclear test moratorium,[72] and on June 12 promptly after its tests, Pakistan also declared that it would observe a moratorium.[73] Despite the mutual refraining from further nuclear tests, only eight months passed before the two countries were embroiled in a major crisis, known as Kargil, which again brought them close to war. The United States worried that the crisis might perhaps end in nuclear war. In the summer of 1999, clashes broke out between Indian and Pakistani troops deployed on the line of control (LoC), which delineates Indian from Pakistani-controlled Kashmir, near the Siachen glacier and the town of Kargil in Kashmir at heights up to 17,000 feet. In May, Pakistan initially advanced into a 500-square-mile area up to 5 miles beyond the LoC, into positions from which India had withdrawn. In June, India responded with a massive retaliation bringing in several divisions. There was heavy fighting at these high elevations, and the Pakistani positions beyond the LoC were becoming untenable. Fearing that Pakistan might escalate to nuclear weapons, the United States put heavy pressure on Pakistan to withdraw. President Clinton in a meeting with Sharif in Washington insisted on immediate action, and eventually Sharif agreed. In withdrawing, the Pakistani troops suffered more casualties than in the entire conflict, resulting in considerable anger and humiliation for Pakistan, which denied any intent to escalate to nuclear weapons. India's position on the nuclear weapons issue was never disclosed. The crisis was over by July, but it remains the most controversial event in the recent history of the region. And in October 1999, Pakistani Army Chief Musharraf overthrew Prime Minister Sharif's government and made himself president of the country.

On December 13, 2001, five suicide terrorists attacked the Indian Parliament with guns and grenades. Nine people were killed, including the terrorists. The next day, India blamed Lashkar-e-Taiba, a Pakistani-based terrorist organization waging jihad in support of Kashmiri freedom. This led to another huge crisis. By January 3, 2002, India had mobilized 500,000 troops, their largest mobilization since the 1971 war. Pakistan counter-mobilized, and the scale of confrontation on the Indo-Pakistan border was unprecedented since the 1971 conflict. India recalled its ambassador (designated the high commissioner), demanded the extradition of twenty alleged Pakistani terrorists, deployed its Prithvi ballistic missiles, and announced its largest military exercise in fifteen years to be carried out near the border. On January 25, India proceeded to flight test its Agni missile, dubbing it the "Pakistan-specific" missile. Pakistan put its troops on full alert but uncharacteristically did not flight test its missile.[74]

By May 2002, the situation had calmed down. Nevertheless, following a major Hindu-Muslim clash in the Indian state of Gujarat in mid-May, another major terrorist attack took place in an Indian army camp in Kashmir, killing thirty-one. India blamed Pakistan and demanded that the Pakistani ambassador depart. The two sides again moved close to war with bellicose statements on both sides. At the time, Pakistan chose to flight test its three principal ballistic missiles: Haft V Ghauri, composed of liquid fuel (the North Korean No-Dong) with a range of 1,300–1,500 kilometers; Haft III Ghaznavi, composed of solid fuel with a range of

280 kilometers; and Haft II Abdali, composed of solid fuel with a range of 180-200 kilometers. General Khan referred to this practice of conducting missile tests during a time of crisis as a "new norm of signaling deterrence," a form of sending messages to adversaries.[75] General Pervez Musharraf later explained in a speech on June 17, 2002:

> We were compelled to show them in May 1998, that we were not bluffing and in May 2002, we were compelled to show that we do not bluff. . . . By testing with outstanding success the delivery systems of our strategic capability. . . . We need to ensure that the three basic ingredients of deterrence—capability, credibility, and resolve—never got compromised.[76]

During this last crisis, there was significantly reduced rhetoric about nuclear weapons, and neither side put its nuclear forces on alert. In June, US Defense Secretary Rumsfeld and Deputy Secretary of State Armitage traveled to the region, and gradually tensions began to subside. This confrontation lasted ten months, and it had two intense phases where the two sides came close to war but fortunately did not engage. Much of the time, from December 2001 to October 2002, when this crisis finally ended, major US military campaigns against the Taliban and al-Qaeda were also occurring along the Afghan-Pakistan border, which added to Pakistan's perceived instability and insecurity. The speech by General Musharraf on June 17, 2002, quoted above, came in the middle of all this.[77] As is well known, immediately after the 9/11 attacks, the US government commandeered several Pakistani air bases and some two-thirds of Pakistani air space from which to conduct the aerial part of its campaign to destroy the Taliban regime in Afghanistan. The long war inside Afghanistan led to considerable conflict and antagonism between the United States and Pakistan.

In 2012, when General Khan was writing his book, Pakistan's nuclear weapon arsenal was close to one hundred weapons. By 2017, this number had increased to between one hundred and thirty and one hundred and forty,[78] while at the same time US-Pakistani relations had fallen to an all-time low, for three reasons: (1) a CIA contractor killed two Pakistan citizens at a traffic stop in Lahore early in 2011; (2) a US Navy SEAL team successfully raided Abbottabad where Osama bin Laden was hiding (without notice to Pakistan) and killed Osama bin Laden, an operation that was regarded as a serious breach of Pakistan's sovereignty; (3) US Army forces mistakenly attacked a Pakistani checkpoint on the Afghan border on November 16, killing twenty-seven soldiers and officers.

This brings us to a discussion about Pakistan's nuclear policy. After the US-India nuclear deal was announced in 2005 and became operational in 2008, India was able to expand its uranium enrichment capabilities for its submarine program and complete its reprocessing facilities for production and breeder reactors. General Khan asserts that the combination of this deal and the India Cold Start doctrine forced Pakistan to increase its plutonium production capability by beginning work on three additional reactors, bringing the Pakistani total to four. But he says that Pakistan has no plan for battlefield nuclear weapons. The introduction of Haft IX (a variant of Nasr ["vengeance" in Arabic], tactical nuclear weapon system, solid fuel, range 60 kilometers) is regarded as a purely defensive measure meant to bolster conventional deterrence. As Khan elaborates:

> In the Pakistani strategic belief, as of 2001 and 2002 the country had restored the strategic balance in the region; it was disturbed by India's military doctrine of limited war under the nuclear overhang and nuanced through the Cold Start Doctrine. Nasr, therefore, re-restores "the strategic balance by closing in the gap at the operational and tactical level." Pakistan's security managers surmise that in India's calculations, Pakistan would not have used the "big strategic weapons if the attacks were shallow and occurring in the vicinity of the battlefield close to the border." So in their assessment "Nasr pours cold water to Cold Start . . . thus this is a weapon of peace. It restores the balance; it should convince India to think long before deciding to attack."[79]

There is another view of this issue in Pakistan. As two prominent nuclear scientists, A. H. Nayyar of Pakistan and Zia Mian, a dual Pakistani/American citizen, warn in an article included in Pervez Hoodbhoy's book:

> While Pakistani leaders have issued no formal nuclear doctrine, it is widely understood that they are prepared to initiate the use of nuclear weapons in a conflict. Pakistan has consistently rejected suggestions that it adopt a policy of no-first use of nuclear weapons, and has instead reinforced the notion that its nuclear weapons are meant, in part, to counter India's larger conventional military forces. In 2011 Pakistan tested the Nasr missile, which has a reported range of 60 km and is intended to deliver nuclear weapons on the battlefield.[80]

General Khan was an important participant in and chronicler of the Pakistani nuclear weapon program. Citing the general once more, Pakistan nuclear policy is likely to evolve into one of two futures, depending on: the evolution of the struggle against terrorism; the regional power balance between India and Pakistan; how the United States acts in Asia—toward China, India, and the

Islamic world (particularly Iran); and Pakistan's own domestic progress after the end of military rule.

> The first future is moderate and pragmatic and would occur if Pakistan has a moderate government that ensures balanced civil-military relations. This course would perpetu-ate the national security establishment's perception of nuclear force as purely a national security instrument. . . . The other nuclear future is a radical shift away from Pakistan's traditional approach to international relations. Such an outcome is more likely if a radi-cal right-wing government assumes power. A domestic change of this nature could shift the emphasis of nuclear weapons from a purely national security tool to a more ideo-logically-based power instrument. . . . At the time of this writing Pakistan has shown tendencies that reveal potential to move toward either future described above. . . . The country stands divided between moderates, with a liberal outlook of a modern state, and conservatives who have a vision of a theocratic state. This division has brought the nature of Pakistan into question, pointing to the potential for the second future of radical tendencies, raising concerns in the international community. By the end of 2011, however, Pakistan has shown maturity in its policies. Civil-military relations are better, and relations with India have begun to improve. . . . Should this trend gain momentum, the Pakistani trajectory could well be toward the first future.[81]

We must all hope that General Khan's positive alternative for the future in Pakistan is realized. As said above, India and Pakistan are vastly less secure since the introduction of nuclear weapons and associated delivery systems into the region. India and Pakistan are fully integrated nuclear weapon states. Both coun-tries have short- and long-range ballistic missile systems as well as cruise missiles with associated nuclear weapon types to be carried by the various missiles. The nuclear warheads, while perhaps of less yield than some of the weapons in the West, are undoubtedly capable of wreaking incalculable damage. Both sides have highly capable bomber aircraft and associated nuclear bomber systems. India has a submarine-based nuclear deterrent, and Pakistan is working on one.

Nuclear war between these two adversaries would be the greatest human trag-edy in history. Nearly 1.5 billion people live in South Asia; in the case of nuclear war, many millions would die and many cities would be destroyed. The degree of debris and soot ejected into the atmosphere would sweep around the world in the so-called nuclear winter effect, causing plants and animals to die from lack of sunlight and precipitous temperature drops. This would result in a catastrophic worldwide famine that would affect millions outside of South Asia.

South Asia is the only one of the three additional regions into which the NWFZ movement must move to bring the world close to nuclear disarmament, where nuclear war is a short-term risk. Thus it is the region where a negotiated NWFZ is most needed and where it would be most beneficial. With enlightened leadership, it may someday be possible.

And there is cause for optimism. On March 1, 2016, I attended a presentation by Sartaz Aziz, the last foreign minister of Pakistan before the Musharraf coup and in recent times the advisor to the prime minister on foreign affairs, an important figure in the government of Pakistan. He said that Pakistan has lost in the range of 60,000 people to terrorism in recent years, but in the last few years many things have improved. Over 35,000 terrorists have been arrested. The attack by the Taliban in 2014 on a children's school was a turning point; it unified the nation against terrorism and terrorist groups. In a year or two, a corner will have been turned on terrorism. There now is a broad national consensus that there is no place in Pakistan for groups that would carry out such terrorist actions and that not only should the Taliban disappear from Pakistan, but also it should never be allowed to come back into power in Afghanistan. Pakistani security forces must be strong, and there must be a hand extended to dissidents for reconciliation. There is an active dialogue among Afghanistan, China, Iran, and Pakistan on this subject, and Aziz believes that serious peace talks could begin in the near future. He noted that 95 percent of the FATA have been cleared of terrorists by the Pakistani army. Also, relations with India are steadily improving. If these sorts of things can truly be realized in both India and Pakistan, perhaps the highly dangerous situation that the presence of nuclear weapons has created in South Asia can be put on the table as well. With a unified national consensus in both countries and wise and strong leadership in both capitols, it is within the realm of possibility that one day nuclear weapons will be eliminated from South Asia. This would be not only in the best interests of the peoples of South Asia but also a huge step forward toward peace in the world.

Chapter 12
The P-5 and the Future

And so we have come to the end of our analysis of the nuclear weapon–free zone movement and its potential for expansion. Already NWFZ treaties cover a significant part of the globe, including Latin America up to the US-Mexican border; the South Pacific and most of the land areas therein; Southeast Asia, which brings the nuclear weapon–free zone to the Pacific shores of the Eastern Hemisphere; Africa, including near- and offshore islands; and central Asia. Three other major areas are potential candidates for additional NWFZs: the Middle East, northeast Asia, and South Asia. We have examined the enormous difficulties that would have to be overcome to establish NWFZs in these regions, with perhaps the problems of South Asia being the greatest. Nowhere else does the possession of nuclear weapons become so strongly influenced by anticolonial, racial, and religious politics. Without a doubt, the introduction of nuclear weapons into South Asia has made both India and Pakistan immeasurably less secure. Likewise, all the countries of the Middle East would be far more secure if nuclear weapons could be verifiably banned from this region. The situation in northeast Asia is a bit more muddled with the one problem state in the region, North Korea, apparently believing that it cannot survive, at least in its present form, without nuclear weapons.

Should all the barriers within these three regions somehow be overcome, what would then stand between the world community and the worldwide elimination of nuclear weapons would be the still considerable issue of China, the NATO states (and European neutrals), and Russia. Practically speaking, what would remain is the P-5.

When NWFZ treaties cover the globe except for the P-5 area—should this outcome be achieved—the world environment likely would be far different from that which exists today. Climate change will have advanced to the point that several former states, such as Bangladesh, will be partly underwater; deserts will have dramatically expanded virtually everywhere; and, because of these developments and others, many less powerful countries will be contemplating nuclear weapons as equalizers vis-à-vis more powerful states in order to protect the remaining arable land they still possess. To head off the risk of multiple conflicts involving nuclear weapons, nuclear disarmament may have become an immediate imperative and the P-5 more amenable to negotiation.

The United States built 72,000 nuclear weapons during the Cold War and once had 32,500 in its stockpile. The Soviet Union built some 55,000 weapons and kept in the range of 45,000 deployed for many years. The other three nuclear states—Britain, China, and France—each have never had more than around 500 weapons in their arsenals. In 2015, the United States had 1,597 strategic nuclear warheads on 785 land-based intercontinental ballistic missiles (ICBMs), submarine-launched ballistic missiles (SLBMs), and strategic bombers. The US non-deployed strategic arsenal is estimated to be about 2,800, and the US tactical weapon arsenal numbers around 500 warheads. The April 2017 New Start declaration by the United States reported 1,411 strategic warheads and in a January 2017 speech, Vice President Biden reported a total of 4,108 acrive and inactive nuclear warheads.

Russia has 1,582 strategic deployed warheads on 515 ICBMs, SLBMs, and strategic bombers. It has been estimated that Russia has several thousand nondeployed strategic warheads and around 2,000 tactical warheads. An additional 3,200 warheads are awaiting dismantlement. The total likely is in the range of 7,700. The United Kingdom has 120 strategic warheads, no more than 40 are deployed at any one time, and the total stockpile is 225 weapons. France has a total of 300 total warheads and China about 260.[1]

If the world community does reach this final stage of nuclear weapons control through the NWFZ process, even though the arsenals of the P-5 likely will have changed drastically during the many years of this process, some final steps will still need to be taken. Recognizing the hugely speculative nature of this conjecture, let us assume that the nuclear weapon stockpiles of the P-5 many years in the future will not have drastically changed. The United States is, after all, planning a thirty-year modernization for its nuclear weapon force, costing some $1 trillion, and Russia and China have ambitious modernization programs as well.

The United States would still have to lead in taking the final step of achieving the worldwide elimination of nuclear weapons. A first part could be that the United States and Russia could reduce to three hundred weapons total each on a verifiable basis, with the other three nations perhaps going to seventy-five each. This would require agreement to worldwide intrusive onsite inspection and probably security guarantees to a number of states on the edge of conflicts.[2]

Then, after some time had passed and after intense, long-lasting negotiations, all could reduce *verifiably* to virtual zero—that is, possessing small stockpiles of HEU and plutonium under national and international safeguards but no weapons. Perhaps each state might retain enough fissile material in its stockpile for reconstitution into fifteen bombs each for the United States and Russia and five each for the United Kingdom, France, and China as a hedge against failure of the disarmament agreement. This virtual-zero arrangement would remain under close supervision, perhaps for many years until solutions to relevant technical problems are developed.

Such an agreement would involve a truly overwhelming degree of unprecedented international on-site inspection. Agreement to a broad array of international sanctions—not excluding military action—by the UN Security Council against any nation in violation of the final nuclear disarmament treaty would be indispensable. But at this stage in the struggle against climate change, it might not be so unprecedented and therefore perhaps not as difficult to achieve as it appears now. And at this stage of virtual disarmament the threat of nuclear war would have been almost completely eliminated.

The chance of one day achieving the verifiable worldwide elimination of nuclear weapons is essential to the preservation of the Nuclear Non-Proliferation Treaty, the cornerstone of international security. This treaty has been largely successful in preventing the proliferation of nuclear weapon stockpiles all over the world—a proliferation that was President John F. Kennedy's great fear. Despite some predictions at the time of the Kennedy presidency of twenty-five to thirty nuclear weapon states by 1975 and with there being perhaps up to forty to forty-five today, the current actual number of states possessing nuclear weapons is only nine. If the NPT and related NWFZ treaties should fail and President Kennedy's fears be realized, nuclear disarmament would become impossible.

But the NPT is based on a strategic bargain in which most of the states of the world agreed never to acquire nuclear weapons in exchange for the pledge of the five states allowed to keep them under the NPT to eventually negotiate away those weapons and also to engage in peaceful nuclear commerce. The principal quid pro quo for establishment of this bargain—for states giving up forever the world's most powerful weapon—was the promise by these five states that they would seek an agreement prohibiting the further testing of nuclear weapons.

But now, nearly fifty years later, this promise goes unfulfilled. The principal reason is the inability of the United States of America, the first nation to sign the Comprehensive Nuclear-Test-Ban Treaty (CTBT) in 1996, to ratify the treaty and remove the major impediment to its coming into force. The US Constitution provides that two-thirds of the members of the US Senate must authorize the president to ratify a treaty such as this. The Republican Party, the majority party in the Senate most years since 1996, has consistently prevented this from happening. Because a two-thirds vote is required, it takes but thirty-four Republicans to prevent ratification of this treaty, which is overwhelmingly in the national security interests of the United States. As a result, there appears to be no possibility that the CTBT will be approved for ratification in the foreseeable future, if ever, despite its immense value to the United States and the world community.

Meanwhile, the NPT grows steadily weaker largely because of the lack of balance in the treaty in the absence of the CTBT in force, but also for other reasons such as the unrestrained nuclear weapon programs in the Middle East, northeast Asia, and South Asia. There is no guarantee that the NPT can survive these difficulties for many more years. The end of the NPT regime would also mean the end of all chances for removing the sword of destruction that has been hanging over the head of humankind for more than seventy years.

But perhaps there is a partial solution to preserving the NPT. Specifically, the UN Security Council, under Chapter Seven of the UN Charter, could "determine" that any nuclear weapon test anywhere by anyone would be "a threat to international peace and security" and therefore "decide" that no state may conduct nuclear weapon tests. In addition, pursuant to Article 25 of the UN Charter, all members agree to "accept and carry out" the decisions of the Security Council. This resolution would become binding international law on all states and would make a nuclear weapon test by any state contrary to international law and subject to sanctions. Such a measure might hold the line for the NPT in the short to medium term in that it would at least provide balance to the international non-proliferation regime if not to the NPT itself, pending one day the actual entry into force of the CTBT. This step was at least considered during the Obama administration, but one must admit it is quite unlikely today.

Passing such a Security Council resolution would advance the entry into force of the CTBT. Whereas the resolution would prohibit further testing, the CTBT in force would institutionalize and make permanent the organizational structure to monitor and verify conduct. The council has the power under the UN Charter to pass such a ban on nuclear testing and has taken such action in the past.

In 2015, thirteen of the fifteen members of the Security Council had already ratified the CTBT (including three of the five permanent members: France, Russia, and the United Kingdom), and supporting such a resolution therefore would have been consistent with their national law. The ten nonpermanent members were also all CTBT parties. The fourteenth, China, has a history of not wanting to be isolated politically and therefore would have been likely to support such a resolution. The fifteenth member is the United States. This balance, with five new members of the Security Council replacing (in June 2016) five retiring nonpermanent members, likely will not change.

In October 2013, I gave a speech advocating consideration of such a course on the margins of the United Nations. In June 2014, I published an article in *WMD Junction*, an online publication of the Monterey Institute, urging the same,[3] and in 2015, Professor David Koplow of the Georgetown Law School published an article in the *Georgetown Journal of International Law* setting forth the full legal argument supporting such a course of action.[4]

Following these steps, a small group of citizens pressed the case for action on such a UN Security Council resolution in the summer of 2015. Five nonpermanent members of the Security Council were approached on this measure. They all supported the idea, and one of them, Chile, was prepared to table a draft resolution. If it had been tabled, it stood a good chance of passage, and the United States, given its rhetorical support of the CTBT for many years, could not have opposed it.

This small group of concerned citizens sent detailed memoranda to high officials of the National Security Council, but the State Department opposed such a step without providing a persuasive argument why. Essentially, it was argued that an attempt to pass such a resolution would be unsuccessful and would inhibit the (slim to nil) possibility of favorable Senate CTBT action in the future. Chile approached the office of the US ambassador to the United Nations in November 2015 and asked if there would be any objection by the United States to Chile's tabling a draft resolution on this subject. A few days later, Washington instructed the US UN Mission to tell Chile that pursuing such a resolution at this point would not be timely. Some of the State Department objections were passed on. There were unsubstantiated rumors that the real reasons for Washington's objection might be fears that Israel or Pakistan would make trouble over this issue. In any case, the attempt to secure a Security Council resolution prohibiting further nuclear weapon tests was abandoned. One can only hope that this idea will be revisited, as it appears to be, for the foreseeable future, the only step available thereby to strengthen the NPT and protect the world community from further nuclear weapon tests.

Pursuing measures to control nuclear weapons is difficult even when they appear relatively easy to accomplish and to create great benefits. Also difficult is the pursuit of measures to reduce nuclear weapons even in the United States itself, a country with a wealth of experience in the field of nuclear arms control, non-proliferation, and disarmament.

Nuclear disarmament is a cause that must not be abandoned; nuclear weapons remain a great threat to humanity. If the traditional route of US-Russia reductions followed by the other states with nuclear weapon stockpiles is not available—and will not be available for many years, as appears to be the case—the course discussed in this book could be considered. Perhaps a well-organized and highly motivated United States can help lead the world community through the treacherous waters of further regional nuclear weapon disarmament and expand the nuclear weapon–free zone movement so that it covers most of the earth and brings the goal of nuclear weapon elimination much closer to realization than it is today.

Notes

Chapter 1. Another Way Forward

1   Rhodes, *Making of the Atomic Bomb*, 713.

2   Ibid., 710–11.

3   Ibid., 732–33.

4   Ibid., 733.

5   Ibid., 742.

6   Ibid.

7   Dallek, *Unfinished Life*, 615.

8   Accounts of the Norwegian rocket incident can be found in Geoffrey Forden, "False Alarms in the Nuclear Age," *NOVA*, accessed April 9, 2017, http://www.pbs.org/wgbh/ nova/military/nuclear-false-alarms.html; "Norwegian Rocket Incident," Wikipedia, accessed April 3, 2014, last modified on March 31, 2016, https://en.wikipedia.org/wiki/ Norwegian_rocket_incident; and David Hoffman, "Shattered Shield: Cold-War Doctrines Refuse to Die," *Washington Post*, March 15, 1998, A01.

9   Blight and Blanton, "Cuban Missile Crisis," 3.

10 McNamara, "Forty Years after 13 Days," 8.

11 Ibid., 6.

12 Blight and Blanton, "Cuban Missile Crisis," 4.

13 McNamara quoting from Kennedy tapes, "Forty Years after 13 Days," 5.

14 McNamara, "Conversation in Havana," 3.

15 Hoffman, *Dead Hand*, 6–11.

16 Ibid., 23.

17 Ibid., 152.

18 Ibid., 24, 152–53.

19 Taubman, *The Partnership*, 40–41.

20 Ibid., 9.

21 Ibid., 256.

22 Blix, *Why Nuclear Disarmament Matters*, 55.

23 Shultz et al., "World Free of Nuclear Weapons," 4, 5, 8. See also *Wall Street Journal*, January 4, 2007, A15.

Chapter 2. The NPT and Nuclear Weapon–Free Zones

1   US Arms Control and Disarmament Agency, *Arms Control and Disarmament Agreements*, 83.

2   US Arms Control and Disarmament Agency, *Documents on Disarmament*, 694.

3   Shaker, *Nuclear Non-Proliferation Treaty*, 37.

4   Ibid., 904.

5   Graham and LaVera, *Cornerstones of Security*, 114.

6   Ibid.

7   Shaker, *Nuclear Non-Proliferation Treaty*, 920.

8   Ibid., 923–24.

9   Ibid.

10 Singh, "Against Nuclear Apartheid," 1.

11 Shaker, *Nuclear Non-Proliferation Treaty*, 924.

12 Alfonso Garcia Robles, quoted in UN General Assembly, *First Committee Provisional Verbatim Record*, 13 and 32; Michael Hamel-Green, "Peeling the Orange: Regional Paths to a Nuclear-Weapon-Free World," accessed February 16, 2015, http://nwp.ilpi. org/wp-content/uploads/2011/10/Peeling-the-orange_-regional-paths-to-a-nuclear-weapon-free-world.pdf.

13 Barack Obama, "Remarks Regarding Prague, Czech Republic," Office of the Press Secretary, White House, April 5, 2009.

14 Newhouse, *Cold Dawn*, 2–3.

15 Obama, "Remarks Regarding Prague, Czech Republic."

16 Vladimir Putin, quoted in Katie Saunders, "Did Vladimir Putin Call the Break-Up of the USSR 'the Greatest Geopolitical Tragedy of the 20th Century?'" *Punditfact*, March 6, 2014, http://www.politifact.com/punditfact/statements/2014/mar/06/john-bolton/did-vladimir-putin-call-breakup-ussr-greatest-geop/.

17 "Putin: No External Pressure on Russia Will Go Unchallenged," *RT*, February 20, 2015, http://on.rt.com/ap1q93.

18 Tom Parfitt, "Seven Reasons to Explain Vladimir Putin's Popularity Cult," *Telegraph*, November 27, 2014, http://www.telegraph.co.uk/news/worldnews/vladimir-putin/11257362/Seven-reasons-to-explain-Vladimir-Putins-popularity-cult.html.

19 David Remnick, "Watching the Eclipse," *New Yorker*, August 11 and 18, 2014, http://www.newyorker.com/magazine/2014/08/11/watching-eclipse.

20 Ibid.

21 Ibid.

22 Vladimir Putin, as quoted in ibid.

23 Ibid.

24 Michael McFaul, quoted in ibid.

25 Michael Birnbaum, "Russia's Anti-American Fever Goes beyond the Soviet Era's," *Washington Post*, March 8, 2015, https://www.washingtonpost.com/world/europe/russias-anti-us-sentiment-now-is-even-worse-than-it-was-in-soviet-union/2015/03/08/b7d534c4-c357-11e4-a188-8e4971d37a8d_story.html?utm_term=.9eb87db6b798.

26 Ibid.

27 Evgeny Tarlo, quoted in ibid.

28 Myers, *New Tsar*, 474.

29 Birnbaum, "Russia's Anti-American Fever."

30 Rossiyskaya Gazeta, "Military Specialists Advised Using All Means of Deterrence in 'Crimean Spring' Documentary," *Russia Beyond the Headlines*, March 16, 2015, http://www.rbth.com/news/2015/03/16/military_specialists_advised_using_all_means_of_deterrence_in_crimean_sp_44520.html.

Chapter 3. Treaty of Tlatelolco

1 Sotomayor, *U.S.-Latin American Nuclear Relations*, 2.

2 Ibid., 4.

3 Ibid., 10–11.

4 Ibid., 11–12.

5 Alfonso Garcia Robles, "The Latin American Nuclear-Weapon-Free Zone," Nobelprize.org, accessed April 15, 2016, http://www.nobelprize.org/nobel_prizes/peace/laureates/1982/robles-lecture.html.

6 Serrano, *Common Security in Latin America*, 6. The following paragraphs draw from Serrano's account.

7 Ibid., 8–9.

8 Ibid., 11–14.

9 Ibid., 13.

10 Ibid., 13–14.

11 Ibid., 14–15.

12 Ibid., 19.

13 Ibid., 19–20, citing Khrushchev from Dinersten, *Making of a Missile Crisis*, 82.

14 Serrano, *Common Security in Latin America*, 20.

15 Ibid., 21.

16 Allison, *Essence of Decision*, 39.

17 Serrano, *Common Security in Latin America*, 22–24.

18 Ibid., 26.

19 Garcia Robles, "Latin American Nuclear-Weapon-Free Zone."

20 Ibid.

21 Ibid.

22 "Article 5, Treaty for the Prohibition of Nuclear Weapons in Latin America (Tlatelolco Treaty)," International Atomic Energy Agency website, accessed April 17, 2016, https://www.iaea.org/publications/documents/treaties/ treaty-prohibition-nuclear-weapons-latin-america-tlatelolco-treaty.

23 "Article 17, Treaty for the Prohibition of Nuclear Weapons in Latin America (Tlatelolco Treaty)," International Atomic Energy Agency website, accessed June 8, 2017, https://www.iaea.org/publications/documents/treaties/ treaty-prohibition-nuclear-weapons-latin-america-tlatelolco-treaty.

24 Garcia Robles, *Latin American Nuclear-Weapon-Free Zone*, 18–19.

25 Ibid., 18.

26 Serrano, *Common Security in Latin America*, 78.

Chapter 4. The Treaty of Rarotonga

1 US Central Intelligence Agency, "French Nuclear Weapons Program," Current Intelligence Weekly Summary, September 18, 1958, 6 as quoted in Richelson, *Spying on the Bomb*, 206.

2 "Gerboise Bleue," Wikipedia, accessed April 19, 2016, https://en.wikipedia.org/wiki/ Gerboise_Bleue.

3 Charles de Gaulle quoted in Gaddis, "Nuclear Statesman," 231.

4 Richelson, *Spying on the Bomb*, 206. The paragraphs that follow draw heavily on Richelson's account.

5 Ibid., 207.

6 Ibid.

7 Ibid., 207–8.

8 Ibid., 208–9.

9 Ibid., 209–10.

10 Maclellan, "Public Opposition Resistance to Nuclear Testing," 10.

11 Ibid.

12 Tish Falco, "French Nuclear Testing in the South Pacific," ICE Case Studies: Mururoa, Case #4, Trade and Environment Database, accessed April 19, 2016, http://mandal-aprojects.com/ice/ice-cases/mururoa.htm.

13 Maclellan, "Public Opposition Resistance to Nuclear Testing," 5.

13 Ibid.

14 Ibid., 6.

15 Weyler, *Greenpeace*, 134.

16 Stanley, *South Pacific Handbook*, 262.

17 Angelique Chrisafis, "French Nuclear Tests 'Showered Vast Area of Polynesia with Radioactivity,'" *The Guardian*, US ed., July 3, 2013, http://www.theguardian.com/world/2013/jul/03/french-nuclear-tests-polynesia-declassified.

18 "'Nuclear Reaction': French Polynesia to Demand Nearly $1bn from Paris over Tests," RT, November 25, 2014, http://rt.com/news/208599-french-polynesia-nuclear-tests/.

19 Barnes, *French Nuclear Tests in the South Pacific*, 3.

20 Ibid., 4.

21 Hamel-Green, *South Pacific Nuclear-Free Zone Treaty*, 1.

22 Hamel-Green, "Antinuclear Campaigning," 52.

23 Ibid.; the Menzies quotation is from *Commonwealth Parliamentary Debates, House of Representatives*, May 15, 1962, 2318–29.

24 Hamel-Green, "Antinuclear Campaigning," 53–54.

25 Ibid., 54.

26 Hamel-Green, *South Pacific Nuclear-Free Zone Treaty*, 82–84.

27 Ibid., 83–87.

28 Hamel-Green, "Antinuclear Campaigning," 55.

29 Ibid.

30 Hamel-Green, *South Pacific Nuclear-Free Zone Treaty*, 73-74.

31 Ibid., 74.

32 Ibid., 74-75.

33 Ibid., 69-70.

Chapter 5. Treaty of Pelindaba

1   Richelson, *Spying on the Bomb*, 243.

2   Ibid.

3   Ibid., 243–44.

4   Ibid., 244–45.

5   Steyn et al., *Nuclear Armament and Disarmament*, 13.

6   Ibid., 13–14.

7   Ibid., 14.

8   Ibid., 39–40.

9   Richelson, *Spying on the Bomb*, 277.

10 Ibid., 278.

11 Ibid., 278–81.

12 Ibid., 281.

13 Ibid., 283.

14 Ibid., 286.

15 Ibid., 294–304. Richelson details the work of the Ruina panel.

16 Ibid., 304.

17 Ibid., 309.

18 Ibid., 313–16.

19 Steyn et al., *Nuclear Armament and Disarmament*, 42.

20 Richelson, *Spying on the Bomb*, 370.

21 Ibid.

22 Ibid., 371.

23 Ibid., 372–73.

24 Ibid., 373.

25 Ibid., 325.

26 Ibid., 32–27.

27 Adeniji, *Treaty of Pelindaba*, 2.

28 Ibid., 8.

29 Ibid., 35.

30 "Israeli Friends," Institute for Science and International Security, May 1994, accessed April 22, 2016, http://isis-online.org/uploads/isis-reports/documents/Israeli_friends.pdf. See also Richelson, *Spying on the Bomb*, 283.

31 Adeniji, *Treaty of Pelindaba*, 52–54.

32 Ibid., 60–62.

33 Ibid., 63–69.

34 Ibid., 71–74.

35 Ibid., 75–101.

36 Ibid., 109.

37 Ibid., 149.

38 Ibid., 142.

39 Ibid., 154–55.

Chapter 6. Treaty of Bangkok

1 Haacke, *ASEAN's Diplomatic and Security Culture*, 1.

2 Ibid., 53.

3   Ibid., 54–56.

4   Ibid., 57.

5   Ibid., 59–60.

6   Ibid., 65–68.

7   "Southeast Asian Nuclear-Weapon-Free-Zone [SEANWFZ] Treaty [Bangkok Treaty]," NTI, September 22, 2016, http://www.nti.org/treaties-and-regimes/southeast-asian-nuclear-weapon-free-zone-seanwfz-treaty-bangkok-treaty/.

8   Laursen, *Southeast Asia and Nuclear Weapons.*

9   Graham, *Disarmament Sketches,* 296–301.

10 Ibid., 301.

11 Laursen, *Southeast Asia and Nuclear Weapons.*

12 Haacke, *ASEAN's Diplomatic and Security Culture,* 246n25.

13 Laursen, *Southeast Asia and Nuclear Weapons.*

14 Ibid.

15 Ibid.

16 Crail and Liang, "Southeast Asia Nuclear-Weapon-Free Zone and the Nuclear-Weapon States."

17 "Southeast Asian Nuclear-Weapon-Free-Zone [SEANWFZ] Treaty."

18 Laursen, Southeast Asia and Nuclear Weapons.

19 Haacke, *ASEAN's Diplomatic and Security Culture,* 164.

Chapter 7. Treaty of Semipalatinsk and Mongolia as a Single-State Nuclear Weapon–Free Zone

1   Graham, *Disarmament Sketches,* 285.

2   Ibid., 134-35

3   Burk, "Nuclear-Weapon-Free Zones," 311.

4   Roscini, "Something Old, Something New," 595.

5   Burk, "Nuclear-Weapon-Free Zones," 312.

6   Ibid.

7   Roscini, "Something Old, Something New," 596.

8   Ibid.

9   William Potter, Togzhan Kassenova, and Anya Loukianova, "Central Asia Becomes a Nuclear-Weapon-Free-Zone," Middlebury Institute of International Studies at Monterey website, December 11, 2008, http://www.nonproliferation.org/central-asia-becomes-a-nuclear-weapon-free-zone/.

10 Roscini, "Something Old, Something New," 596.

11 Scott Parrish and William Potter, "Central Asian States Establish Nuclear-Weapon-Free-Zone Despite U.S. Opposition," James Martin Center for Nonproliferation Studies (September 5, 2006), cited in "Central Asian Nuclear Weapon Free Zone," Wikipedia, last updated September 4, 2015, accessed April 24, 2016, https://en.wikipedia.org/wiki/Central_Asian_Nuclear_Weapon_Free_Zone.

Chapter 8. Where We Are, and Where and How We Must Go

1 Graham, "A Farewell to ACDA," 24.

2 Ibid. 25.

3 Ibid.

4 Ibid.

5 Ibid., 28.

6 Ratz, *Organizing for Arms Control*, 18.

7 Ibid., 4.

8 Ibid., 26.

9 Ibid., 23.

10 Ibid., 21.

Chapter 9. The Middle East

1 Mandy Katz, "Do We Divide the Holiest Holy City?," *Moment Magazine*, June 3, 2008, http://www.momentmag.com/do-we-divide-the-holiest-holy-city/.

2 Cohen, *Israel and the Bomb*, 236.

3 Ibid., 236–40.

4 Ibid., 31.

5 Cirincione et al., *Deadly Arsenals*, 264.

6 Richelson, *Spying on the Bomb*, 240.

7 Cohen, *Israel and the Bomb*, 231.

8 Ibid., 273–74.

9 Ibid, 116.

10 Ibid., 88.

11 Ibid., 90, 101.

12 Jeffrey Lewis, "Israel, Nuclear Weapons and the 1973 Yom Kippur War," *Arms Control Wonk*, October 21, 2013, http://www.armscontrolwonk.com/archive/206909/israel-nuclear-weapons-and-the-1973-yom-kippur-war/#_ftn1.

13 Cohen, *Israel and the Bomb*, 361-67.

14 Cohen, *Worst Kept Secret*, 26, 27, 31. See also Cohen, *Israel and the Bomb*, 336–37.

15 Takeyh, *Hidden Iran*, 136.

16 Ibid., 121.

17 Ibid., 128–29.

18 Graham, *Unending Crisis*, 40.

19 Gates, Duty, 190–93, and "Why Give Iran a Reason Not to Fear a Military Attack," *Washington Post*, November 18, 2010, http://www.washingtonpost.com/wp-dyn/content/article/2010/11/18/AR2010111805728.html.

20 Thomas Erdbrink, "Post-Deal Iran Asks if U.S. Is Still 'Great Satan,' or Something Less," *New York Times*, September 17, 2015, http://www.nytimes.com/2015/09/18/world/middleeast/post-deal-iran-asks-if-us-is-still-great-satan-or-something-less.html. A print version of this article appeared September 18, 2015, on page A1 of the New York edition with the headline "Post-Deal Iran Reappraising 'Great Satan.'"

21 Richelson, *Spying on the Bomb*, 322.

22 Ibid., 334.

23 Ibid., 448–69.

24 Blix, *Disarming Iraq*, 156.

25 Lauren Johnston, "Powell '01: WMDs Not Significant," *CBS News*, last modified September 28, 2003, http://www.cbsnews.com/news/powell-01-wmds-not-significant/.

26 Suskind, *Way of the World*, 362–69.

27 Graham and Hansen, *Preventing Catastrophe*, 75.

28 Robin Wright, "N. Korea Taped at Syrian Reactor," *Washington Post*, April 24, 2008, http://www.washingtonpost.com/wp-dyn/content/article/2008/04/23/AR2008042302906.html.

29 Randall Mikkelsen, "Update 2—Syrian Reactor Capacity Was 1-2 Weapons/Year," *Reuters*, UK ed., April 29, 2008, http://uk.reuters.com/article/korea-north-usa-idUKN2820597020080429.

30 Associated Press, "IAEA Chastises U.S., Israel over Syrian Reactor: Lack of Information Sharing, Unilateral Arrack Anger Nuclear Watchdog," *NBCNews.com*, last updated April 25, 2008, http://www.nbcnews.com/id/24306434/ns/world_news-mideast_n_africa/t/iaea-chastises-us-israel-over-syrian-reactor/#.Vx-516MrJoI.

31 Peter Crail, "US Shares Information on NK-Syrian Nuclear Ties," *Arms Control Today*, June 11, 2008, https://www.armscontrol.org/act/2008_05/NKSyria.

32 Spector and Cohen, "Israel's Airstrike on Syrian Reactor."

33 Richelson, *Spying on the Bomb*, 324–27.

34 Corera, *Shopping for Bombs*, 108–9, 179.

35 Ibid., 176–94.

36 Mark Urban, "Saudi Nuclear Weapons 'On Order' from Pakistan," *BBC News*, November 6, 2013, http://www.bbc.com/news/world-middle-east-24823846.

37 Ibid.

38 Ibid.

39 Ibid.

40 "Algeria," Nuclear Threat Initiative website, accessed April 26, 2016, http://www.nti. org/learn/countries/algeria/.

41 "Egypt," Nuclear Threat Initiative website, accessed April 26, 2016, http://www.nti.org/ learn/countries/egypt/nuclear/.

42 "WMD-Free Middle East Proposal at a Glance," Arms Control Association website, last accessed April 26, 2016, https://www.armscontrol.org/factsheets/mewmdfz.

43 Ibid.

44 Ibid.

45 Associated Press, "Diplomats: Mideast Nuke Talks Called Off," *USA Today*, last updated November 11, 2012, http://www.usatoday.com/story/news/world/2012/11/11/ mideast-nuke-talks-npt/1697215/.

46 Lianet Vazquez, *Toward the 2015 NPT Review Conference: Attitudes and Expectations of Member States in the Middle East* (London: British American Security Information Council, October 2014), http://www.basicint.org/sites/default/files/ LVazquez_2015NPTRevCon_Oct2014.pdf.

47 "WMD-Free Middle East Proposal at a Glance."

48 Dexter Filkins, "Shot in the Heart," *New Yorker*, October 26, 2015, http://www.newyorker.com/magazine/2015/10/26/shot-in-the-heart.

Chapter 10. Northeast Asia

1 Jake Adelstein, "New Evidence of Japan's Effort to Build Atom Bomb at the End of WWII," *Los Angeles Times*, August 5, 2015, http://www.latimes.com/world/asia/la-fg-japan-bomb-20150805-story.html.

2 Wikipedia, s.v. "Japanese Nuclear Weapon Program," accessed April 27, 2016, https:// en.wikipedia.org/wiki/Japanese_nuclear_weapon_program.

3 Ibid.

4 Ibid., citing Park, *U.S. and the Two Koreas*, 111.

5 K. J. Kwon, "Under Threat, South Koreans Mull Nuclear Weapons," *CNN*, March 18, 2013, http://www.cnn.com/2013/03/18/world/asia/south-korea-nuclear/.

6 Phillip Iglauer, "Nuclear Weapons for South Korea: Under Threat of a Possible Fourth North Korean Nuclear Test, Should South Korea Develop Its Own Nuclear Weapon?," *The Diplomat*, August 14, 2014, http://thediplomat.com/2014/08/ nuclear-weapons-for-south-korea/.

7 Wikipedia, s.v. "South Korea Nuclear Research Programs," accessed April 27, 2016, https://en.wikipedia.org/wiki/South_Korean_nuclear_research_programs, citing Troy

Standarone, "Why South Korea Won't Develop Nuclear Weapons," *The Peninsula*, May 13, 2013, http://blog.keia.org/2013/05/why-south-korea-wont-develop-nuclear-weapons/.

8   Chant and Hogg, *Nuclear War in the 1980's?*, 58-59.

9   "South Korean Nuclear History," Wilson Center Digital Archive, accessed April 27, 2016, http://digitalarchive.wilsoncenter.org/collection/128/south-korean-nuclear-history.

10   Ibid.

11   Wikipedia, s.v. "South Korea Nuclear Research Programs," citing "South Korea Special Weapons," GlobalSecurity.org, accessed April 27, 2016, http://www.globalsecurity.org/wmd/world/rok/index.html.

12   William Burr, "Stopping Korea from Going Nuclear," George Washington University National Security Archive, March 22, 2017, http://nsarchive.gwu.edu/nukevault/ebb582-The-U.S.-and-the-South-Korean-Nuclear-Program,-1974-1976,-Part-1/.

13   Chen Kane, Stephanie C. Lieggi, and Miles A. Pomper, "Time for Leadership: South Korea and Nuclear Nonproliferation," *Arms Control Today*, March 3, 2011, https://www.armscontrol.org/act/2011_03/SouthKorea.

14   Ibid.

15   Ibid.

16   Wikipedia, "South Korea Nuclear Research Programs," citing "South Korea Special Weapons," GlobalSecurity.org.

17   Ibid.

18   Richelson, *Spying on the Bomb*, 332.

19   Ibid., 333.

20   For details on IAEA inspections, see ibid., 517-23.

21   Reiss, *Bridled Ambition*, 240-52.

22   Ibid., 251–80.

23   Chinoy, *Meltdown*, 9–10.

24   Ibid., 19.

25   Ibid., 20, 25–26.

26   Ibid., 35.

27   Ibid., 43.

28   Ibid, 50.

29   Ibid, 55.

30   Ibid, 59.

31   Ibid, 77–78.

32   Pritchard, *Failed Diplomacy*, 35.

33   Ibid., 38–39.

34 Glen Kessler, "Far Reaching U.S. Plan Impaired North Korea Deal," *Washington Post*, September 26, 2008, http://www.washingtonpost.com/wp-dyn/content/article/2008/09/25/AR2008092504380.html.

35 David E. Sanger and William J. Broad, "U.S. Concludes North Korea Has More Missile Sites," *New York Times*, December 14, 2010, http://www.nytimes.com/2010/12/15/world/asia/15nukes.html?_r=0.

36 Uzi Mahnaimi, Michael Sheridan, and Shota Ushio, "Iran Steps Deep into Kim's Nuclear Huddle," *London Sunday Times*, February 17, 2013, http://www.thesundaytimes.co.uk/sto/news/world_news/Middle_East/article1215608.ece.

37 Ibid.

38 Ibid.

39 James M. Acton, "Focus on Nonproliferation—Not Disarmament in North Korea," Carnegie Endowment for International Peace website, February 14, 2013, http://carnegieendowment.org/2013/02/14/focus-on-nonproliferation-not-disarmament-in-north-korea.

40 Ibid.

41 Foster Klug, "Nuclear Weapons Are 'Life of the Nation', says North Korea," *Independent*, March 31, 2013, http://www.independent.co.uk/news/world/asia/nuclear-weapons-are-the-life-of-the-nation-says-north-korea-8555615.html.

42 Alexandre Y. Mansourov, "Kim Jong Un's Nuclear Doctrine and Strategy: What Everyone Needs to Know," *NASPNET Special Reports*, December 16, 2014, http://nautilus.org/napsnet/napsnet-special-reports/kim-jong-uns-nuclear-doctrine-and-strategy-what-everyone-needs-to-know.

43 Ibid.

44 Ibid.

45 Ibid.

46 Ibid.

47 Cha, *Impossible State*, 468.

48 Daryl G. Kimball, "North Korea and Nuclear Testing," *Arms Control Today*, January/February 2016, http://www.armscontrol.org/ACT/2016_0102/Focus/North-Korea-and-Nuclear-Testing.

49 Ju-min Park and Tony Munroe, "WRAPUP 6-South Korea Calls for 'Bone-Numbing' Sanctions on North for Nuclear Test," *Reuters*, January 13, 2016, http://www.reuters.com/article/northkorea-nuclear-idUSL2N14X0222016013.

50 Somini Sengupta, David E. Sanger, and Choe Sang-Hun, "Security Council Condemns Nuclear Test by North Korea," website of the *New York Times*, January 6, 2016, https://www.nytimes.com/2016/01/07/world/asia/north-korea-hydrogen-bomb-claim-reactions.html.

51 Greg Miller and Anna Fifield, "U.N. Condemns North Korean Launch after an Emergency Meeting," *Washington Post*, Press Reader, February 7, 2016, https://www.

washingtonpost.com/world/national-security/un-condemns-north-korean-launch-after-an-emergency-meeting/2016/02/07/01a89d9a-cdb4-11e5-88cd-753e80cd29ad_story.html?utm_term=.7e22f704e2a2.

52 "North Korea 'Expands Plutonium Production,' says US," *BBC News*, February 9, 2016, http://www.bbc.com/news/world-asia-35534995.

53 Jack Kim, "North Korea Leader Tells Military to Be Ready to Use Nuclear Weapons," *Reuters*, March 4, 2016, https://ca.news.yahoo.com/north-korea-leader-tells-military-ready-nuclear-weapons-002910835.html.

54 Joel S. Wit, "How 'Crazy' Are North Koreans?," *New York Times*, January 10, 2016, http://www.nytimes.com/2016/01/10/opinion/sunday/how-crazy-are-the-north-koreans.html.

55 Jim Walsh and John Park, "To Stop the Missiles, Stop North Korea, Inc.," *New York Times*, March 10, 2016, http://www.nytimes.com/2016/03/10/opinion/to-stop-the-missiles-stop-north-korea-inc.html.

56 Victor Cha and Robert L. Gallucci, "Stopping North Korea's Nuclear Threat," *New York Times*, January 8, 2016, http://www.nytimes.com/2016/01/08/opinion/stopping-north-koreas-nuclear-threat.html.

57 Hiromichi Umebayashi, "A Possible Approach for Establishing a Northeast Asia Nuclear-Weapon-Free Zone," Research Center for Nuclear Weapons, Nagasaki University, January 30 to February 1, 2013, http://www.recna.nagasaki-u.ac.jp/recna/eyes/n02.

58 "Supreme Leader Kim Jong Un's Report to the Seventh Congress of the Workers' Party of Korea on the Work of the Central Committee," accessed April 29, 2017, http://www.ncnk.org/resources/news-items/kim-jong-uns-speeches-and-public-statements-1/KJU_Speeches_7th_Congress.pdf.

59 Anna Fifield, "N. Korea Carries Out Nuclear Test, Experts Say," *New York Times*, September 9, 2016, PA-1.

60 Max Fisher, "North Korea Crazy? Worse. It's Calculating," *New York Times*, September 11, 2016, PA-6.

61 Joby Warrick, "Anxiety Grows over North Korea's Arsenal: 'Danger Is Now Miscalculation,'" *Washington Post*, March 11, 2017, http://www.baltimoresun.com/news/nation-world/ct-north-korea-weapons-arsenal-20170311-story.html.

62 Ibid.

Chapter 11. South Asia

1 Perkovich, *India's Nuclear Bomb*, 16.

2 Richelson, *Spying on the Bomb*, 219.

3 Perkovich, *India's Nuclear Bomb*, 16-17.

4 Richelson, *Spying on the Bomb*, 219.

5 Perkovich, *India's Nuclear Bomb*, 19–20.

6 Ibid., 20.

7 Ibid., 17.

8 Ibid., 14.

9 Ibid., 36.

10 Richelson, *Spying on the Bomb*, 220–21.

11 Ibid., 221.

12 Ibid., 223.

13 Ibid., 223–24.

14 Perkovich, *India's Nuclear Bomb*, 175.

15 Ramanna, *Years of Pilgrimage*, 89.

16 Perkovich, *India's Nuclear Bomb*, 178.

17 Richelson, *Spying on the Bomb*, 231–33.

18 Ibid, 232.

19 Ibid., 427–28.

20 Perkovich, *India's Nuclear Bomb*, 243.

21 Ibid., 248–49.

22 Ibid., 253–54.

23 Ibid., 263, 276.

24 Ibid., 281.

25 Ibid., 283.

26 Ibid., 286.

27 Ibid., 293–295.

28 Richelson, *Spying on the Bomb*, 429.

29 Ibid., 430–32.

30 Ibid., 432.

31 Ibid., 434.

32 Ibid., 438–39, 445–46.

33 Ibid., 446.

34 Metcalf and Metcalf, *Concise History of Modern India*, 293.

35 Ibid., 295.

36 Ibid., 294.

37 Hensman, "Why India and Pakistan Should Denuclearize," 25–26.

38 Arundhati Roy, website of *Frontline: India's National Magazine* 15, No. 16 (August 1–14, 1998), http://www.frontline.in/navigation/?type=static&page=archiveSearch&aid=151 60040&ais=16&avol=15.

39 Jayshree Bajoria and Esther Pan, "The US-India Nuclear Deal," Council on Foreign Relations website, November 5, 2010, http://www.cfr.org/india/us-india-nuclear-deal/ p9663.

40 Tellis, *Atoms for War?*

41 Jimmy Carter, "A Dangerous Deal with India," *Washington Post*, March 28, 2006, http://www.cartercenter.org/news/documents/doc2335.html.

42 Brahma Chellaney, "India's Retarded Nuclear Deterrent: The Impotent Bomb," *Stagecraft and Statecraft,* September 21, 2008, https://chellaney.net/2008/09/21/ indias-retarded-nuclear-deterrent/.

43 Rashid, *Descent into Chaos*, 34.

44 Ibid., 35.

45 Ibid.

46 Ibid.

47 Ibid., 33.

48 Khan, *Eating Grass*, 7.

49 Ibid., 7–8.

50 Ibid., 8.

51 Ibid., 7.

52 Hoodbhoy, "Nationalism and the Bomb," 135–36.

53 Rashid, *Descent into Chaos*, 38.

54 Ibid., 38–39.

55 Ibid., 265.

56 Corera, *Shopping for Bombs*, xiii.

57 Franz and Collins, *Nuclear Jihadist,* 208–10.

58 Ibid., 169–71.

59 Rashid, *Descent into Chaos*, 40.

60 Richelson, *Spying on the Bomb*, 331.

61 Khan, *Eating Grass*, 254.

62 Ibid.

63 Reiss, *Bridled Ambition*, 187–88, 192.

64 Corea, *Shopping for Bombs*, 48–49.

65 Richelson, *Spying on the Bomb*, 435.

66 Khan, *Eating Grass*, 271.

67 Ibid., 275–77.

68 Ibid., 278.

69 Ibid., 279–82.

70 Richelson, *Spying on the Bomb*, 436.

71 Ibid., 440.

72 Michael Krepon, "Looking Back: The 1998 Indian and Pakistani Nuclear Tests," Arms Control Today, May 2008, https://www.armscontrol.org/act/2008_05/lookingback.

73 "Pakistan Announces Testing Moratorium, Seeks Talks with India," *Chicago Tribune*, June 12, 1998, articles.chicagotribune.com/1998-06-12/news/9806120113_1_nuclear-escalation-india-and-pakistan-test-ban.

74 Khan, *Eating Grass*, 346–48.

75 Ibid., 350.

76 Ibid., 350–51.

77 Ibid. See also Smith, "The 2001-2002 Standoff." See also Khan, "Nuclear Signaling."

78 "Nuclear Weapons: Who Has What at a Glance," Arms Control Association Website, last updated July 2017, accessed July 28, 2017, https://www.armscontrol.org/factsheets/Nuclearweaponswhohaswhat.

79 Khan, *Eating Grass*, 396.

80 Nayyar and Mian, *Limited Military Utility of Pakistan's Battlefield Use of Nuclear Weapons*.

81 Khan, *Eating Grass*, 389–90.

Chapter 12. The P-5 and the Future

1 "Nuclear Weapons: Who Has What at a Glance," Arms Control Association Website, last updated July 2017, accessed July 28, 2017, https://www.armscontrol.org/factsheets/Nuclearweaponswhohaswhat.

2 Graham, "Nuclear Weapons Elimination," 20–21.

3 Thomas Graham Jr., "A New Pathway to Prohibiting Nuclear Testing," *WMD Junction*, June 3, 2014, http://wmdjunction.com/140603_prohibiting_nuclear_testing.htm.

4 Koplow, "Nuclear Arms Control by a Pen and a Phone", 475–518.

Bibliography

Adeniji, Oluyemi. *The Treaty of Pelindaba on the African Nuclear Weapon Free Zone.* Geneva: United Nations, 2002.

Allison, Graham T. *Essence of Decision: Explaining the Cuban Missile.* Boston: Little, Brown, 1971.

Barnes, Bruce E. *The French Nuclear Tests in the South Pacific: Case Study of an International Environmental Dispute.* Honolulu: University of Hawaii, Spark M. Matsunaga Institute for Peace and Conflict Resolution, 1987.

Blight, James, and Tom Blanton. "The Cuban Missile Crisis: Revisited on the Anniversary." *Arms Control Today* 32, no. 9 (November 2002): 3.

Blix, Hans. *Disarming Iraq.* New York: Pantheon Books, 2004.

———. *Why Nuclear Disarmament Matters.* Cambridge: Massachusetts Institute of Technology Press, 2008.

Burk, Susan. "Nuclear-Weapon-Free Zones." In *Routledge Handbook of Nuclear Proliferation and Policy,* edited by Joseph F. Pilat and Nathan E. Busch, 306-16. New York: Routledge, 2015.

Cha, Victor. *The Impossible State: North Korea Past and Future.* New York: Harper Collins, 2012.

Chant, Christopher, and Ian Hogg. *Nuclear War in the 1980's?* New York: Harper & Row, 1983.

Chinoy, Mike. *Meltdown: The Inside Story of the North Korean Nuclear Crisis.* New York: St. Martin's Press, 2008.

Cirincione, Joseph, Jon B. Wolfsthal, and Miriam Rajkumar. *Deadly Arsenals: Nuclear, Biological, and Chemical Threats.* 2nd ed. Washington, DC: Carnegie Endowment for International Peace, 2005.

Cohen, Avner. *Israel and the Bomb.* New York: Columbia University Press, 1998.

———. *The Worst Kept Secret: Israel's Bargain with the Bomb.* New York: Columbia University Press, 2012.

Corera, Gordon. *Shopping for Bombs: Nuclear Proliferation, Global Insecurity, and the Rise and Fall of the A. Q. Khan Network.* Oxford: Oxford University Press, 2006.

Crail, Peter, and Xiaodon Liang. "Southeast Asia Nuclear-Weapon-Free Zone and the

Nuclear-Weapon States." *Asian Pacific Bulletin* 148 (2012): 1-2. https://www.ciaonet. org/attachments/20720/uploads.

Dallek, Robert. *An Unfinished Life: John F. Kennedy, 1917-1963*. New York: Little, Brown, 2003.

Dinersten, Herbert S. *The Making of a Missile Crisis*. Baltimore: Johns Hopkins University Press, 1976.

Franz, Douglas, and Catherine Collins. *The Nuclear Jihadist: The True Story of the Man Who Sold the World's Most Dangerous Secrets . . . and How We Could Have Stopped Him*. New York: Hachette, 2007.

Gaddis, John Lewis. "Nuclear Statesman." In *Cold War Statesmen Confront the Bomb: Cold War Diplomacy Since 1945*, edited by John Lewis Gaddis, Philip H. Gordon, Earnest R. May, and Jonathan Rosenberg. Oxford: Oxford University Press, 1999.

Garcia Robles, Alfonso. *The Latin American Nuclear-Weapon-Free Zone*. Occasional Paper 19. Muscatine, IA: Stanley Foundation, 1979.

Gates, Robert M. *Duty: Memoirs of a Secretary at War*. New York: Alfred A. Knopf, 2014.

Graham, Thomas, Jr. "A Farewell to ACDA," *Foreign Service Journal* 76, no. 9 (September 1999): 24.

———. "A New Pathway to Prohibiting Nuclear Testing," *WMD Junction* (June 3, 2014). http://wmdjunction.com/140603_prohibiting_nuclear_testing.htm.

———. *Disarmament Sketches*. Seattle: University of Washington Press, 2002.

———. "Nuclear Weapons Elimination: A Process." In *Implications of the Reykjavik Summit on Its Twentieth Anniversary*, edited by G. P. Shultz and S. Drell. Stanford, CA: Stanford University, 2006.

———. *Unending Crisis: National Security Policy after 9/11*. Seattle: University of Washington Press, 2012.

Graham, Thomas, Jr., and Keith A. Hansen. *Preventing Catastrophe: The Use and Misuse of Intelligence in Efforts to Halt the Proliferation of Weapons of Mass Destruction*. Stanford: Stanford University Press, 2009.

Graham, Thomas, Jr., and Damien J. LaVera. *Cornerstones of Security: Arms Control Treaties in the Nuclear Era*. Seattle: University of Washington Press, 2003.

Haacke, Jürgen. *ASEAN's Diplomatic and Security Culture, Origins, Development, and Prospects*. London: Routledge, 2003.

Hamel-Green, Michael. *The South Pacific Nuclear-Free Zone Treaty: A Critical Assessment*. Canberra: Peace Research School on Pacific Studies, Australian National University, 1990.

———. "Antinuclear Campaigning and the South Pacific Nuclear-Free Zone (Rarotonga) Treaty, 1960-85." In *Proceedings of the 14th Biennial Labour History Conference*, edited by Phillip Deery and Julie Kimber, 51-62. Melbourne: Australian Society for the Study of Labour History, 2015. https://labourhistorymelbourne.files.wordpress.com/2015/02/antinuclear-campaigning-and-the-south-pacific-lh-proceedings2.pdf.

Hensman, Rohini. "Why India and Pakistan Should Denuclearize and Sign the Comprehensive Test Ban Treaty." *Bulletin of Concerned Asian Scholars* 31, no. 2 (April–June 1999): 23-36.

Hoffman, David E. *The Dead Hand.* New York: Random House, 2009.

Hoodbhoy, Pervez. "Nationalism and the Bomb." In *Confronting the Bomb, Pakistani and Indian Scientists Speak Out,* edited by Pervez Hoodbhoy and J. C. Polanyi, 90-116. Oxford: Oxford University Press, 2013.

Khan, Feroz Hassan. "Nuclear Signaling, Missiles, and Escalation Control in South Asia." In *Escalation Control and the Nuclear Option in South Asia,* edited by Michael Krepon, Rodney W. Jones, and Ziad Haider, 75-100. Washington, DC: Henry L. Stimson Center, 2004.

———. *Eating Grass: The Making of the Pakistani Bomb.* Stanford, CA: Stanford University Press, 2012.

Koplow, David A. "Nuclear Arms Control by a Pen and a Phone: Effectuating the Comprehensive Test Ban Treaty without Ratification." *Georgetown Journal of International Law* 46, no. 2 (Winter 2015): 475-518.

Laursen, Halle Winge. *Southeast Asia and Nuclear Weapons: An Introduction to the Issue of Nuclear Weapons in Southeast Asia.* Oslo, Norway: International Law and Policy Institute (ILPI). http://nwp.ilpi.org/wp-content/uploads/2015/12/Southeast-Asia-nuclear-weapons.pdf.

Maclellan, Nic, ed. "Public Opposition Resistance to Nuclear Testing and the Build-up of Nuclear Arms." In *Banning Nuclear Weapons: A Pacific Island Perspective.* Australia: International Campaign to Abolish Nuclear Weapons, 2014. http://studylib.net/doc/18465042/banning-nuclear-weapons---a-pacific-islands-perspective.

McNamara, Robert. "A Conversation in Havana." *Arms Control Today* 32, no. 9 (November 2002): 6-7.

———. "Forty Years after 13 Days." *Arms Control Today* 32, no. 9 (November 2002): 4-8.

Metcalf, Barbara D., and Thomas R. Metcalf. *A Concise History of Modern India.* 2nd ed. Cambridge: Cambridge University Press, 2006.

Myers, Steven Lee. *The New Tsar: The Rise and Reign of Vladimir Putin.* New York: Alfred A. Knopf, 2016.

Nayyar, A. H., and Zia Mian. *The Limited Military Utility of Pakistan's Battlefield Use of Nuclear Weapons in Response to Large Scale Indian Conventional Attack.* Brief Number 61. Bradford, UK: Pakistan Security Research Unit, 2010. https://www.princeton.edu/sgs/faculty-staff/zia-mian/Limited-Military-Utility-of-Pakistans.pdf.

Newhouse, John. *Cold Dawn: The Story of SALT.* New York: Holt, Rinehart and Wilson, 1973.

Park, Tong Whan. *The U.S. and the Two Koreas: A New Triangle*. Boulder, CO: Lynne Rienner, 1998.

Perkovich, George. *India's Nuclear Bomb: The Impact on Global Proliferation*. Berkeley: University of California Press, 1999.

Pihaatae, Francois. "A United Pacific Voice to Ban Nuclear Weapons" (Preface). In *Banning Nuclear Weapons: A Pacific Island Perspective*," edited by Nic Maclellan. Australia: International Campaign to Abolish Nuclear Weapons, 2014.

Pritchard, Charles L. *Failed Diplomacy: The Tragic Story of How North Korea Got the Bomb*. Washington, DC: Brookings Institution Press, 2007.

Ramanna, Raja. *Years of Pilgrimage: An Autobiography*. New Delhi: Viking, 1991.

Rashid, Ahmed. *Descent into Chaos: The U.S. and the Disaster in Pakistan, Afghanistan, and Central Asia*. New York: Penguin, 2009.

Ratz, Leon. *Organizing for Arms Control: The National Security Implications of the Loss of an Independent Arms Control Agency*. Discussion Paper 2013-06. Cambridge, MA: Belfer Center for Science and International Affairs, Harvard Kennedy School, September 2013. http://belfercenter.ksg.harvard.edu/files/Organizing%20for%20Arms%20Control%20-%20Web%203.pdf.

Rhodes, Richard. *The Making of the Atomic Bomb*. New York: Simon and Shuster, 1986.

Richelson, Jeffrey T. *Spying on the Bomb, American Nuclear Intelligence from Nazi Germany to Iran and North Korea*. New York: W. W. Norton, 2006.

Roscini, Marco. "Something Old, Something New: The 2006 Semipalatinsk Treaty on a Nuclear Weapon-Free Zone in Central Asia." *Chinese Journal of International Law 7*, no. 3 (2008): 539-624.

Russ, Mitchell. *Bridled Ambition: Why Countries Constrain Their Nuclear Capabilities*. Washington, DC: Woodrow Wilson Center Press, 1995.

Serrano, Monica. *Common Security in Latin America*. London: University of London Institute of Latin American Studies, 1992.

Shaker, Mohamed I. *The Nuclear Non Proliferation Treaty, Origin and Implementation, 1959-1979*. London: Oceana, 1980.

Shultz, George P., William J. Perry, Henry A. Kissinger, and Sam Nunn. "A World Free of Nuclear Weapons." In *Implications of the Reykjavik Summit on Its Twentieth Anniversary*, edited by Sidney D. Drell and George P. Shultz, 3-8. Stanford, CA: Hoover Institution Press, 2007.

Singh, Jaswant. "Against Nuclear Apartheid." *Foreign Affairs* (September/October 1998): 41-52.

Smith, David. "The 2001-2002 Standoff: A Real-Time View from Islamabad." In *The India-Pakistan Military Standoff: Crisis and Escalation in South Asia*, edited by Zachary S. David, 187-212. New York: Palgrave Macmillan, 2011.

Sotomayor, Arturo. *U.S.-Latin American Nuclear Relations: From Commitment to Defiance.* Monterey, CA: Naval Postgraduate School and Center on Contemporary Conflict, 2012.

Spector, Leonard, and Avner Cohen. "Israel's Airstrike on Syrian Reactor: Implications for the Nonproliferation Regime." *Arms Control Today* (July-August 2008). http://www.armscontrol.org/act/2008_07-08/SpectorCohen.

Stanley, David. *South Pacific Handbook.* 7th ed. Emeryville, CA: Avalon Travel Publishing, 2000.

Steyn, Hannes, Richardt Van Der Walt, and Jan Van Loggerenberg. *Nuclear Armament and Disarmament, South Africa's Nuclear Experience.* Shanghai: iUniverse, 2007.

Suskind, Ron. *The Way of the World: A Story of Truth and Hope in an Age of Extremism.* New York: Harper Collins, 2008.

Takeyh, Ray. *Hidden Iran: Paradox and Power in the Islamic Republic.* New York: Henry Holt, 2006.

Taubman, Philip. *The Partnership.* New York: Harper Collins, 2012.

Tellis, Ashley J. *Atoms for War? U.S.-Indian Civilian Nuclear Cooperation and India's Nuclear Arsenal.* Washington, DC: Carnegie Endowment for International Peace, 2006. http://carnegieendowment.org/files/Atoms_for_War_Final.pdf.

UN General Assembly, *First Committee Provisional Verbatim Record of the Two Thousand and Eighteenth Meeting.* Document A/C.1/PV.2018. New York: United Nations, 1974.

US Arms Control and Disarmament Agency. *Documents on Disarmament.* Washington, DC: US Government Printing Office, 1961.

———. *Arms Control and Disarmament Agreements.* Washington, DC: US Government Printing Office, 1980.

Vazquez, Lianet. *Toward the 2015 NPT Review Conference: Attitudes and Expectations of Member States in the Middle East.* London: British American Security Information Council, October 2014.

http://www.basicint.org/sites/default/files/LVazquez_2015NPTRevCon_Oct2014.pdf.

Weyler, Rex. *Greenpeace: How a Group of Ecologists, Journalists, and Visionaries Changed the World.* Emmaus, PA: Rodale, 2004.

Index